Psychology

for AS Level

ERIKA COX

OXFORD
UNIVERSITY PRESS

OXFORD
UNIVERSITY PRESS

Great Clarendon Street, Oxford OX2 6DP

Oxford University Press is a department of the University of Oxford. It furthers the University's objective of excellence in research, scholarship, and education by publishing worldwide in

Oxford   New York

Athens   Auckland   Bangkok   Bogotá   Buenos Aires
Calcutta   Cape Town   Chennai   Dar es Salaam   Delhi
Florence   Hong Kong   Istanbul   Karachi   Kuala Lumpur
Madrid   Melbourne   Mexico City   Mumbai   Nairobi   Paris
São Paulo   Singapore   Taipei   Tokyo   Toronto   Warsaw

with associated companies in Berlin   Ibadan

Oxford is a registered trade mark of Oxford University Press in the UK and in certain other countries

British Library Cataloguing in Publication Data

Data available

ISBN 0 19 832824 9

Typeset by Hardlines, Charlbury, Oxon
Printed in Italy by G. Canale & C. S.p.A. - Turin

The author and publishers would like to thank the following for permission to reproduce photographs and other copyright material:

Cover Science Photo Library; p 13 Professor Albert Bandura, Stanford University; p 48 Tografox/Bob Battesby; p 55 Harlow Primate Laboratory, University of Wisconsin; p 57 Science Photo Library; p 92 Science Photo Library/Martin Dohrn; p 107 Mary Evans Picture Library; p 129 Professor Phillip G. Zimbardo, Stanford University; p 132 Moviestore Collection; p 134 Popperfoto; p 135 from the film 'Obedience' by Stanley Milgram.

Illustrations by Bill Piggins, diagrams by Hardlines.
Special thanks to Bexhill Photographic for their assistance.

Contents

Preface

This textbook is precisely targeted at the AQA (formerly AEB) AS Psychology A syllabus. It will also be of interest to those who are new to psychology, and who want to get a flavour of the kinds of topics in which psychologists are interested.

It aims to be a user-friendly text which explains the material clearly and in simple language, while at the same time giving good coverage to the sometimes complex ideas psychologists have put forward. There are frequent summaries (marked by ● symbols) throughout each chapter; these can be used to provide an overview of each topic and should also be useful when it comes to revision.

The text contains a range of activities (questions, short tests, mini-practicals, and so on) to encourage you to engage with the material. Many of these activities are designed to help you remember the information being put across and check your understanding of it. The mini-practicals will help you get a feel for how psychologists go about their research, and experience for yourself some of their findings.

I would like to thank Julie Harris for her useful contributions to chapters 2 and 5, and Nick Oliver for his many helpful suggestions, which I am sure have made the book much better than it would otherwise have been. I would also like to thank Helen Kara, for her patience in editing the constantly changing versions of the text, and Sue Cave and Clive Barrett for help in tracking down elusive references. Last buut not least, my thanks to Robert as an endless source of support and cups of tea.

Psychology is a fascinating subject. I hope you enjoy using this book as an introduction to what it can offer.

Erika Cox
Fakenham, February 2000

An Introduction to Psychology

In this chapter we will be looking at:

1.1   WHAT IS PSYCHOLOGY?

What is psychology? The general view of what psychology is all about is often rather narrow. When I tell people I am a psychologist, I often get one of two responses. One is: "I'll have to be careful what I say to you". The other is: "I hope you're not going to psychoanalyse me".

The first response seems to imply that psychologists have developed skills which allow them to read people's minds and easily unearth their deepest secrets in a casual conversation. It is true that when you start to study psychology, you are likely to notice and think about behaviour, and perhaps what people say, and relate it to what you have learned, in the same way that someone starting to learn about geology might notice different rock formations. But psychology is not a basis for reading people's minds.

The second response assumes that psychology and psychoanalysis are the same thing. This is understandable in a way, since Freud is probably the best-known name in psychology. Many of his ideas (though perhaps in a distorted form, such as 'Freud is all about sex') are widely known, and some terms associated with psychoanalytic theory have filtered down into general use. You may perhaps have heard of the **Oedipus complex**, the **ego** or **repression**. But there is a vast amount of psychology beyond Freud.

The *Concise Oxford Dictionary* defines psychology as 'the scientific study of the human mind and its functions, especially those affecting behaviour in a given context'. This definition is not without its problems. There are very many different kinds of psychologist. As we will see, each of these concepts – 'scientific', 'mind' and 'behaviour' – can be considered to be either more or less important, depending on what kind of psychologist you are. As a working definition, though, this gives us some general idea of what psychology is about. But what exactly does this study entail?

As you have chosen to study psychology, you probably have an idea of some of the kinds of questions in which psychologists are interested. We will look at this a little more closely in Activity 1:

◗ ACTIVITY 1: topics in psychology

Which of these topics do you think psychologists might be interested in?

- ◆ why people help others (or don't)
- ◆ treatments for depression
- ◆ how children learn language
- ◆ the relationship between stress and illness
- ◆ the behaviour of animals
- ◆ astrological signs and personality
- ◆ why some people are more outgoing than others
- ◆ the causes of schizophrenia
- ◆ extra-sensory perception
- ◆ how people solve logical problems
- ◆ improving performance in sport

When you have finished, see page 18.

This activity should have given you some idea of the broad range of topics in psychology. Obviously not all psychologists are interested in all of them; just as in other disciplines, psychologists specialise.

There are six main topic areas with which most psychologists are concerned. **Cognitive** psychologists are interested in the ways in which we process information – for example, when we use our memory. **Developmental** psychologists are mainly interested in the ways in which children develop – for example, the way that they become attached to their caregivers, and how their thought processes and personality develop. More recently, the developmental approach has also looked at changes across the lifespan. **Physiological** psychologists are interested in the way in which the body functions, and how these physiological processes can be linked to psychological experience and behaviour. Emotion, stress and the effects of brain damage are examples of the kinds of topic in which they are interested.

While these three areas are interested in establishing general laws – the functioning of people in general – psychologists are also interested in **individual differences** – for example, personality, intelligence and mental disorders. **Social** psychologists focus on the idea that people are essentially social creatures, and that therefore much of a person's behaviour is influenced by others. They are interested in topics such as relationships, helping behaviour and obedience. Finally, **comparative**

psychologists study animal behaviour, both as a subject that is interesting in its own right – for example, predator-prey behaviour – and because an understanding of animals may help to establish general principles which also apply to humans. Theories of learning fall into this category, as we will see later in this chapter. Each of the following five chapters covers one topic from the first five areas.

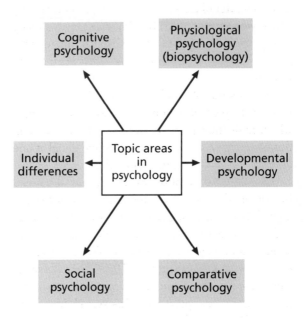

Psychologists vary in their basic beliefs about the nature of people, the questions they think are important and the methods which they think are appropriate to the study of psychology. To get some idea of how these differences have come about, we need to turn now to the history of psychology as a discipline.

- ● Psychology covers a wide range of topic areas. It can be generally defined as 'the science of mind and behaviour'.
- ● The boundaries of the subject are not clear-cut. Some topics are seen as marginal by some psychologists.
- ● The six main areas of psychology in which psychologists are interested are cognitive, developmental, physiological, individual differences, social and comparative.

1.2 THE PHILOSOPHICAL ROOTS OF PSYCHOLOGY

Psychology has its roots in philosophy, going back at least as far as the ancient Greeks. Plato argued, for instance, that we need to make a distinction between mind and body (this belief is known as **dualism**). He also believed that we have innate ideas and knowledge, so that learning is not so much a matter of experience, but rather a process by which we reveal to ourselves knowledge we already have. The motivation to do this is also innate. This general approach is known as **rationalism** or **nativism**.

In your study of psychology, you will come across many examples of modern psychological theories which have their roots in rationalist ideas. Later in this chapter, we will be looking in some detail at one of them, Freud's psychodynamic theory.

Aristotle was a pupil of Plato, but disagreed fundamentally with Plato's belief in innate ideas. He argued that all learning must come from experience, and that we learn by associating aspects of the world which commonly occur together. This approach is known as **associationism**. These general ideas were taken up by a group of seventeenth century philosophers, in particular Locke, Hobbes and Hume. They argued that **experience** is the basis of all knowledge of the world. They are referred to as **empiricists**, from Greek words meaning 'from experience'. In other words, we find out about the world not because of innate knowledge, but through our experience of it. Again, you will come across many examples of modern psychological theories which have their roots in associationism, notably the learning theory of Skinner, which we will be discussing later.

A further tradition in psychology, bringing together rationalism and associationism, has its roots in the rather more recent ideas of the eighteenth-century philosopher, Immanuel Kant. In his *Critique of Pure Reason* (1781), he agreed with the associationist position that experience is important to learning. At the same time, he argued, something must already be present in the mind if we are to make any sense of reality. In brief, we have an innate rule-forming capacity which enables us to *construct* models of reality on the basis of this experience. For this reason, this point of view is known as **constructivism**. A major theorist whose work has its roots in this philosophical position was Jean Piaget (1896–1980), who was interested in the development of thinking in children.

Psychology, then, did not emerge from a vacuum; many of the beliefs that psychologists have and the ideas which they explore go back a long way. At the same time, producing philosophical arguments is far removed from modern psychology. In order to provide a framework for the kind of psychology you will find in this course, we now need to turn to the end of the nineteenth century, to the time when psychology became a discipline in its own right, separate from philosophy.

● Psychology has its roots in philosophy, starting with the ideas of Plato and Aristotle.
● The three different philosophical positions – **rationalism**, **associationism**, **constructivism** – are reflected in the different beliefs of modern psychologists about the nature of people.

1.3 THE BEGINNINGS OF MODERN PSYCHOLOGY

In 1879, Wilhelm Wundt opened the first psychology laboratory at the University of Leipzig in Germany. This is usually thought of as the beginning of psychology as we know it.

While philosophy involves speculation about the mind, Wundt was aiming to do something rather different. He and his co-workers were attempting to analyse the workings of the mind in a rather more structured way, with the emphasis being on **measurement** and **control**.

Participants were exposed to a standard stimulus (e.g. a light or the sound of a metronome) and asked to report their sensations. Asking people to report on their mental processes is known as **introspection**. The aim here was to record thoughts and sensations, and to analyse them into their constituent elements, in much the same way as a chemist analyses chemical compounds, in order to get at the underlying structure. For this reason, the school of psychology founded by Wundt is known as **structuralism**.

Around the same time, other psychologists were also investigating mental experience. The American psychologist William James published *The Principles of Psychology* in 1890. He was opposed to the structuralist approach, believing that we ought to study mental experience as a whole. Like Wundt, however, he used the introspective method. His work covered a wide range of topics in psychology, among them the perceptual experience of newborn babies, human instincts and emotion. Many of his ideas can still be related to modern-day theories.

The German psychologist Hermann Ebbinghaus published *Concerning Memory* in 1885. He carried out a considerable amount of research into human memory, using nonsense syllables in an attempt to eliminate the effect of meaning in memory, and with himself as the sole participant. His work is covered in more detail in chapter 2. While still generally within the introspectionist tradition, his work is also notable for its carefully controlled experimental approach.

◗ ACTIVITY 2: evaluating introspection

Introspection involves asking people to report on their mental processes. Can you think of any problems which might arise in relying on this kind of information to form theories and test ideas? When you have finished, see page 18.

Because of the problems with introspection, a new kind of psychology emerged with J. B. Watson (1878–1958), whose ideas have their roots in the **associationism** mentioned above. He argued that psychology should be like any other science, and that its methods should be those of a science.

◗ ACTIVITY 3: the scientific method

What procedures do scientists go through to collect information, and form and test theories? You will need to think about the methods of investigation you are familiar with from your study of chemistry, physics or biology. When you have finished, see page 18.

Watson argued that if psychology is to be a science, the scientific method should be adopted. The introspective data produced by psychologists like Wundt and James were inappropriate, since they were not **objective**. He asserted that psychology could find its objective data in behaviour, which is observable, public information, and therefore this should be central to the study of psychology. For this reason, the school of thought started by Watson is known as **behaviourism**, and we will be coming back to it in more detail in the next section. He believed that all human functioning can be studied in this way, even claiming (mistakenly) that thinking is expressed in tiny movements of the vocal cords.

But not all psychologists have gone along this route. Sigmund Freud (1856–1939) started to develop his **psychodynamic theory** around 1900. For him, the unconscious mind is central. Although unconscious factors can be inferred from behaviour, his methods relied very much on talking to patients with problems. Necessarily this involved quite a lot of interpretation of the information the patients supplied, and so was quite different from the methods of a behaviourist.

Freud's method of studying the individual in depth is known as a **case study**, which will be discussed in more detail in chapter 7. Up to a point it can be regarded as scientific; Freud thought of himself as a scientist, and he was trained as a neurologist. The case study method has some of the features of the scientific method: the careful collection of data, and analysis (though not necessarily statistical analysis) of those data. It can also be used to support a hypothesis or a theory.

While an experimental approach has been the dominant tradition within psychology, more recently several different approaches to psychology have emerged. They vary in what they see as the proper subject matter of psychology, the kinds of questions which they believe to be important and their 'model of the person', i.e. the assumptions they make about the nature of people. Given these differences, the methods they use also vary. In the next section we shall be looking more closely at these distinctions and how they relate to different models.

- Modern psychology began with researchers like Wundt, whose methods relied heavily on **introspection**.
- Watson criticised introspection as being **subjective**. He argued that psychology should be a science and adopt the methods of other sciences. The study of behaviour would supply **objective** data. The movement he started is known as **behaviourism**.
- Not all psychologists have accepted Watson's model. Different approaches to psychology have emerged, each with its own **model of the person**. They vary in their assumptions, aims and methods.

1.4 PERSPECTIVES IN PSYCHOLOGY

Different approaches in modern psychology can be summarised under five major headings: psychodynamic; behaviourist; physiological; cognitive; and humanistic.

The psychodynamic perspective

The **psychodynamic** or **psychoanalytic** model is based on the work of **Freud**. Freud was a major theorist, and probably the most widely known in psychology. Although they are controversial, his ideas have been applied to many areas of psychological investigation – for example, aggression, gender development, moral development, mental disorders and personality – so we will look at his theory in some detail.

There are a number of fundamental ideas which formed the basis of Freud's theory: the principle of **psychological determinism**, the role of the **unconscious**, and the importance of **childhood** in determining adult behaviour.

Psychological determinism refers to the idea that all behaviour is motivated, and the reasons we behave as we do are often unconscious. Unconscious motivation can be illustrated by Freudian slips or **parapraxes**, where a person says or does something which they had not consciously intended to say or do. Here is a parapraxis reported by Freud:

ACTIVITY 4: a parapraxis

Read through this description of the behaviour of one of Freud's patients:

A young man who was rather cautious about commitment finally proposed to his girlfriend and was accepted. When he had taken her home, he got on a tram to go home himself, and asked the conductress for two tickets.

Six months after his wedding, he was not entirely happy with married life. He missed his friends and did not get on with his parents-in-law. One evening he fetched his wife from her parents' house, got on a tram with her and asked for one ticket.

What unconscious reasons might the young man have had for the mistakes he made in asking for tram tickets?

When you have finished, see page 18.

The concept of the **unconscious** is one of the unique contributions Freud made to psychology. This was not in itself a new idea, but before Freud, the unconscious was seen as a dumping ground for experiences which were no longer of any importance, and so the unconscious itself had no particular status. Freud conceived of a **dynamic unconscious**, an active force, motivating much of our behaviour. He believed that a lot of material in the unconscious, far from being unimportant, is there because it is too painful for us to acknowledge consciously, and that this kind of material can only be accessed using the special techniques of the therapy he developed called **psychoanalysis**. The unconscious can be contrasted with the preconscious, ideas of which we are not at the moment conscious but which we can recall if we want to – for example, a friend's telephone number. There is also the conscious, those ideas we are currently aware of.

The idea of **unconscious conflict** is central to Freud's theory. It can show itself as parapraxes, as disturbing emotional states, and can also be revealed in dreams, where conflict expresses itself through the use of symbols.

Freud believed that adult behaviour is shaped by our experiences in **childhood**. He saw instinctual needs such as hunger, thirst and sex as being very important sources of motivation; at the same time, however, he thought that the social environment, which constrains the gratification of these instincts, was crucial to a child's development. He placed particular emphasis on the conflict between instinctual needs and the demands of society as the basis of personality development and the development of mental disorders.

The experiences of the first five years of life and the conflicts which arise during this time are seen as particularly important to the development of an individual's personality, and we will be coming back to Freud's ideas about children's development later in this section.

The structure of the mind

Freud proposed a theoretical (i.e. non-anatomical) account of the structure of the mind. He believed it consisted of three parts: the **id**, the **ego** and the **superego**.

> ### Figure 1: the structure of the mind
>
> **id**   The id is present at birth. It is the seat of our instincts, and is unconscious. It operates on the **pleasure principle**, in that it tries to get immediate gratification and to avoid pain. It is the source of psychic energy, the **libido**.
>
> **ego**   This develops in childhood out of the id, as children learn that immediate gratification is not always possible and that pain cannot always be avoided. The ego works on the **reality principle**. It decides what actions are appropriate, and which id impulses will be satisfied, and how. The ego tries to balance the demands of the id, the realities of life, and the demands of the **superego**. Many ego processes are conscious, but some are preconscious and

others, especially the **ego defences** we shall come to later, are unconscious.

superego   This consists of the values and morals of the child, and develops around the age of five. It is the child's **conscience** and **ego-ideal**, a model of what the child would like to be.

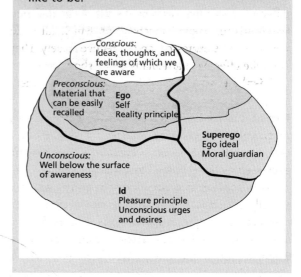

The forces of the superego and the id are often in opposition, with the superego curbing the primitive impulses of the id when they don't fit in with socially acceptable behaviour. For example, your superego would find it socially unacceptable if you decided to have sex on a crowded bus, no matter how frustrated your id was. So your ego would then decide that the action was inappropriate and must wait until later, or be expressed in some other more socially acceptable way. The dynamics of personality, according to Freud, are rooted in this conflict, originating in the id and fuelled by the libido. The way conflict is resolved is a crucial part of the way people develop.

● One major principle of Freud's theory is **psychological determinism**; all behaviour is seen to be motivated. This idea can explain **parapraxes**. Another central idea is the **dynamic unconscious**. **Childhood experience** is seen as being crucial to later development.

● The mind consists of the **conscious**, the **preconscious** and the **unconscious**.

● Freud suggested that personality is made up of the theoretical constructs of the **id**, the **ego** and the **superego**. **Unconscious conflict** between them is important to personality development.

Defence mechanisms

States of conflict may lead to the unpleasant sensation of anxiety developing, and people deal with this in different ways. One way is by the use of ego **defence mechanisms**, coping mechanisms which allow id impulses to be expressed, and so reduce anxiety. They are quite effective, particularly in the short term.

Displacement is one defence mechanism: where feelings cannot be expressed towards their real targets, substitute objects on which feelings can be taken out are chosen. For example, if a child is angry with its mother, these unacceptable feelings may be expressed by being unkind to a younger sibling.

Sublimation is a type of displacement where a socially acceptable activity is found to express an unacceptable impulse. For example, you might play squash to re-channel either your aggressive impulses, or sexual energy which lacks a sexual outlet. This is the only defence mechanism which can be effective long-term.

There are several other defence mechanisms. In **denial**, a fact which is too painful to cope with – such as the knowledge that you have a life-threatening illness – is denied. **Repression** is motivated forgetting (discussed in the section on **forgetting** in chapter 2). A person may unconsciously 'forget' something that is too distressing to remember, such as memories of being abused as a child, or the death of a relative. **Rationalisation** involves finding superficially acceptable reasons for a behaviour. You might, for example, blame your awful exam results on the fact that you had a cold on the day you sat the exam, to protect yourself from feelings of inadequacy. In **reaction formation**, a person consciously feels or thinks the exact opposite of their unconscious feelings or thoughts. For example, a person who is deeply prejudiced against a minority group could protect themselves from these unacceptable feelings by becoming actively involved in the Campaign for Racial Equality. **Regression** involves a symbolic return to an earlier stage of development, for example, sucking your thumb to comfort yourself.

Psychosexual development

As we saw earlier, the importance of childhood is central to Freud's theory, and he describes how children progress through a sequence of **psychosexual stages**. Everyone goes through these stages in the same order, and their experience of them is crucial not only to the child, but also to the adult. At each stage, interest is focused on the pleasurable sensations associated with different **erotogenic** (pleasure-giving) zones.

The **oral stage** lasts from birth to around one year. During this time, the source of pleasurable sensations is the mouth. You may have noticed that babies and very young children automatically put anything new into their mouths, and seem to derive pleasure from doing so. This stage is divided into two sub-stages. In the first few months, in the **incorporative** sub-stage, the baby is relatively passive; activity is largely focused on sucking and swallowing. This is followed by the **aggressive** sub-stage, when biting and chewing become important.

The **anal stage** lasts from around one to around three. Once weaned, the libido focuses on the anus and the muscles of the urinary system. Again, there are two sub-stages. In the **expulsion** sub-stage, the child gets great pleasure from defecating, while in the **retention** sub-stage, there is pleasure from holding in faeces. During this stage, the child comes up against external restrictions in terms of where and when defecation is acceptable, and will find that this aspect of behaviour has social implications in terms of pleasing parents, or not.

The **phallic stage** lasts from around three to around five. In this stage, pleasure centres on the genitals, and the stage is experienced differently by boys and by girls.

The young boy goes through a crisis which Freud called the **Oedipus complex**, during which he develops unconscious sexual feelings towards his mother. He is envious of his father, and jealous of the love and attention he gets from his mother. The way in which the boy's feelings for his mother and rivalry with his father is resolved is crucial for development. Similarly, a girl will experience the **Electra complex**.

In the **latency period**, from five to puberty, children turn aside from their sexuality, concentrating instead on developing socially and intellectually. This continues until the onset of adolescence. At adolescence, the child moves into the **genital stage**. In this stage, recognisably adult sexual feelings develop, and mature love becomes possible.

Freud suggested that the developmental stages which a child goes through help to form the personality of that child as an adult. The adult personality is determined not only by the interaction of id, ego and superego, together with the use of particular defence mechanisms, but also by **fixation**, an unconscious preoccupation with a particular psychosexual stage. This causes problems with adult personality if the child experiences frustration or overgratification while passing through a stage. If this happens, these early fixations are expressed symbolically in adult behaviour.

● Unconscious conflict causes **anxiety**, which can be dealt with using ego **defence mechanisms**. Only the mechanism of **sublimation** is effective in the long term. People differ in the kinds of mechanisms they use, and the extent to which they use them.
● Children develop through **psychosexual stages: oral, anal, phallic, latency** and **genital. Fixation** in one of these stages has implications for adult personality characteristics.

Overview of the psychodynamic model
The basic model here is of behaviour being shaped by **unconscious** forces. The idea of **conflict** is also central, with problems being created as the result of conflict between different parts of the personality. These in turn are determined by the **psychosexual development** which takes place in childhood, considered to be an extremely important time within this tradition, since our experiences at this time can affect us throughout our lives. Freud's is a **nativist** theory, since psychosexual development is determined by the sex into which we are born. On the basis of our sex, we are shaped by early childhood experiences.

The aims of this approach are twofold. Firstly, Freud seeks to explain development and behaviour within this general framework. However, this is not only a theory, but also a therapy: **psychoanalysis**. The aims here are to uncover unconscious conflict and help the patient understand its causes. They

can then come to terms with their problems.

In developing his theory, Freud used a clinical method known as the **case study**. Talking to patients and exploring their problems allowed him to understand the course of development which he claimed we all go through. Psychoanalysis is often referred to as the 'talking cure'. The methods here involve asking patients to talk about their concerns (**free association**) and to describe their dreams. This material allows the analyst to uncover unconscious conflict and start the process of curing the patient.

The behaviourist perspective

As we have seen, behaviourism had its roots in the ideas of **Watson**. Watson argued that if psychology was to be carried on in a scientific way, and to gain wide acceptance as a science, it needed to be objective. It must use the same methods and collect the same kinds of data as other sciences. The contents of a person's consciousness were not objectively measurable and were therefore not valid data; studying behaviour would provide observable, measurable events. He therefore saw behaviour as the only acceptable data.

Darwin's evolutionary theories had already suggested that there was a continuity between humans and other animals. This meant that animal behaviour could be studied in psychology experiments, and would provide valid, objective, measurable data which could also throw light on human behaviour.

▷ ACTIVITY 5: using animals in experiments

Many psychologists have used animals in experiments, instead of humans.
What advantages does this have?
When you have finished, see page 18.

In proposing what a science of psychology should be, Watson was concerned with the connection between an event in the environment (e.g. touching something hot, or a voice saying your name) and the behaviour which follows (e.g. taking your hand away quickly, or turning your head towards the sound of the voice). The environmental event is called a

stimulus, and what a person does as a result of the stimulus is called a **response**. For this reason, the behaviourist approach to psychology is sometimes called stimulus-response (or S-R) psychology. Watson saw learning as the process of associating stimulus and response, and believed this would prove a fertile area for psychological research. These ideas were developed by others interested in the nature of learning, and their theories are grouped together as **learning theory**.

Classical conditioning

Watson's ideas tied in with research being carried out by Pavlov (1849-1936), a Russian physiologist interested in the digestive processes of dogs, in particular the salivation reflex. A **reflex** is a fixed and automatic response to a particular stimulus; the response cannot be controlled. Pavlov was interested in accurate measurement of the relationship between the **stimulus** of food in the mouth and the **response** of salivation. In the course of his research (which won him a Nobel prize), Pavlov developed a technique for collecting the saliva secreted by the dog as part of the digestive process, and this made accurate measurement of the strength of the salivary reflex possible.

Pavlov noticed that the dog would salivate not only when it could taste the food, but also when it could only see it. The experiments he carried out demonstrate a phenomenon known as **classical conditioning**, one of the two kinds of learning processes in the behaviourist tradition. The other is **operant conditioning**, which we shall come to later.

Box A: Pavlov (1927)

Procedure: A dog was held in a harness so that little movement was possible. A bell, which the dog had not heard before, was rung to check that the dog didn't have an automatic salivary response to this sound. Pavlov called the bell a **neutral stimulus (NS)**, because there was no automatic response to it. The experimenter then rang the bell and immediately afterwards presented food to the dog. The pairing of bell and food was repeated several times. Finally, the bell was rung on its own.

Results: The paired presentation of bell and food automatically produced the response of salivation on each presentation. Finally the bell alone also produced salivation.

Conclusion: The bell which had previously not produced salivation eventually did so because of its repeated pairings with food. This response came about as the result of an **association** being formed between bell and salivation.

We need now to look at a few technical terms. Pavlov referred to the food in this experiment as the **unconditional stimulus** (**UCS** or **US**) because it automatically or unconditionally causes salivation. Salivation in response to the food is referred to as the **unconditional response** (**UCR** or **UR**), for the same reason. The bell is originally referred to as a **neutral stimulus** (see Box A). After its pairing with food, it becomes a **conditional stimulus** (**CS**), because it can only cause salivation *on condition* that it has been paired with food. The salivation caused by the bell on its own is the **conditional response** (**CR**), because it only occurs on condition that the bell-food pairings have taken place.

With the dog salivating to the sound of the bell, we have an objectively measurable change in behaviour, so the dog can be said to have *learned* to salivate to the sound of a bell.

It is possible to condition any reflex. Humans as well as animals have reflex responses – for example, the knee-jerk or patellar response. We also show the reflex response of blinking when air is blown into our eyes.

Watson was enthusiastic about Pavlov's work, since it was an example of the scientific study of behaviour he wanted to see in psychology. He used Pavlov's procedure for experiments into human learning. A classic study is shown in Box B:

Box B: Watson and Rayner (1920)

Procedure: An eleven-month-old child known as Little Albert was the participant in this study. Two months earlier, his reactions to various stimuli had been tested: a white rat, a rabbit, various other animals, cotton wool and burning newspapers. He showed no fear of any of these, and seems to have been a rather unemotional child. However, hardly surprisingly, he did show a fear reaction to a loud noise behind him, a hammer hitting a steel bar. The experimenters made this noise several times, at the same time presenting him with a white rat.

Results: Albert developed a fear of the white rat. The fear response to the rat became less extreme over time, but was still evident a month later.

Conclusion: Classical conditioning is one way of explaining fear responses. This is an example of a **conditioned emotional response** (CER). It is possible that people develop phobias through forming this kind of association.

ACTIVITY 6: questions on 'Little Albert'

Read through the Little Albert experiment in Box B and answer these questions:
a Identify the NS, UCS, UCR, CS and CR.
b What are the ethical problems here, and how might they be overcome?
When you have finished, see the notes on page 19.

The case of Little Albert shows that Pavlov's findings do have some relevance to human learning. Psychologists have made use of this in various ways, most notably in **behaviour therapy**. If behaviour is learned, it can also be unlearned, and more appropriate behaviours learned instead. These ideas have been used to help people who suffer from disorders such as phobias, and are discussed in a little more detail in chapter 5.

● Watson wanted a scientific psychology, using objective methods. He saw behaviour as the only legitimate data for psychology.
● Studies of **animals** have often been carried out within the behaviourist tradition. Their use has several advantages.
● Watson was interested in the relationship between a **stimulus** to which an animal is exposed and its **response**. His ideas have been incorporated into **learning theory**.
● Pavlov's work on the salivary reflex in dogs led him to demonstrate what has come to be known as **classical conditioning**. His ideas can also be used to condition humans. The principles of classical conditioning are used in **therapy**.

Operant conditioning

The most famous name in operant conditioning is Skinner (1904–1990). The term 'operant' means an action: the animal operates on its environment. While sharing some general principles of classical conditioning – the emphasis on observable behaviour and explaining behaviour in terms of learning theory – operant conditioning is a move away from looking at associations between stimulus and response. In operant conditioning, what is important is the association between **behaviour** and the **consequences** of that behaviour. The basic principle behind Skinner's theory is that behaviour is shaped and maintained by its consequences.

While Pavlov's work related to reflex behaviour, Skinner's theory applies to any behaviour. He believed that all behaviour is learned, apart from the few reflexes we have at birth, and that any organism, human or animal, could be taught to produce any behaviour of which it was physically capable by the use of appropriate techniques.

Two key terms in Skinner's theory are reinforcement and shaping. **Shaping** is a way of gradually changing behaviour. **Reinforcement** refers to a positive consequence of a behaviour, which makes the behaviour likely to be repeated. To understand the theory, we will need to look at what he meant by these terms in a little more detail.

Shaping

If you wanted to train a rat to produce a behaviour, you might have quite a long wait before the rat produced the desired behaviour spontaneously. To shorten this time, Skinner used **shaping**. For example, if you want a rat to press a lever, you would reinforce a hungry rat with food when it moved in the direction of the lever. Once this behaviour was established, the rat would have to come a bit closer to what was required before being reinforced – for example, it might have to touch the lever. You would then require the rat to get even closer to lever-pressing – perhaps a slight lever press – to receive food, and then finally only reinforce when the rat produced a full lever press. In this way, you would be reinforcing **successive approximations** to the behaviour you were aiming at. Skinner himself managed to train pigeons to play table tennis using these methods!

Reinforcement and punishment

Although most of his original work was carried out on rats and pigeons, Skinner also applied his ideas to humans, and his research into the effect on learning of both reinforcement and punishment is of considerable relevance to human behaviour. He distinguished between positive and negative reinforcement. **Positive reinforcement** is when something with pleasurable consequences, which is likely to encourage a particular behaviour, is introduced into a situation. An example could be food for a hungry animal. It could also be praise or attention; it doesn't have to be anything tangible, just something which is pleasurable for the animal (or human) who is being reinforced. **Negative reinforcement** is when something aversive is removed from a situation. An example could be taking your hand away when you have accidentally touched a hot iron.

Both positive and negative reinforcement *strengthen* a particular behaviour. **Punishment**, on the other hand, weakens behaviour. It also differs from both positive and negative reinforcement, because it involves introducing something aversive into a situation, or taking something pleasurable away from it.

These distinctions are summarised in Figure 2. In discussing ways of changing behaviour, Skinner himself was strongly in favour of the use of positive reinforcement, and to a lesser extent negative reinforcement. Punishment may be necessary to put an immediate stop to dangerous behaviour, like stopping a child playing with a knife, but otherwise Skinner was very much against it.

One of the reasons for this was practical: if you try to use punishment to change behaviour, initially it seems to work. What typically happens, however, is that this change is only temporary, and the undesired behaviour comes back, perhaps even more strongly than before. Although punishment may not be a good way of stopping a behaviour once and for all, it is very effective in temporarily suppressing unwanted behaviour. It could perhaps be useful, then, in stopping unwanted behaviour for long enough to allow desired behaviour to occur; this desired behaviour could then be shaped and reinforced, using positive reinforcement.

Figure 2: reinforcement and punishment

term	what happens	effect	examples
positive reinforcement	something pleasurable is added to a situation	behaviour is strengthened	praise, food if hungry
negative reinforcement	something aversive is removed from a situation	behaviour is strengthened	pain stops
punishment	something aversive is added to a situation	behaviour is weakened	physical punishment
	something pleasurable is removed from a situation	behaviour is weakened	pocket money taken away

The implications of operant conditioning

Skinner and his followers believed that all behaviour is learned, apart from the few reflexes we have at birth. This is true both for animals and for humans. Our behaviour is shaped and maintained by its consequences. It therefore follows that, in theory, anyone can be taught to do anything which is physically possible.

Skinner considered that the principles of behaviour change which he had established could be very widely used well beyond the laboratory. His principles have been applied in many areas; for example, helping children with learning difficulties to acquire skills, and behaviour management in the classroom.

● **Operant conditioning** is the term used to refer to the work of Skinner and his followers. Skinner explained learning as the association between a behaviour and its consequences. He believed all behaviour except reflexes is learned through **shaping** and **reinforcement**.

● Behaviour is **reinforced** when the consequences are positive. **Shaping** allows behaviour to be developed which would not occur spontaneously.

● Skinner distinguished between **positive reinforcement**, **negative reinforcement** and **punishment**. He strongly advocated the use of positive reinforcement as a way of changing behaviour. Punishment is an ineffective long-term measure, but it may have a place in behaviour change if it is used alongside positive reinforcement.

● The principles of operant conditioning have been applied in a variety of contexts.

Social learning theory

Social learning theory is based on the principles of operant conditioning, in that it suggests that all behaviour (including social behaviour) is learned, and is likely to be repeated if it is positively reinforced.

Bandura, one of the foremost proponents of this theory, claims that all social behaviour is learned through **modelling**. He suggested that there were three main sources of models: the family, the subculture (the people we mix with outside the immediate family) and the mass media.

Social learning theory: sources of models

We learn through observing the behaviour of others, and seeing the results of their behaviour. This is called **observational learning**. Modelling is rather more than just imitation, since Bandura sees the psychological effects of modelling as being much broader than just copying what we see; it is general rules and principles which are learned. This theory therefore also introduces cognitive factors to behavioural theory, such as attending to relevant features of the modelled behaviour, and remembering its critical features so that they can be accurately reproduced. He and his co-workers have shown this effect in a series of studies. One is described in Box C:

Box C: Bandura *et al.* (1963)

Procedure: Children observed an adult behaving aggressively towards a large, inflatable Bobo doll. The adult attacked the doll in unusual ways (e.g. hitting it with a hammer, and saying things like 'Pow ... boom ... boom'). The children were then left in the playroom and their behaviour was observed. A control group of children also played in the playroom with the same toys, but did not observe the adult model attacking the doll.

Results: The behaviour of the experimental group was very similar to that of the adult model. The control group did not display similar behaviour.

Conclusion: Children imitated the behaviour of the adult model they had observed.

In a later study (Bandura, 1965), one group of children went straight into the playroom after they had observed the adult model. A second group saw the adult being rewarded for aggressive behaviour before they were let into the playroom, while a third group saw the adult punished. There was little difference in the number of imitated aggressive behaviours shown by the first two groups, but the third group showed significantly fewer imitated behaviours.

This seems to suggest that seeing a model punished leads to less learning. However, Bandura then offered rewards to the children who had seen the adult punished if they could reproduce the behaviour they had observed. The number of imitated aggressive behaviours shown by this group then rose to the level of the other two groups. Bandura concluded from this that **modelling** is sufficient for behaviour to be *learned*, but **reinforcement** is necessary for behaviour to be *performed*.

● **Social learning theory** is a development of operant conditioning which introduces a cognitive element. It proposes that all behaviour is learned through **modelling**.
● **Observation** of models is sufficient for learning to take place, but **reinforcement** is necessary if it is to be reproduced.

Overview of the behaviourist model

The behaviourist model claims that behaviour can be accounted for within the framework of **learning theory**, with S-R associations being learned within a classical conditioning framework, and behaviour which is reinforced being strengthened and therefore likely to recur within an operant conditioning framework.

Behaviourism emphasises the continuity between humans and other animals, since the same principles of learning are believed to apply in both cases. It assumes that very little is innate, and that therefore most of our behaviour needs to be learned. It is fundamentally an **associationist** approach.

Its aims are to establish by experimentation the rules which establish and change behaviour. This is often done by studying **animal behaviour** to establish basic principles. This has the advantage of control, in that animal behaviour is very much less complex than human behaviour, so it is easier to isolate particular variables. These principles may then be helpful in understanding human behaviour.

Human behaviour has also been studied directly using behavioural methods. These methods are also relevant to therapies; since all behaviour is learned, it can be unlearned and more appropriate behaviour learned in its place. This principle forms the basis of behavioural attempts to help people with problems, for example those suffering from phobias.

The physiological perspective

All the wide range of behaviour and experience which adds up to being human must have a physiological basis. Some psychologists therefore believe that to understand human functioning, we need to focus on the basic physiological processes which underlie it. We will look briefly at some of the topics with which biopsychologists are concerned.

One area of interest is **localisation of function**, i.e. how the functioning of different areas of the brain relates to behaviour and experience. In chapter 2, for example, some of the areas of the cerebral cortex which are known to be involved in different kinds of memory are discussed.

Biopsychologists are also interested in biochemical processes. **Neurotransmitters**, for example, are chemical messengers which allow neurons (nerve cells) to communicate with each other. In chapter 4, the role of neurotransmitters in the stress response is discussed. These substances are also implicated in mental disorders; for example, an excess of the neurotransmitter dopamine has been offered as one explanation for the development of schizophrenia. **Hormones** are another kind of biochemical; it has been suggested that the hormone CCK-8 may be related to the development of eating disorders. This is discussed in chapter 5.

Genetics is another area of interest. Physical characteristics (such as eye colour) and some physical disorders (such as cystic fibrosis) are passed on through the genes from parent to child. Biopsychologists have investigated the possibility that psychological characteristics (such as intelligence)

Can psychological characteristics be inherited?

and mental illnesses (such as schizophrenia) can be inherited in the same way.

These are just a few of the topics in which biopsychologists are interested, but this should have given you a flavour of the kinds of areas with which they are concerned. The aims of this approach are to provide a detailed picture of aspects of physiology related to psychology, and to see how they relate to behaviour and experience. Given the nature of this approach, the scientific method is used. As in the behaviourist approach, animal research can often be a starting point.

The cognitive perspective

While behaviourism was a very popular approach in the 1940s and 1950s, some psychologists have pointed out that internal mental processes play a large part in many human functions, and therefore study of these processes should have a place in psychology. While behaviourists acknowledge the existence of processes such as thinking and emotion, they do not consider them an appropriate focus of study since they are not directly observable. Many psychologists believe, however, that to focus entirely on observable behaviour and ignore the mental processes which lead to the behaviour being produced provides an unecessarily limited account of psychological functioning.

Cognitive psychologists are particularly interested in the mental processes involved in perception, attention, memory, language and thinking. They propose that the human mind can be compared to a computer, where information is taken in, processed in some way, and in turn affects behaviour and experience. The underlying model here is of people as **information processors**, and the aims are to establish the rules which govern our cognitions.

While it is not possible to observe cognitive processes directly, they can be observed indirectly by looking at the *results* of processing information. As you will see in chapter 2, much research into memory asks people to carry out memory tasks in controlled conditions; the results of these studies have helped psychologists to understand the nature of the cognitive processes involved in memory. Most research into memory is carried out using scientific methods. These methods are also common in research into other areas of cognition.

A recent development has been **artificial intelligence**, combining cognitive psychology with computer science. This has focused on the development of computer programs which can carry out the kinds of complex cognitive tasks typical of human functioning. The most recent theoretical framework taking this approach is **connectionism**, which has been influential in such areas as explaining how children develop language and why they make particular kinds of linguistic errors.

The cognitive approach is a move away from the use of animals, since some of our cognitive functions, such as the spontaneous development of language, are not shared by animals, and in any case human cognitions are vastly more complex than those of animals.

This approach has also been influential in the development of **therapies**, which try to help people with problems by encouraging them to reappraise the ways they think about themselves and others. This is discussed in chapter 6.

The humanistic perspective

The humanistic approach grew out of dissatisfaction with the rather piecemeal approach of the other perspectives we have described. In particular, some psychologists were unhappy with the behaviourist approach, with its disregard for conscious experience, as well as the rather pessimistic view of the psychodynamic approach, which saw people as being at the mercy of unconscious forces. In response to the huge influence of behaviourism and psychodynamic psychology, humanistic psychology therefore emerged as a third force, concerned with people's conscious experience and their ability to direct their lives.

Humanistic psychologists also question the use of the scientific method as the most useful one for psychologists to follow. This method has been dominant in much of psychology, and aims at objectivity. It is interested in the measurement of behaviour and exploring cause and effect relationships through rigorously controlled experiments. In contrast, humanistic psychologists argue that what is important is the experience of being a person, and that the methods used in the more traditional sciences are inappropriate for this kind of study. A rigorously scientific approach constrains our understanding of the individual. Like Freud, humanistic psychologists prefer to use a **case-study** method, and to make use of **introspective** data, which allows the psychologist to understand the individual in depth.

There are three basic principles of humanistic psychology. Firstly, what is important is the **experience** of being human. Instead of analysing people in an objective way, the humanistic psychologist is interested in people's experience. This is known as a **phenomenological approach**. An important aspect of this is that we are aware of our own existence as distinct individuals, moving through life towards old age and death.

The second principle is that we should take a **holistic approach** – in other words, look at the **person as a whole**. You will remember from earlier in the chapter that a similar viewpoint was put forward at the end of the nineteenth century by William James. Instead of studying specific psychological processes in isolation, the focus should be on the whole person, the physical person with thoughts and feelings, within a particular social context.

The final principle is that we all have **personal agency**. In most situations, we are aware of having choices. There may well be social constraints on our choices, and we may not be fully aware of the alternatives open to us. We may even be afraid of the consequences of making particular choices. Nonetheless, we do have the potential to choose. An extension of this principle is that we can play a part in the kind of person we become. Humanistic psychologists believe that people can be helped to change and develop by becoming as aware as possible of their feelings and motivations and the influences upon them. This process of change is referred to as **personal growth**.

The aims of humanistic psychology are to explore the experience of the individual, and to facilitate personal growth. Perhaps the major figure in humanistic psychology is Carl Rogers (1902–

1987), whose work is particularly relevant to **therapies**. The aim of humanistic therapy is to help a person explore the changes they wish to make in their lives, and thus help them to grow as individuals.

▷ ACTIVITY 7: identifying perspectives

Try to match each of the following statements to one (or more) of the perspectives described above **psychodynamic behaviourist physiological cognitive humanistic**

1 It is important to study what makes an individual unique.

2 Like any other science, psychology needs to use scientific methods.

3 Animal research can be useful in helping us to understand how people function.

4 The principles of psychology can be used in therapies.

5 It is important to focus on people's unconscious processes.

6 We need to understand how the body works if we are to understand behaviour and experience.

7 We have no direct access to internal psychological processes; we should therefore concentrate on what is observable.

When you have finished, see the notes on page 19.

This section should have given you some insight into the different ways in which psychology can be carried out. As you study different topics, you can consider each perspective: what its assumptions are, what its aims are, and what methods are used. You may also find it useful to come back to this section later, when you have more knowledge to which these distinctions can be related.

● There are five major approaches to psychology: **psychodynamic, behaviourist, physiological, cognitive** and **humanistic**.

● They vary in their assumptions, aims and methods.

1.5 PSYCHOLOGY AND COMMON SENSE

It may seem questionable whether psychology has much to tell us which is not just a matter of common sense. After all, we all observe what is going on around us and how people behave, and we draw conclusions about what people are like from what we observe. We seem to understand people quite well without the help of psychologists. So what does psychology have to offer?

One way of looking at this is to think of psychology as *organised* common sense. Psychology can give us a more detailed understanding of people, supported by evidence. This evidence has been reached in a systematic way, compared with the rather sporadic observations we may make of a very limited number of cases.

Common sense also has its problems. We may assume, for example, that what is true for us is also true for everybody else. Given the nature of Western society, for example, we could assume that people are 'naturally' competitive. Research in other cultures, which are based more on co-operation, suggest that this may not be the case. These assumptions, then, may have come about because we are particular individuals, who live in a particular community, in a particular culture, at a particular time. In a different setting, common sense could let us down. Psychology can take a wider view.

Some of the subject matter of psychology may not be within the experience of all of us. The physiological basis of behaviour is an obvious example, if we are not trained physiologists. For example, common sense can tell us little about the relationship between brain damage and behaviour.

Finally, common sense is sometimes wrong. For example, common sense tells many of us that if you punish someone for doing something, they will not do it again. (We know this in spite of prisons being full of people who have reoffended!) The findings of behaviourists, such as Skinner, however, show that punishment is not the best way of stopping behaviour, and can also suggest more effective ways of changing behaviour.

Common sense can of course be useful. It may give us useful insights, which start us off on a more precise psychological investigation. At the same time, psychology can extend and organise our understanding.

● Psychology can be thought of as organised common sense. It can provide evidence for common sense theories, and can take a wider perspective than the individual.
● Sometimes the findings of psychologists may contradict common sense.

1.6 WHAT DO PSYCHOLOGISTS DO?

Psychology is one of the most popular subjects at A-level, and also at university, with large numbers of students graduating each year. What can a psychology graduate do with their degree once they have it? Of course many psychology graduates, like graduates in other disciplines, work in areas where a degree may be required, but the subject of the degree is not really important. But what about jobs in psychology?

Psychology **teaching** is one possibility. Psychology graduates can train to teach GCSE or A-level psychology in schools or colleges of further education. They can also combine teaching with research in a university department. Most people working in a university psychology department will have taken a PhD after their first degree.

Educational psychology is another option. Educational psychologists have teaching experience, and a masters degree in educational psychology. Most are employed by the local educational authority, and work with 5–16 year olds. Their work includes testing and assessing children with learning difficulties, and planning remedial programmes.

Postgraduate training is also necessary to become a **clinical psychologist**. Clinical psychologists work in general and psychiatric hospitals, often as part of a team of healthcare professionals, which includes a psychiatrist and a psychiatric social worker. Psychiatrists are *not* psychologists; they have medical training first, and then further training in psychological medicine. They assess patients with psychological problems, and plan and carry out therapy. **Forensic psychology** is a branch of clinical psychology. Forensic psychologists are employed by the prison or probation service. They may work with young offenders, running courses on anger management, or carry out risk assessment when certain prisoners are being considered for release. Another area related to clinical psychology is **counselling**. Many diploma courses in counselling are now available.

Another major area is **industrial** or **occupational psychology**. Occupational psychologists are often employed by large firms, though some work on a consultancy basis. They work in the personnel field, assessing people for job suitability, training people for jobs and retraining people for a new career after accident or redundancy. They are also involved in **ergonomics**, which involves designing machinery and equipment to optimise the working environment and maximise productivity. Specialised areas within this field include **advertising** and **sports psychology**.

The **British Psychological Society (BPS)** is the professional body for psychologists. Suitably qualified psychologists can apply for **Chartered Psychologist** status under its charter.

● Psychology graduates work in a range of fields, not always directly related to psychology.
● Some psychologists **teach** psychology. In a university department, teaching is combined with research.
● Professional psychologists work in three other main areas: educational, clinical and industrial or occupational psychology.
● Suitably qualified psychologists can apply for Chartered Psychologist status.

Notes on activities are on page 18.

Notes on activities

1 You would be right in thinking that psychologists are interested in nearly all these topics. There are some areas, though, which are controversial. An interest in animal behaviour is one example. Many psychologists believe that since animals and people are all living creatures, insight into the behaviour of rats and dogs may give us a head-start in understanding human behaviour. Others argue that people are unique, and we therefore need to concentrate directly on the behaviour and experience of people.

The relationship between astrological signs and personality is *not* a topic in psychology, though perhaps psychologists could be interested in the relationship between personal characteristics and a *belief* in astrology. There are also some areas (e.g. extra-sensory perception) which many psychologists would not regard as psychology, and others would regard as being, at best, on the fringes of psychology.

2 One obvious drawback is that you are relying on the skill (and honesty) of the person you are testing. The participants Wundt tested were carefully trained to try to overcome this problem, but they would still be dependent on their own level of awareness, and their ability to turn this awareness into words. It is also possible that describing a sensation may actually interfere with that sensation. In addition, reporting is always retrospective – you are describing something which has happened, not something which is happening, and this may present further difficulties.

It may well be possible to get useful information when the sensations which are to be reported are relatively straightforward and relate to simple events. All the problems outlined, though, are likely to become more serious as the stimulus to which a person is exposed becomes more complex.

A key point here is that introspection is essentially **subjective** – only the individual concerned can observe these internal processes. The accuracy of a subjective account cannot be checked, and it does not lend itself easily to measurement and precise analysis.

3 First of all, a precise area to be studied needs to be identified. This is followed by **observation** of a phenomenon, and from this observation, a general explanation or **theory** can be produced (though in practice, much new research is triggered off by an existing theory or research). This in turn will lead to a specific and testable **hypothesis**: a precise prediction of what the results of an experiment will be.

An **experiment** or test must then be set up, which isolates the factor in which you are interested, and controls other factors which are not relevant to your research. Information or **data** must be collected. This needs to be **objective**, so that someone else running a similar experiment could check their results against the results you have found. This is in contrast to the **subjective** data produced by introspection. **Conclusions** can then be drawn on the basis of the findings.

4 Freud believed that on the first occasion, the young man asked for two tickets because he wished his fiancée was with him. Asking for only one ticket on the second occasion expressed the unconscious wish for her *not* to be there, as he was dissatisfied with his marriage.

5 There are various ideas here which you could have come up with:

a Animals can be bred for laboratory experiments. This means that animals who are genetically identical can be bred, and their environment from birth onwards can be closely controlled. It is therefore possible to eliminate confounding variables from the study.

b It is also possible to treat animals in ways that would not be allowed if humans were to be tested – for example, keeping them hungry, or rearing them in isolation. There are ethical problems here, but national bodies like the British Psychological Society (BPS) have laid down guidelines which must be strictly followed.

c Animals are less likely to be affected by demand characteristics, i.e. to change their behaviour in line with what they think the purpose of the study might be.

d The kinds of animals which are used in laboratories, such as rats and pigeons, have much shorter lives than humans. This makes it easier to study learning at different stages of the lifespan.

e There are no problems in finding enough participants for a study, they don't drop out and they don't need paying!

6 You should have identified the NS (and later the CS) as the rat. The initial UCS–UCR bond here is between noise–fear. The final CS–CR bond is between rat–fear.

There are serious **ethical problems** here. Researchers have a duty of care to protect participants from short-term stress and long-term harm, and this research fails on both counts. Albert obviously could not give his informed consent to what was to happen in this experiment, and it is not clear whether Watson had explained the experiment fully to his mother. Albert and his mother moved away soon after this study, before Watson had done anything to remove the fear response. Extinguishing Albert's learned fear would have gone at least some way to addressing the ethical concerns this study raises.

7 The first statement very much describes the humanistic approach. Scientific methods are a major feature of behaviourist, physiological and cognitive psychology. Remember, though, that Freud thought of his methods as scientific. Animal research has been important in behaviourist and physiological psychology. All five perspectives can have therapeutic applications. You should have identified the emphasis on unconscious processes as being associated with psychodynamic psychology, and how the body functions with a physiological perspective. The final statement typifies the behaviourist view, though it could also relate to physiological and to some extent cognitive psychology.

Human Memory

In this chapter we will be looking at:

2.1 THE NATURE OF MEMORY

Imagine life without memory! You wouldn't be able to talk, to read this chapter, to use a knife and fork... Nor would you be able to learn anything from experience – you would in effect spend your whole life as a new-born baby. You use memory to get dressed in the morning, carry on a conversation, pass exams, know people's telephone numbers, recognise faces – the list is endless. So studying memory is an area of psychology that seems relevant to all our lives. The ultimate goal of memory research is to apply its findings to practical problems such as helping people to use their memory more effectively and improving eye-witness accounts of crimes.

The three main processes involved in memory are **registration**, **storage** and **retrieval**. Registration is the process by which your sense organs detect information and enter that information in the memory system; storage is the process by which information is kept or stored in the memory; and retrieval is the process by which information in memory can be recovered or recalled. All these aspects are considered in the theories and research we will be looking at in this chapter.

2.2 EARLY STUDIES OF MEMORY

Psychologists have studied memory experimentally for more than 100 years. In 1885, Ebbinghaus's research was published, research in which he was the only participant. The study in Box A is only one of many that he carried out to look at such things as how the position of a word in a list affects its recall:

Box A: Ebbinghaus (1885)

Procedure: Ebbinghaus used **nonsense syllables** of three letters such as KED and MOZ. He read a long list of these syllables at a steady pace, then covered up the list and tried to recite it from memory. He counted the syllables he remembered correctly, then read the list again, and repeated the procedure until he could recall the whole list. He tested his memory of the lists at various times after he had learned them.

Results: Ebbinghaus discovered that forgetting the syllables occurred quite quickly at first, but gradually slowed down.

Conclusion: The first, quick forgetting is the loss of material from a short-term memory system. The more gradual forgetting is their loss from a more long-term system.

▷ Activity 1: evaluating Ebbinghaus

Having read Ebbinghaus' study, now evaluate its design. Try to think about the advantages and disadvantages of the way in which he carried out his research.

When you have finished, see the notes on page 50.

Although criticisms can be made of Ebbinghaus' work, he carried out a series of pioneering pieces of research, and was the first to suggest that memory consists of more than one system or store. His distinction between a short-term memory system and a longer-term memory system is similar to that made by William James (1890) between **primary memory** and **secondary memory**. The modern terms for such a distinction are **short-term memory (STM)** and **long-term memory (LTM)**.

Ebbinghaus believed that memory depends on the association of ideas, so that the process of learning a list of words or numbers consists of forming associations between the items. Another early theorist called Bartlett, whose work we will be looking at later in the chapter, published a book called *Remembering* (1932) in which he argued against the associationist standpoint. He took a **constructivist** approach to memory, seeing memory as a reconstructive process, and what we recall as a reconstruction rather than an exact copy of the original information. He believed that to get a clearer picture of how memory works, we should investigate memory using meaningful material.

● Memory involves **registration**, **storage** and **retrieval**.
● Ebbinghaus took an **associationist** approach to memory. He was the first to distinguish between a **short-term memory** store and a **long-term memory** store. William James described these as **primary** and **secondary** memory.
● Bartlett took a **constructivist** approach to memory. He saw remembering as **reconstruction** rather than reproduction.

2.3 MODELS OF MEMORY

Sometimes in psychology, a **model** of a particular process is used. A model is a sort of metaphor – a way of representing a process that makes it easier to understand, and for this reason models are often drawn up to try to produce a framework that explains complicated processes such as memory, and which enables us to investigate the processes involved.

The multi-store (structural) model of memory

This model is also often called the two-process model because of the importance attached to the two stores of **short-term memory (STM)** and **long-term memory (LTM)**. You may also find it referred to as the modal model; 'modal' here means 'most frequently occurring', and this model shares a number of common features with other, similar, models.

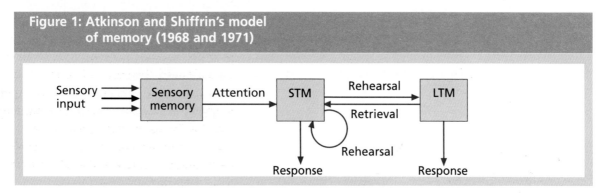

Figure 1: Atkinson and Shiffrin's model of memory (1968 and 1971)

This model describes memory in terms of information flowing through a system. In Figure 1, you can see that information is detected by the sense organs, and enters the **sensory memory** (**SM**). If we attend to this information, it enters the **STM**. Information from the STM is transferred to the **LTM** only if that information is rehearsed. If **rehearsal** does not occur, then the information is forgotten.

There are different types of rehearsal. Craik and Watkins (1973) distinguished between **maintenance rehearsal**, where, for example, you repeat a word out loud a number of times to keep it in STM, and **elaborative rehearsal**, in which information is processed in terms of its meaning. They suggested that maintenance rehearsal may be enough to keep information in STM, while elaborative rehearsal is the type necessary to transfer information from STM to LTM.

Psychologists often contrast memory stores in terms of how much information they can hold (their **capacity**), how long they can hold that information (the **duration** of the storage), and how information is coded (**encoding**). The characteristics of the different stores in the Atkinson and Shiffrin model are shown in Figure 2:

Figure 2: comparing SM, STM and LTM

	SM	STM	LTM
Capacity	small	7±2 items	unlimited
Duration	0.25–2 seconds	up to 30 seconds	indefinite period of time
Encoding	modality specific	mainly acoustic	semantic/ visual/acoustic

Sensory memory

SM is what happens after information has reached the sense organs, and it travels to the brain for interpretation. This lingering of information in the nervous system (very briefly) gives the brain time to interpret it. There are two types of sensory storage: **iconic storage**, the store associated with visual information, and **echoic storage**, associated with heard, or auditory information. You can probably imagine iconic storage if you remember what happens when someone takes your photograph with

a flash – you often see an after-image of the flash for a brief moment, and this is iconic storage. Box B explores the nature of SM:

Box B: Sperling (1960)

Procedure 1: Replicating many previous studies, Sperling asked participants to look at an array of letters. He used a device called a tachistoscope, a machine which can display letters or numbers on a screen for very short and accurately controlled periods of time. In one trial, the participants were shown three rows of four letters (such as that shown below) for 50 milliseconds. They were then asked to recall as many letters as they could from the whole display.

sample display:

G	B	T	F
S	R	D	W
E	N	Z	X

Results: Participants could recall on average about 4.5 of the 12 items.

Procedure 2: Sperling then introduced his own idea, a partial report condition in which the participant was asked to recall only part of the display. A tone was played just after the display – if the tone was a high-pitched tone they should recall the top row of the display, a low-pitched tone indicated the bottom row, and a medium-pitched tone indicated the middle row.

Results: When the participants were cued to recall one row of the display immediately after the display was switched off, their average recall was 3.3 letters. As the tone was increasingly delayed, the average number of letters recalled decreased as the after-image faded.

Conclusion: Since the proportion of items remembered was greater in the partial report condition than for the total display, participants must have been reading the letters from an after-image – their iconic stores. Iconic storage lasts approximately half a second.

A study by Averbach and Coriell (1961) has provided a more sensitive measure of the capacity of SM, with information about how material is lost from this store:

Box C: Averbach and Coriell (1961)

Procedure 1: Participants were shown two rows, each of 8 letters chosen at random, for 50 milliseconds. A small mark then appeared just above one of the letter positions. Participants were asked to state which letter had been in the position of the marker.
Results: Letter identification was 75% accurate.
Conclusion: 12 letters can be held in SM, i.e. 75% of the 16 letters shown.

Procedure 2: Using a tachistoscope, participants were shown a letter, followed after a short time interval by another letter. They were asked to identify the first letter.
Results: If the time interval between the presentation of the two letters was less than 100 milliseconds, **superimposition** occurred (e.g. F followed by L was reported as E). If the time interval was longer than 100 milliseconds, backward visual masking (**displacement**) occurred (e.g. F followed by L was reported as L).
Conclusion: The iconic store forgets by displacement; the second letter displaces the first. For this to occur, there must be at least 100 milliseconds between the original stimulus and the displacing stimulus.

Treisman (1964) found that echoic memory has similar characteristics.

Short-term memory (STM)

If you look back to Figure 2, you will see that the capacity of STM is said to be 7±2 items. This idea was put forward by Miller (1956). '7±2' means 'seven plus-or-minus two', so Miller was suggesting that STM can store between 5 and 9 pieces of information. STM can store only a limited number of items because it has only a certain number of 'slots' in which items can be stored. But Miller didn't specify the amount of information that could be held in each slot – indeed, his idea was that we can increase that amount by **chunking** the material; for example, by grouping letters together into words or into abbreviations that have meaning for us.

▶ Activity 2: chunking

Write the letters listed below on a large piece of paper, and test some volunteers to see how many of the letters they can recall in a free recall task (they should try to remember as many as they can, in any order):

M S C G N V Q G C S E P H D B S C A S

Now group the letters so that they form the chunks below, and write them on a second large piece of paper. Test a different set of volunteers to see how many of the letters they can recall.

MSC GNVQ GCSE PHD BSC AS

Which task led to greater recall?

You probably found that the second condition allowed people to recall significantly more letters than the first. In terms of Miller's idea, the first set of letters (19 items) would be too many for the 7±2 slots of STM to hold. But if we group the letters so that they form the chunks MSC, GNVQ, GCSE, PHD, BSC and AS, they give six 'chunks' of information (at least to English-speaking people who know something about the English education system) which is within the range of STM.

A further task to investigate STM which you could try on your participants is what is known as the **Brown-Peterson technique**. Peterson and Peterson (1959) asked their participants to remember **trigrams** – groups of three consonants like KMG or PNS. But to prevent the participants from rehearsing the trigrams, they were asked to count backwards aloud in threes, from a number such as 176. This is a very effective way of preventing rehearsal (try it!) and they found that information was rapidly forgotten; they concluded that without rehearsal, material in STM is forgotten within 6-12 seconds. Although Atkinson and Shiffrin believe it lasts rather longer (see Figure 2), these findings give a general indication of the **duration** of STM, and show that **rehearsal** is necessary to enable information to be transferred to LTM.

Activity 3 investigates how material is encoded in STM:

▶ Activity 3: coding in STM

You will need to find some participants to help you carry out this activity.

Draw each of the letters listed below on to a separate piece of white card, in large clear lettering. Put the letters into two piles – list 1 and list 2.

List 1:	B V T C D G E P
List 2:	M R W L Z Y Q A

Now show each letter of list 1 to your participants and ask them to look at each letter carefully and try to memorise it. When all the letters have been shown, ask them to write down as many of the list of letters as they can.

Next, repeat the procedure with list two. To make it a better test, you should really present half your participants with list 1 first and list 2 second; the other half of the participants should be presented with list 2 first and list 1 second. This technique is known as **counterbalancing**. It eliminates **order effects**, such as practice, fatigue or boredom, and is discussed in more detail in chapter 7.

Work out which list was remembered most accurately. What is the difference between the two lists?

You may have noticed that the letters in list 1 all sound like each other – they are acoustically similar. You may have found that your participants were far more likely to make errors when recalling the letters that were acoustically similar than when recalling different sounding letters, so made more mistakes when they tried to recall list 1 than with list 2. Bear in mind that this happened even though the letters were presented visually – you didn't read the letters out loud and in doing so show that list 1 letters all sounded similar. The results of this study imply that information stored in STM is stored in an **acoustic code**. Other studies have given similar results:

Box D: Conrad (1964)

Procedure: Participants were shown sequences of 6 letters, chosen from B C F M N P S T V X. They were asked to write them down as they appeared, but presentation was too fast for participants to keep up, so the information had to be held in STM. The errors made were analysed.

Results: The errors were generally acoustic confusion errors, where the original letters were replaced by ones with a similar sound, e.g. S for X or M for N.

Conclusion: Coding in STM is acoustic, even when material is presented visually.

Long-term memory (LTM)

Figure 2 shows that according to the multi-store model, LTM can hold unlimited amounts of information for an indefinite period of time, and that this store uses mainly **semantic coding** (i.e. based on the meaning of information) together with **visual** and **acoustic** coding.

Box E: Baddeley (1966)

Procedure: Participants were presented with a short list of words which were semantically similar (e.g. neat/clean/tidy/smart). He also gave them a list of words that were acoustically similar (e.g. heat/sweet/greet/sheet). Recall was tested immediately, and again after a period of time had elapsed.

Results: When testing immediate recall, there was acoustic confusion between acoustically similar words, while those with similar meanings were easily remembered. When participants were tested again later, however, the words with similar meanings caused problems.

Conclusion: The confusion on semantically similar lists after a period of time is evidence that LTM mainly uses a semantic code. The confusion on lists that sounded similar is evidence that encoding in STM is acoustic.

- Atkinson and Shiffrin's **multi-store model** described information flowing through a memory system composed of **sensory memory (SM)**, **short-term memory (STM)** and **long-term memory (LTM)**.
- **SM** is **modality-based** and lasts up to 2 seconds.
- **STM** uses an **acoustic code** and has a capacity of 7±2 items. It lasts between 6 and 12 seconds, but can be extended by **rehearsal**.
- **LTM** has unlimited **capacity** and can potentially last indefinitely. It mainly uses a **semantic code**.

Evidence for the multi-store model of memory

Evidence for this model comes from a number of sources, one of which you can test for yourself in Activity 4.

▷ Activity 4: a free recall task

You can try this activity on a few friends or on members of your family. The more people you try it on, the better the test will be.

Read out the following instructions to your participants: 'I am going to read you a list of words. I would like you to listen carefully to the words. When I have finished, I would like you to write down as many of the words as you can remember, in any order.'.

Now read out the following list of words in order (first 'scissors' then 'file' etc) to your participants – slowly and clearly, with a gap of a second or two in between each word. (Don't read out the numbers!)

1. scissors	2. file	3. grass	4. lion
5. computer	6. carpet	7. room	8. knife
9. book	10. dish	11. idea	12. sand
13. card	14. cushion	15. parrot	16. fire
17. milk	18. house	19. pencil	20. wall

Then say to your participants: 'Now please write down as many of the words as you can remember, in any order.'.

To analyse your results, write down a list of the 20 words in the order in which you read them out. Now go through your participants' recall lists, and count up how many people recalled each word. Your results table should look something like this:

word	position of word in list	number of people who recalled that word
scissors	1	3
file	2	2
grass	3	3
lion	4	0

When you have finished the table, plot a graph like the one below:

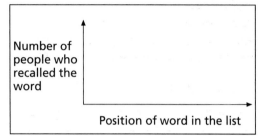

Was the position of the word in the list related to the number of people who recalled it?

You may have found no particular pattern in your graph, especially if you were limited to only a couple of participants. On the other hand, you may have a curve that looks like the one in Figure 3:

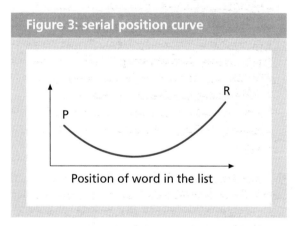

Figure 3: serial position curve

Your participants performed what is called a **free recall task** – that means that they recalled the words in any order. Similar experiments were carried out by Ebbinghaus whose work on nonsense syllables was mentioned earlier. He had similar results to those shown in Figure 3. Displaying results in this way is known as a **serial position curve**. Typically, words near the beginning and end of the list are better recalled than those in the middle. The effect whereby the first few words are well recalled is known as the

primacy effect (**P** on the graph) and the effect whereby the last few words are well recalled is known as the **recency effect** (**R** on the graph).

◗ **Activity 5: interpreting the serial position curve**

Look carefully at the serial position curve above. What does it show? Try to explain what the shape of the curve means. How does it support the two-process model?

When you have finished, see the notes on page 50.

Evidence that the recency effect is due to retrieval from STM is given by Glanzer and Cunitz (1966) who found that the recency effect occurs only if the last items on the list are recalled immediately; if recall is delayed, then the recency effect disappears. You could try this as a further experiment, if you still have willing participants!

Clinical evidence also supports the two-process model:

Box F: Milner (1966)

Scoville and Milner described the now classic case study of HM, a man who had drastic brain surgery to cure his epilepsy. One consequence of this procedure was that he suffered from **anterograde amnesia** – he could recall events that happened before the operation, such as details of friends he knew before the surgery, but very little of what occurred afterwards. He re-read newspapers unaware that he had just read them, and only knew what time it was for about 15 seconds after he looked at the clock. All the people he met after the surgery had to be 're-met' each time they visited him, as he couldn't remember who they were.

The case of HM supports the two-process model, because it supports the idea that the brain uses different mechanisms for holding information for a short time, and for holding it relatively permanently. HM could remember a lot from before the surgery, so presumably his LTM was unaffected by the operation, but he did not seem able to transfer new information from his STM into his LTM.

Further clinical evidence for the idea of separate STM and LTM processing systems comes from cases of amnesia resulting from the type of brain damage caused by chronic alcoholism. This is called the **Korsakov syndrome** and patients suffering from it have a fairly intact LTM but a severely faulty STM.

One other piece of evidence for the two-process model is that different types of coding are used in STM and LTM, as previously discussed (see Box E). The fact that short-term coding is so different from long-term coding supports the idea that there are two distinct stores.

Criticisms of the multi-store model of memory

Atkinson and Shiffrin's model affected psychological research into memory for many years. It has made a valuable contribution to memory research as it clearly distinguishes between the *structures* and the *processes* of memory. However, the model is no longer accepted as entirely plausible, and has been criticised on many counts.

One problem is that it implies that to reach LTM, information needs to flow through STM. Shallice and Warrington (1970) carried out a case study of KF, who suffered brain damage as the result of a motorcycle accident. His STM was seriously impaired, but his LTM was relatively intact, including memory for information *after* his accident. This suggests that information does not have to flow through the STM in order to reach LTM.

The multi-store model can also be criticised for its lack of detail about the nature of LTM; it does not go beyond defining capacity, the coding involved and duration of storage.

Another major problem with the model is that there is evidence that neither STM nor LTM is a unitary store. Each may more usefully be seen as being made up of different subsystems. This approach has been taken in the theory of **working memory** which we shall be looking at in the next section.

Similarly, Tulving (1972) suggested that there are two systems within LTM: **semantic memory**, consisting of facts, such as that Lima is the capital of Peru, and **episodic memory**, personal memories such as where you went on holiday last year, and public events which have happened in your lifetime, such as earthquakes or assassinations. He also described **procedural memory**, memory for complex skills such as how to type, and how to combine words appropriately when speaking your native language. Evidence for these distinctions comes from clinical evidence, such as the study reported by Blakemore (1988) of Clive Wearing. After suffering brain damage as the result of a brain infection, Clive Wearing's semantic and episodic memory were severely affected, while his procedural memory was relatively intact.

A further problem is that the multi-store model takes no account of the *nature* of information to be recalled, concentrating only on *quantity* of information. It treats all information as the same, whereas we know intuitively that *what* we are trying to remember is very important in whether or not it is remembered. Some people find it very easy to remember golf scores or astronomy facts, for example, but cannot for the life of them recall capital cities or relatives' birthdays.

The importance of the nature of the information to be recalled is shown by the phenomenon of **flashbulb memories**. This is where people have a particularly strong and often detailed memory of where they were and exactly what they were doing when a specific major event occurred. For example, you may know people who remember in great detail where they were on VE day at the end of the second world war when the Germans surrendered unconditionally (1945) or when the American president John F Kennedy was shot (1963) or when Mrs Thatcher resigned as Prime Minister (1990) or when they heard that Diana, Princess of Wales had died (1997), depending on their age.

Brown and Kulik (1977) found that people were likely to remember six kinds of information in memories of this kind: where they were when they heard the news; what they were doing at the time; the person who gave them the news; how they felt about it; how others felt about it; and the aftermath of the event. The most important factors in triggering a flashbulb memory were that the event

was surprising, was seen to be important and was associated with a high level of emotional arousal. These ideas were demonstrated in their findings that of the 80 people asked about their memories of the Kennedy assassination – an unexpected event of national importance in the USA, and about which most people had very strong feelings – 79 remembered where they were and what they had been doing at the time. Similarly, very high levels of flashbulb memory for the resignation of Mrs Thatcher were found by Conway *et al.* (1994).

A further study has produced similar findings:

Box G: Pillemer (1984)

Procedure: In this American research, people were asked about their memory for the attempted assassination of the American president Ronald Reagan in 1981. They were asked about this event a month after it happened, and again six months later.

Results: People had vivid memories of where they were when they heard the news, and who told them about it. They reported strong visual images. The amount of emotional arousal people experienced was related to the vividness, elaboration and consistency over time of the memory.

Conclusion: Flashbulb memories are associated with an event being unexpected, seen as important, and creating strong emotional arousal.

As well as public events, we can also have flashbulb memories of personal events. Rubin and Kozin (1984) asked people to describe their three clearest memories. Many of these memories related to accidents or injuries to themselves or those close to them, while others related to love affairs, sports, animals and their experiences when starting college. National events, such as those described above, made up only three per cent of the sample. As with the other research in this area, surprise was an important factor; the number of times people had rehearsed the memory, i.e. gone over it in their minds, was also important.

Activity 6: investigating flashbulb memories

Carry out a small-scale replication of the Rubin and Kozin study. Use your own three clearest memories as a starting point.

a Do they include the kinds of events Rubin and Kozin describe?

b Was there a strong element of surprise associated with these memories?

c Have you often thought about these events since they happened?

Ask other people the same questions, and compare what they say with your own answers and the findings of the Rubin and Kozin study.

One of the factors associated with flashbulb memories is **distinctiveness**: the fact that an event is so unusual means that it stands out from our everyday memories. Distinctiveness is a factor in memory which applies more widely than just to flashbulb memories, a phenomenon which is known as the **von Restorff effect**.

More everyday personal factors are also important:

Box H: Morris *et al.* (1985)

Procedure: Participants were asked to fill in a soccer knowledge questionnaire. They were then asked to memorise that day's football results and a set of simulated scores.

Results: There was a high positive correlation (0.82) between soccer knowledge and memory for the real scores. For simulated scores, the correlation was only 0.36.

Conclusion: Interest and knowledge are factors in whether or not information is retained.

● The **primacy** and **recency effects**, the case of **HM**, the **Korsakov syndrome** and the fact that different **codes** are used in **STM** and **LTM** are all evidence for the multi-store model.

● This model has been criticised for being too simplistic in its assumption that memory flows in one direction through the different stores.

● This model gives little detail of **LTM**.

● There is evidence that neither the **STM** nor the **LTM** is a unitary store.

● This model does not take into account the nature of the material to be remembered.

In the light of the criticisms made of the multi-store model, several other models of memory have been suggested. The **working memory** model of Baddeley and Hitch (1974) offers an alternative explanation of STM. **The levels of processing** model of Craik and Lockhart (1972) moves away from an emphasis on separate stores, while providing insight into the importance of how material is processed for retention.

Working memory

In contrast to the multi-store model, the working memory model of Baddeley and Hitch (1974) deals only with STM and recently activated parts of LTM. The working memory model concentrates on systems by which information is processed in STM, and emphasises the idea of an **active processor**. If you look back to the work by Atkinson and Shiffrin, you will see that the stages of their model are passive stores through which information flows, in strong contrast to this idea of memory as an active process.

Baddeley and Hitch suggested that working memory consists of a **central executive** which controls three **slave systems**. The central executive is used when you are dealing with difficult mental tasks such as problem solving. Information can be briefly held within a slave system while new information is being processed. In doing a complicated addition sum, for example, the number to be carried forward from one column of figures can be held while the next column is added up. The central executive also acts as a sort of attention system, deciding which information entering from the sense organs should have attention allocated to it, and directing the work of the slave systems.

The central executive is the most important part of the system as it controls all the other systems. It is very flexible: it can process information from any of the senses, and can even store information for a short period of time. The three slave systems are the **visuo-spatial scratch pad**, the **articulatory loop** and the **primary acoustic store**.

Figure 4: working memory (Baddeley Hitch, 1974)

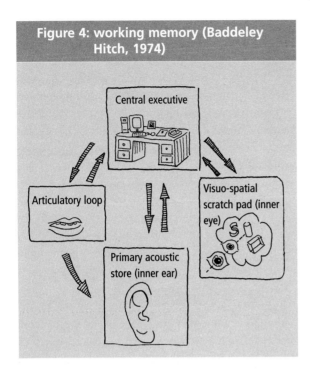

The **visuo-spatial scratch pad**, also known as the **inner eye**, uses a visual code and deals with visual and spatial information, such as the layout of the inside of your house or where the plants are situated in your garden. Activity 7 looks at the ways information is coded using the visuo-spatial scratch pad and the articulatory loop:

Activity 7: coding in working memory

You will need to draw carefully the display grid below on a large piece of paper. You also need to draw a number of blank grids, exactly the same as the first one but without the letters in. Then you will need to draw two patterned grids similar to the one shown below, each with a slightly different pattern of squares coloured in.

Display grid

M			K	
		Z		
			A		G
F		R		

Patterned grid

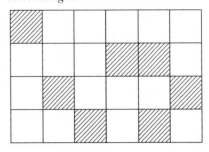

Half your participants will be performing a verbal task in between seeing the display and recalling it; the other half will perform a visual task.

Show half your participants the display for 10 seconds. Then ask them to count backwards aloud from 100 and time this counting for 10 seconds. (This is the **verbal task**). Finally, ask them to fill in one of the blank grids you prepared earlier, to see how much of the display they can recall.

If they remember a letter but not where it went, they should put it anywhere. If they remember there was a letter in a particular square, but can't remember what it was, they should put any letter in the square.

Repeat this procedure with the rest of your participants, but instead of the verbal task, ask them to look at two of the patterned grids you prepared earlier, and tick which parts of the two grids match (time them doing this for 10 seconds) – this is the **visual task**.

You should score your participants' answers separately in two ways. For each condition each participant should have a score out of 7 for number of letters recalled correctly, and a score out of 7 for the number of positions recalled correctly.

Activity 7 is similar to an experiment carried out by Den Heyer and Barrett (1971). You probably found that your participants' recall of the letters was more disrupted by the verbal task, and their recall of the letters' positions in the grid was more disrupted by the visual task. Den Heyer and Barrett suggested that the experiment gives evidence that the letters themselves were encoded acoustically (because the verbal task prevented their recall) and that the position of the letters was encoded visually.

The **articulatory loop** is known as the **inner voice**. It is a **verbal rehearsal loop** which holds words in an articulatory code. It is like an inner voice because you 'hear' in your head the telephone number you are attempting to remember; for example, while you search for a pen and notepad. The capacity of the articulatory loop was discovered when Baddeley *et al.* (1975) showed that people involved in a recall task could immediately recall as many words as they could read out in two seconds, but no more. The articulatory loop therefore works rather like a continuous cassette loop: the amount of information it can hold is determined only by how long it takes that information to be spoken out loud, and not by the number of items.

You may have unwittingly come across evidence for the articulatory loop. Perhaps you have had the experience of asking somebody 'What did you say?' when you thought you hadn't heard them correctly, but in the time it took you to ask the question, you realised that you did know what it was they said. This is your articulatory loop in action; like a cassette loop, the information was played back to you, and you heard what was said.

You can also try out for yourself how the articulatory loop works. If you repeatedly say a phrase out loud, you are occupying your articulatory loop so that it can't be used to hold other information in working memory at the same time. The idea of repeating a phrase at the same time as learning a list of words, or reading a book, is called concurrent verbalisation. If the task being carried out is hampered by the **concurrent verbalisation** task, then you can assume that the task normally utilises the articulatory loop.

▶ Activity 8: a concurrent verbalisation task

Pick a textbook that you sometimes use in your studies, but that you have previously found fairly difficult. Read a page of the text silently, simultaneously saying the phrase 'cognitive psychology' out loud. When you finish reading the page, see how much of the text you can remember.

You may well have found that you could not remember much of the text you had read, because your articulatory loop was being used to repeat the phrase 'cognitive psychology'. This is called **articulatory suppression**. The reason it was suggested that you pick a fairly difficult textbook was because concurrent verbalisation has more effect if the material is quite difficult to understand.

Very little is known about the **primary acoustic store**, or **inner ear**, which was added to the original model in 1982; it is thought to receive auditory information directly from the ears or via the articulatory loop, and to store it in an acoustic code. It was added to the original model when it was found that information which is presented acoustically is not affected by articulatory suppression. This can be contrasted with the silent reading you used in Activity 8.

Evaluation of working memory

Although working memory is one of the most recent models of memory, it is limited in that it considers only STM, and also because comparatively little is known about the central executive, the most important part of the whole system.

However, it seems to make more sense to see STM as a group of processing mechanisms rather than as a single store in which information is passively held. In terms of coding, the working memory model gives more emphasis to the use of visual coding in STM, compared to the multi-store model which sees coding as primarily acoustic.

Its main advantage is the way it portrays memory as an **active process**, and not merely a series of passive stores. Cognitive psychologists also find it useful to see attention and memory as part of the same system, since we tend to use the two processes together. Further research may well provide more information about the nature of the central executive part of the model.

Another strength of the working memory model is that it ties in neatly with PET scan studies of brain activity during different memory tasks, carried out by the Wellcome Foundation. PET stands for Positron Emission Tomography, and this type of scan displays a three-dimensional representation of the brain's structures and provides images which show brain activity in different areas while carrying out different tasks. Activity in different areas corresponds with the four systems the model proposes:

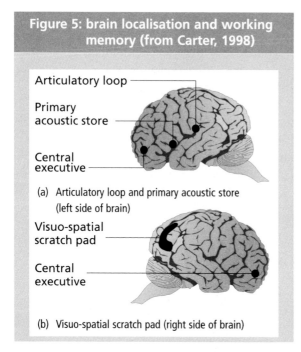

Figure 5: brain localisation and working memory (from Carter, 1998)

Articulatory loop

Primary acoustic store

Central executive

(a) Articulatory loop and primary acoustic store (left side of brain)

Visuo-spatial scratch pad

Central executive

(b) Visuo-spatial scratch pad (right side of brain)

Working memory has potential practical applications – for example, in teaching children to read. If children with normal intelligence are having difficulties learning to read, and they also have trouble in recognising rhyme, it suggests a problem with their articulatory loop. When we understand the systems better, we will be in a better position to help such children and put our theoretical knowledge to good use.

● The working memory model of Baddeley and Hitch is a model of short-term memory.
● This memory system is seen as an active processor, consisting of a **central executive** in control of three slave systems – **the visuo-spatial scratchpad**, the **articulatory loop** and the **primary acoustic store**.

● Concurrent verbalisation tasks give evidence that the articulatory loop is involved in processing information.
● The model places more emphasis on visual aspects of STM.
● The idea of different subsystems is supported by evidence from **PET scans**.
● The working memory model has been criticised on the grounds that the central executive is not fully understood.
● Applications of the working memory model include helping children learn to read.

Levels of processing

The levels of processing model was put forward by Craik and Lockhart (1972), partly as a result of the criticisms levelled at Atkinson and Shiffrin's model. Instead of concentrating on the stores involved, i.e. STM and LTM, this model concentrates on the *processes* involved in memory. The basic idea is that memory is really just what happens as a result of processing information. What is important is what you do with the information to be remembered.

Craik and Lockhart suggested that storage of information varies along a continuous dimension depending on the depth to which it has been encoded. They defined 'depth' in terms of the meaningfulness extracted from material. They proposed that information which has been processed deeply, i.e. more extensively, will be better stored, and is therefore more likely to be recalled; whereas information which has been processed in a more shallow way, i.e. more superficially, is more likely to be forgotten.

Although depth is a continuous dimension, this idea has generally been tested using three levels:

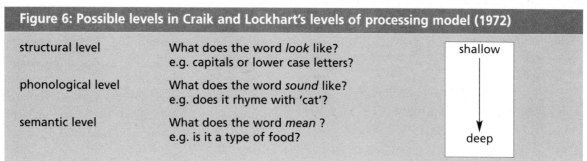

Figure 6: Possible levels in Craik and Lockhart's levels of processing model (1972)

structural level	What does the word *look* like? e.g. capitals or lower case letters?	shallow
phonological level	What does the word *sound* like? e.g. does it rhyme with 'cat'?	
semantic level	What does the word *mean*? e.g. is it a type of food?	deep

An example of a study to test the levels of processing model is shown in Box I:

Box I: Craik and Tulving (1975)

Procedure: Participants were shown a series of words, on each of which they were asked a question. The questions required either **a** structural, **b** phonological or **c** semantic processing, e.g:

a is the word written in capital letters? (e.g. CAT or cat)

b does the word rhyme with 'stable'? (e.g. table or chair)

c does it fit into the sentence 'she climbed up the...' (e.g. stairs or goat)

They were then given an unexpected recall task in which they were asked to pick out the words they had been shown from others they had not seen.

Results: Participants were significantly better at recognising words they had processed semantically.

Conclusion: The effectiveness of recall is related to the level at which material has been processed, with deeper processing producing better recall.

Elias and Perfetti (1973) also tested the levels of processing model. They asked participants to work through a list of words, performing different types of processing on each word (such as thinking of a word that rhymes with each word on the list, or finding a word with a similar meaning). Their participants were not told that they would later have to recall the words, but when they were tested, they recalled significantly more words which had been semantically processed, giving evidence for the levels of processing model.

You can test the levels of processing model for yourself:

Activity 9: testing the levels of processing model

Make up two sets of 18 cards. For each set, each of these words should be written on a separate card:

celery   carrot   plumber   lawyer   ferret
bear   spinach   broccoli   secretary   painter
hamster   hyena   potato   parsnip   doctor
printer   tiger   rabbit

For the first set, write each word in the same kind of writing so that they are as uniform as possible. For the second set, write two vegetables, two professions and two animals in fairly small lower case letters (but so they can still be read easily), two of each group in fairly large lower case letters and the remaining six words in capital letters:

| celery | plumber | FERRET |

For the first set (condition 1), prepare instructions asking participants to sort the cards into three groups of words which are related in meaning. For the second set (condition 2), ask them to sort the cards into three groups by the style of writing in which they are written.

Participants should not be told that this is a memory test; tell them you will explain what the study is about after they have carried out the task. When each participant has carried out the sorting task, remove the cards and ask them to write down as many words as they can remember in any order. You will need to test different participants in each condition. Test as many as you can; if you are working in a group, pool your data.

In which condition did people tend to recall more words correctly?

According to levels of processing theory, you are likely to have found that the people you tested recalled more words if they were asked to sort them by meaning than by writing style.

The distinction Craik and Watkins (1973) made between maintenance rehearsal and elaborative rehearsal, which we mentioned earlier, is relevant here. You will remember that in **maintenance rehearsal**, a word or number is repeated again and again, and this is enough to keep it in STM. For example, if a friend reads out their telephone number to you, you might well repeat that number out loud again and again while you search frantically for a pen and notepad. This is **phonological** processing, and in the levels of processing model it is relatively shallow.

Elaborative rehearsal, on the other hand, is where you elaborate the material to be remembered in terms of its meaning. For example, you might remember the phone number 2954, by thinking: 'Uncle Jim is 29 and he lives at number 54'. This elaborative rehearsal which is necessary to retain information in the LTM involves deeper **semantic** processing.

Evaluation of the levels of processing model

Craik and Lockhart's model of memory has contributed to research in this area of psychology because it concentrates on the *processes* of memory. It emphasises that how likely you are to retrieve a particular item from your memory successfully depends on how you process that piece of information, and not on how hard you try to rehearse it. However, the model is criticised for being descriptive rather than explanatory, and for its failure to explain *why* deeper processing leads to better recall – an opinion which Craik and Lockhart themselves counter by claiming that their idea was not intended to be a theory of memory, but rather a 'conceptual framework for memory research'.

One of the main problems of their approach is that it is very difficult to measure how deeply a piece of information has been processed. It is a circular argument to say that something you remember well is something that you have processed deeply; but the only way to tell whether it has been processed at a deep level is by seeing if you can recall it!

There is also a problem because the levels of processing model makes no distinction between STM and LTM, and you have already read about the evidence which suggests that there are two quite distinct memory processes.

One further problem is that the improved recall of some words could be due to **processing effort** rather than depth of processing:

> ### Box J: Tyler *et al.* (1979)
>
> **Procedure:** Participants were given two sets of anagrams to solve. Some of the anagrams were easy (e.g. FAMIYL); others were difficult (e.g. YMALFI). Participants were later given an unexpected recall test.

> **Results:** Significantly more of the difficult anagram words were remembered than the easy ones.
>
> **Conclusion:** As all words were processed at the same depth (i.e. semantically), recall of the words depended on the effort that was put into processing them, and not the depth of processing.

You can probably see that the participants would also have spent more *time* processing the more difficult anagrams, and this is another potential **confounding variable**. It is impossible for a researcher to work out which variable is having an effect (processing effort, *or* length of time spent processing, *or* depth of processing) if the variables cannot be separated.

There may also be factors other than depth of processing which influence how well something is remembered:

> ### Box K: Craik and Tulving (1975)
>
> **Procedure:** Participants were shown a word and a sentence containing a blank. They were asked whether the word would fit into the sentence. On some trials, the sentence was complex (e.g. 'the great bird swooped down and carried off the struggling ...') and in some trials less so (e.g. 'she cooked the ...').
>
> **Results:** Using cued recall, participants recalled twice as many words accompanying complex sentences.
>
> **Conclusion:** As both kinds of trial required semantic processing, increased recall for the words accompanying more complex sentences can be explained by greater *elaboration* of processing, i.e. the amount of processing of a particular kind.

The **von Restorff effect**, mentioned earlier, suggests that distinctiveness, too, is a factor in whether or not information is recalled.

There is also evidence that semantic processing does not always lead to improved recall:

Box L: Morris et al. (1977)

Procedure: Participants were presented with words and asked to answer questions involving either meaning or rhyme. Recall was tested either by a standard recognition test (see Box H) or by a rhyming recognition test, in which they were asked to pick out words which rhymed with the stimulus words.

Results: On the standard recognition test, recall was better for words which had been processed semantically than for those where questions about rhyme had been asked. On the rhyming recognition test, however, the opposite was true.

Conclusion: Semantic processing does not always lead to superior recall compared with phonological processing. Recall may depend on the relevance of the kind of processing to the memory test.

- Craik and Lockhart's levels of processing model suggested that information is processed at one of three levels – at the **structural** level, the **phonological** level, or the **semantic** level.
- The deeper the information is processed, the better it is recalled.
- The levels of processing model has been criticised on the grounds that it is difficult to measure how deeply information has been processed.
- It has also been suggested that **processing effort** and the time taken to process information, rather than depth of processing, are responsible for improved recall with semantically processed information.
- **Elaboration** and **distinctiveness** are also factors in recall. On some tasks, semantic processing may not be the most effective technique.

2.4 THEORIES OF FORGETTING

To understand the nature of forgetting, it is important to make a distinction between availability and accessibility. **Availability** is whether the information you are trying to recall is still actually stored; **accessibility** is whether or not it can be retrieved at will. Obviously information that is not available (because it wasn't stored in the first place or is no longer stored) will not be accessible.

Inaccessibility

Many years ago, psychologists such as Freud believed that memories were permanent, and forgetting was merely a failure to retrieve information successfully. Evidence for this idea came from Penfield (1969). He stimulated the surface of the brain of epileptic patients on whom he was operating, to try to identify which area of the brain was involved in producing the epileptic attacks:

Figure 7: Penfield (1969)

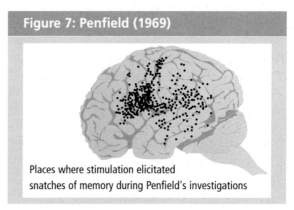

Places where stimulation elicited snatches of memory during Penfield's investigations

He found that this procedure led to some people recalling long-forgotten memories with great clarity. Given this idea, it follows that failure to retrieve information should be because memories are inaccessible.

Theories of forgetting based on the idea that memories are inaccessible include **interference**, **cue-dependent forgetting** and **repression**.

Interference

The idea behind this theory is that memories may be interfered with either by what we have learned before, or by what we may learn in the future. Similarity is the main factor in forgetting. Forgetting increases with time because of interference from competing memories that have been acquired over time.

If you have ever sunburnt your left arm and put your watch on your right wrist for a few days, you are likely to glance at the wrong wrist on the first few occasions you try to tell the time. This is **proactive interference (PI)** – wearing your watch on the left wrist (old knowledge) has interfered with the new knowledge that your watch is actually on your right arm.

When the sunburn heals, you return your watch to the original left wrist. Now you have learned to look at your right wrist, and this new learning will interfere with the old knowledge of where to look for the time. This is **retroactive interference (RI)**.

Figure 8: proactive and retroactive interference
PI: learn A: learn B: interference from A affects recall of B
RI: learn A: learn B: interference from B affects recall of A

This theory is basically associationist. In the example of the watch, the stimulus of wondering 'What time is it?' is associated with the response of looking at your wrist. Interference comes from the very similar responses of looking at your right or left wrist.

McGeoch and Macdonald (1931) found that for participants learning a word list, forgetting was greatest when a subsequent interference task was similar to what had been learned originally. There was little effect on recall from interference when the subsequent task involved unrelated material, but more when it involved antonyms of the original list. Most forgetting occurred when the interference task involved synonyms of the original list.

One problem with this theory, though, is that it doesn't apply very widely to everyday forgetting. As Baddeley has pointed out, PI in particular has been very hard to establish outside the laboratory.

There is some disagreement as to whether interference should be thought of as lack of accessibility or lack of availability. There is some evidence, however, that interference is due to lack of accessibility:

Box M: Tulving (1962)
Procedure: Participants were given a list of words to remember. Recall was tested on three different trials.   **Results:** Participants recalled similar numbers of words on all three trials. What the

specific words were, however, varied from trial to trial. Only about half the words were remembered on all three trials.
Conclusion: Recalling words on later trials which had not been recalled on the first trial suggests that the initial lack of recall could not have been due to lack of availability. It is likely that different retrieval cues were used on each trial.

Cue-dependent forgetting

The term cue-dependent forgetting has been used by Tulving (1974). It refers to two related phenomena: **context-dependent forgetting** and **state-dependent forgetting**.

Research such as that by Abernathy (1940) has shown that it is much easier to remember something if you are in the same context in which you originally learnt it. For example, if you learn a set of A-level facts in a particular room over a long period of time, you would remember those facts significantly better if you were asked to recall the facts in that same room. This has obvious implications for examination technique – unfortunately, it is unlikely that you will be able to sit the exam in the room in which you learnt the material; nor is it practical for you to learn the material in the exam hall! What may help, however, is *imagining* the environment in which you learnt the information. Zechmeister and Nyberg (1982) showed that this can help recreate the conditions in which you learned the information.

An interesting study showing the effect of context is described in Box N:

Box N: Godden and Baddeley (1975)
Procedure: Diver participants learned a list of words either on land or underwater. Later, both groups were tested for their recall either on land or underwater.   **Results:** The divers who learned the words underwater recalled more accurately when tested underwater. The divers who learned the words on land recalled them more accurately when tested on land.   **Conclusion:** Recall is affected by external context.

You may have experienced how memory is related to context if you have ever visited a place where you once lived, or somewhere you regularly went on holiday as a child. Often such a visit helps people recall lots of facts and experiences about the times they spent there – facts that they did not realise were stored in their memory.

To explain why this effect occurs, it has been suggested that information about the environmental context is stored while you are learning. Using that context later on, when you are remembering the information, makes recall easier by providing you with **retrieval cues** which trigger memory for relevant information. Being able to remember something depends on having the information stored (i.e. it being available) *and* having an appropriate cue that brings it back into consciousness. This type of remembering is known as **cued recall**.

While external context has been shown to affect recall, it has also been found that you are much more likely to remember something if you are in the same **internal state** (physical or emotional) in which you learnt it. A good example of this is if you lose something while under the influence of alcohol. You may find it impossible to find the item when sober the following morning, but retrieve it quite easily the next time you drink. Similar results have been shown to be true for mood.

Goodwin *et al.* (1969) found that memory loss was greater for those participants who acquired information while under the influence of alcohol, and were then asked to recall when sober, than vice versa. This shows that physical state does indeed affect recall.

Memory can also be dependent on emotional state:

Box O: Bower *et al.* (1978)

Procedure: Participants were hypnotised, and imagined a happy or unhappy mood while learning information.

Results: Those participants who recalled in the same mood as that created during learning recalled better than those who recalled in a different mood.

Conclusion: The participants were affected by the internal context in which they learned the information.

Repression

Repression also emphasises the role of emotion in forgetting. Freud suggested that we forget because there is great anxiety associated with certain memories, and the psychological pain of recall would be too great to cope with. When this is the case we may use the unconscious defence mechanism of repression to push such memories out of consciousness. The memories continue to exist, but in the unconscious mind. For example, memories of being abused as a child may be too disturbing for a person to cope with, and may be outside conscious recall.

Part of psychoanalytic therapy involves bringing such repressed memories into consciousness. Memories retrieved during therapy are known as **recovered memories**. However, such memories are reconstructed, often long after the event, and so are not always reliable. This has given rise to the concept of **false memory syndrome**. People sometimes 'recall' traumatic childhood abuse, usually with the help of their therapist, which their families claim could not have happened. Loftus (1994) described the case of a woman who 'remembered' during therapy having been involved in a Satanic cult, having sex with animals and watching an eight-year-old friend being murdered. When she left therapy, she realised that these memories were fantasies brought about during therapy.

However, memories accessed during therapy *may* indeed be recovered memories despite the obvious problems in deciding what is true about events many years in the past.

In addition, you will remember that research on **flashbulb memory** found that people have clear memories of events which they found traumatic, and remember in some detail the circumstances in which they became aware of these events. This suggests that high emotional distinctiveness of an event leads to a better ability to recall it, in contrast to Freud's suggestion that if an experience is traumatic, it will be repressed.

Unavailability

Not everybody agrees with Penfield's idea that memories are available but not accessible. In particular, only a small percentage of Penfield's stimulation triggered vivid memories, and it has been suggested that many of the 'memories' were merely fantasies (a bit like dreams) resulting from the stimulation. If this is the case, then forgetting must be due to **unavailability** – because the memory is no longer stored. Theories of forgetting based on the idea that memories are unavailable include **displacement**, **trace decay** and **brain damage**.

Displacement

It has been suggested that forgetting in STM is due to **displacement**. Displacement refers to the limited number of slots in STM – 7±2. When more items are introduced into STM than there are slots, some of the old information must be knocked out of its slot, or 'displaced'. It also follows that this would lead to forgetting: as you put a new piece of information into your STM, the displaced piece of information is lost. This suggests that information in STM must be processed if it is to be retained in LTM.

Evidence for displacement comes from the **Brown-Petersen technique** discussed earlier, where participants were asked to recall trigrams, but

after presentation were asked to count backwards in threes to prevent rehearsal. If this technique is used when participants are asked to learn a list of words, such as that in Activity 4, the recency effect (see Figure 3) is lost. The last few items on the list are displaced from STM by the counting task.

Trace decay

Peterson and Peterson (1959) suggested that forgetting in STM is due to **trace decay**. Learning something creates a memory trace or **engram**, which gradually fades. Rehearsal prevents forgetting because it replenishes the trace before it decays completely. A similar explanation may also explain why some information in LTM is lost.

In a study by Shallice (1967), participants were presented with numbers at different speeds. Forgetting was less when the numbers were presented more rapidly, which suggests that time is a factor, and so supports the idea of **trace decay**. However, what was even more important than speed of presentation was how many numbers followed the ones to be recalled, suggesting that **displacement** is also important.

Brain damage

Sometimes memories may become unavailable because of **brain damage**. Brain damage can cause either **retrograde amnesia** (i.e. loss of memory from the period before the brain damage) or **anterograde amnesia** (i.e. loss of memory for new information after brain damage). Retrograde amnesia can result from electro-convulsive therapy or **ECT**, where a brief electric shock is passed through the brain, which is sometimes used as a therapy for severe depression. Patients often cannot recall what happened immediately before treatment. The **Korsakov syndrome**, which is the result of advanced alcoholism, mentioned earlier in relation to the STM/LTM distinction, is an example of anterograde amnesia, as is the case of HM (see Box F). Changes which occur in the brain as the result of ageing can also lead to amnesia.

Post-traumatic amnesia often follows a blow to the head; for example, as the result of a fall. The person may have retrograde amnesia and often cannot remember what happened immediately before the blow. Yarnell and Lynch (1973) investigated this phenomenon by asking footballers who had been concussed during play what strategy their team had been using immediately before the incident. The footballers could answer this question if asked straight away, but had forgotten if asked twenty minutes later. This suggests that a period of **consolidation** is necessary for something to be remembered.

In contrast, a study by Sacks (1985) showed that brain damage can also lead to remembering rather than forgetting. He described an elderly woman who suffered a mild thrombosis in one of the temporal lobes of her brain, after which she remembered Irish songs which her mother had sung to her when she was a child in Ireland. Unfortunately, as she recovered, these memories also disappeared.

- Information is forgotten because it is not **available** or not **accessible**.
- Theories relating to lack of **accessibility** include **interference**, **cue-dependent forgetting** and **repression**.
- **Interference** theory suggests that similarity between competing memories can result in forgetting.
- **Cue-dependent forgetting** can be divided into state-dependent and context-dependent forgetting. This theory suggests that we cannot recall information without the use of **retrieval cues**.
- Freud believed that forgetting of painful memories may be due to the defence mechanism of **repression**.
- Theories relating to lack of availability include **displacement**, **trace decay** and **brain damage**.

2.5 RECONSTRUCTIVE MEMORY

Bartlett (1932), argued that memory is affected by the store of relevant prior knowledge we have, and not just by what information is presented. He regarded memories not just as reproductions of information but as reconstructions influenced by prior knowledge.

Activity 10: Bartlett's War of the Ghosts (1932)

Read this story, which is the native American story Bartlett used in his research:

One night two young men from Egulac went down to the river to hunt seals, and while they were there it became foggy and calm. Then they heard war-cries and they thought: 'Maybe this is a war-party'. They escaped to the shore and hid behind a log. Now canoes came up, and they heard the noise of paddles, and saw one canoe coming up to them. There were five men in the canoe, and they said: 'What do you think? We wish to take you along. We are going up the river to make war on the people.' One of the young men said: 'I have no arrows'. 'Arrows are in the canoe,' they said. 'I will not go along. I might be killed. My relatives do not know where I have gone. But you,' he said, turning to the other, 'may go with them.' So one of the young men went, but the other returned home. And the warriors went on up the river to a town on the other side of Kalama. The people came down to the water, and they began to fight, and many were killed. But presently the young man heard one of the warriors say: 'Quick, let us go home: that Indian has been hit.' Now he thought: 'Oh, they are ghosts.' He did not feel sick, but they said he had been shot. So the canoes went back to Egulac, and the young man went ashore to his house, and made a fire. And he told everybody and said: 'Behold I accompanied the ghosts, and we went to fight. Many of our fellows were killed, and many of those who attacked us were killed. They said I was hit, and I did not feel sick.' He told it all, and then he became quiet. When the sun rose he fell down. Something black came out of his mouth. His face became contorted. The people jumped up and cried. He was dead.

Now cover up the story and write down as much of it as you can remember.

Bartlett's studies showed that a number of changes occurred to the story as it was recalled by his participants. He found that typically people gave shorter, more simplified versions of the story. You may also have found as you recalled the story that some of your errors made the story sound more like a standard English one, and less like a native American story. For example, you might have written down 'boat' instead of 'canoe'; or said that the man went 'home' rather than 'ashore to his house'. Sometimes new information is introduced to make the story more logical by our standards. For example, some of Bartlett's participants introduced a reason for the fighting, or reproduced 'something black came out of his mouth' as 'blood came out of his mouth'.

This type of reconstruction Bartlett termed **rationalisation**. Such distortions are used to make sense of unfamiliar things. But the most important thing was that the central ideas of the story were not really changed at all. Bartlett suggested that what happens is that people store a few main facts about the story and then **reconstruct** it from those facts. This act of reconstruction Bartlett referred to as **effort after meaning**.

Mr Benson tripped in the refreshment tent and broke his ankle

Old Benson went over in the beer tent and his leg's in plaster

shame

Young Benson was falling about plastered in the bar and now his leg will be in plaster for weeks

Can't hold their beer those lads

Even memories which seem very clear can sometimes be inaccurate. You will remember that earlier in this chapter we discussed **flashbulb** memories, very vivid memories of surprising and emotionally-charged events. Brown and Kulik (1977) believed flashbulb memories to be both long-lasting and very accurate, but there is some evidence that even these memories may become distorted over time. One person interviewed by Linton (1979) gave a vivid account of studying in her college library when told about the Kennedy assassination by a friend. The friend, however, was actually at a different college in a different state at the time. Similar inaccuracies were reported by McCloskey *et al.* (1988) in their study of people's memories of the explosion of the space shuttle Challenger. They also found changes in what people remembered of the event over time, suggesting that their memories were in part a reconstruction.

Bartlett's notion of reconstruction in memory can be linked to **schemas**. A schema is a way of summarising events which enables us to predict what is likely to happen in various situations. Bartlett defined a schema as 'an active organisation of past reactions, or past experiences'. A schema provides the background knowledge that enables us to understand a situation, since we can predict what is likely to happen. For example, if you were asked to say what your schema of 'getting on the bus' involved you would probably include:

> getting on the bus; stating your destination; paying the fare; thanking the driver; finding an empty seat and sitting down.

Schema theory, then, gives us a way of looking at how information is organised in memory: new information is related to what we already know. But while schemas are useful in helping us to organise information, at the same time our reliance on them may lead to distortion of what we remember.

Most memories are at least in part reconstructions. If asked to remember what you were doing three Tuesdays ago at 2 pm, you could probably make an educated guess and might even be correct – but what you remember will in all likelihood be more of a reconstruction of what sort of thing you usually do on Tuesdays rather than an accurate memory of the day in question. This has been shown experimentally:

Box P: Brewer and Treyins (1981)

Procedure: Thirty participants were asked individually to wait in an office while the experimenter supposedly checked the laboratory to see if the previous participant had finished. After 35 seconds, he returned and asked them to go into another room where they were asked to recall everything in the waiting room.

Results: People tended to recall items consistent with an 'office schema'. Nearly everyone recalled the desk and chair, but only eight people recalled the skull, while just one recalled the picnic basket. However, nine people 'recalled' books, which had not been there.

Conclusion: Schemas can produce distorted recall, with items consistent with the schema being incorrectly recalled, and inconsistent items forgotten.

Reconstructive memory can also be affected by stereotypes, leading to distorted memories:

Box Q: Buckhout (1974)

Procedure: Participants were shown a series of counter-stereotypical pictures, each for a very short time. One picture, for example, set in a subway, showed a scruffily dressed white man, holding a razor, threatening a well-dressed black man. It was assumed in this instance that many white people would have a stereotype of black people as having criminal tendencies.

Results: Approximately half the participants remembered the black man as holding the razor.

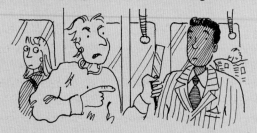

Conclusion: Memory can be distorted by the stereotypes we hold.

Another study tested this idea more naturalistically:

Box R: Duncan (1976)

Procedure: Participants were shown a video of two men having a discussion. They were told it was a live event shown over closed circuit TV. At one point, the discussion became heated, and one man gave the other a shove. At this point the video stopped. Participants were asked to classify the shove, choosing from 'playing around', 'dramatising', 'aggressive behaviour' and 'violent behaviour'. There were several versions of the video, varying the race of the actors.

Results: When the shove was given by a black man, participants were more likely to classify it as 'violent behaviour' than when it was given by a white man. This was particularly true when a black man shoved a white man.

Conclusion: Classification was affected by racial stereotypes. Behaviour is interpreted in line with the stereotypes we hold.

The distortion of recall shown by Duncan's participants could have far-reaching consequences in some contexts. If you forget to buy spaghetti from the supermarket, it is unlikely to be too tragic an event. But in the area of **eye-witness testimony**, where people give evidence in court cases, the accurate recall of events can mean someone's imprisonment or freedom. In the next section we will look at factors which affect the reliability of eye-witness testimony.

- A **schema** is a summary of what happens in a certain situation. Schemas simplify the processing of new information.
- Bartlett used schema theory to suggest that memory is reconstruction. He saw the major determinant of human memory as **effort after meaning**.
- Schemas allow us to predict what is likely to happen in particular situations, but may make us inflexible when we come across something unexpected.
- Reconstructive memory can also be influenced by **stereotypes**.

2.6 CRITICAL ISSUE: EYE-WITNESS TESTIMONY (EWT)

Jurors seem to find eye-witness testimony amongst the most convincing evidence of all. The Devlin Report (1976), which was concerned with eye-witness testimony, found that in more than 300 cases, eyewitness identification was the *sole* evidence of guilt, yet the conviction rate was 74%.

Building on the idea of memory as reconstruction, a lot of research has been carried out, notably by Loftus and her associates, which demonstrates that memory can be affected by the wording of questions testing the memory of an experience. Her studies have shown that people's accounts of events that they have witnessed can be extremely unreliable. One part of a study is shown in Box S:

Box S: Loftus and Palmer (1974)

Procedure: One hundred and fifty participants were shown a film of an accident between two cars, and then asked to fill in a questionnaire about the accident. The important question involved the speed of the cars at the point of impact. The question was phrased differently for different groups of participants – some were asked 'How fast were the two cars going when they *hit* each other'; others were asked the same question but with *smashed, collided, bumped,* or *contacted* replacing the word 'hit'.
Results: The average speeds the participants gave in answer to the question are listed below.

verb used	speed given
hit	34mph
smashed	41mph
collided	39mph
bumped	38mph
contacted	32mph

Conclusion: The speed at which the participants thought the cars were going was affected by the verb used in the question. Recall can be distorted by the wording of a question.

As well as the choice of words, asking **leading questions** which imply that a certain answer is expected can significantly affect a person's testimony. Loftus and Zanni (1975) showed participants a film of a car accident. They found that more participants recalled (incorrectly) seeing a broken headlight if they were asked 'Did you see *the* broken headlight?' than 'Did you see *a* broken headlight?'.

Another part of Loftus and Palmer's study is relevant here:

Box T: Loftus and Palmer (1974)

Procedure: One hundred and fifty participants were shown a film of a car accident. The subsequent questionnaire asked a third of those participants 'How fast were the cars going when they *smashed* into each other?' A third was asked 'How fast were the cars going when they *hit* each other?' The final third (the control group) was not asked about the speed of the cars. One week later, the same people were all asked whether they had seen any broken glass in the film of the accident. (There had been no broken glass shown in the film.)
Results: Twelve per cent of the control group claimed to have seen broken glass in the film and 14% of those who had heard the word *hit* said they had seen broken glass. But 32% of the participants who had heard the word *smashed* remembered seeing broken glass.
Conclusion: The leading question asked a week previously affected the participants' recall. The people who heard the word *smashed* recoded the accident as being more serious than those who heard the word *hit*. This information was added to their earlier memory of the film, and changed it.

So it is clear that leading questions not only affect recall of material, but can actually change information that has previously been stored in memory – they can, in effect, make us **reconstruct** memories. It is argued that this may be what happens in **false memory syndrome**, discussed earlier in the section on **repression**.

At the same time, however, it is less easy to mislead witnesses about something which is central to what they have witnessed than something which is more peripheral. Loftus (1979) found that 98% of people who had watched colour slides of a man stealing a red purse from a woman's bag correctly remembered it as red, even when it was implied that it was brown.

We will look now at research into factors affecting the accuracy of eye-witness testimony in terms of the three processes involved in memory: registration, storage and retrieval.

Registration

Factors which influence people's initial perception of an incident can be categorised as **witness factors** – characteristics of the witness – and **event factors** – factors to do with the situation.

Witness factors

Age can play a part in the accuracy of recall. Several studies (e.g. Dent, 1988) have shown that children typically give fewer details about an event they have witnessed than adults. Similarly, List (1986) found that older people may also recall less than younger people. In terms of responding to misleading information, as in the Loftus studies described in the previous section, Ceci *et al.* (1987) found that children were more likely to be misled than adults, and Loftus *et al.* (1991) found the same to be true of older people, particularly males.

The levels of **stress** experienced when witnessing a crime can also affect accuracy of recall. This relationship can be shown by the Yerkes-Dodson Law (see chapter 4, Figure 1).

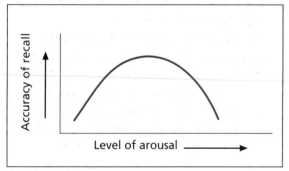

The Yerkes-Dodson Law applied to recall

This law suggests that at very low levels of arousal (i.e. low levels of stress), performance is poor. It improves with moderate levels of arousal, and then falls off again when stress is further increased. The law has been supported by research:

Box U: Peters (1988)

Procedure: People going to a clinic to receive inoculations met a nurse who gave them the injection and another person (the researcher). They were exposed to each person for equal periods of time. They were later asked to identify the nurse and the researcher from a set of photographs.

Results: Participants were significantly better at identifying the researcher than the nurse.

Conclusion: The stress of having an injection, associated with the nurse who gave it, led to comparatively poor memory when asked to pick out her photograph.

However, stress does not always have this effect:

Box V: Yuille and Cutshall (1986)

Procedure: Thirteen people who witnessed an armed robbery in Canada gave evidence to the police. They then agreed to take part in interviews with psychologists between four and five months after witnessing the robbery. During that later interview, participants were asked two misleading questions.

Results: Being asked two misleading questions did not affect the participants' recall four months after the event. There were few, if any, facts recalled by the participants that had been made up or reconstructed. There was no relationship between the levels of stress reported at the time of the crime and accuracy of recall.

Conclusion: In real-life situations, recall is not necessarily inaccurate, or susceptible to misleading questions. The level of stress experienced is not related to accuracy of recall.

This study shows that EWT of events occurring in a real-life situation is not necessarily as inaccurate as laboratory studies might lead us to expect. This is a good example of a study with high **ecological**

validity: it was carried out on people who had witnessed a genuine armed robbery, and not merely watched a video of such an event, and therefore is more convincing as a piece of research.

However, one problem with this study is that those witnesses who experienced more stress were closer to what was going on. It is possible that the higher level of stress they experienced was counteracted by having better access to information, thus improving their recall of the event.

Expectations can also influence the registration of information. In the previous section, the influence of people's beliefs and expectations was shown by the studies in Box Q and Box R.

Event factors

One important factor here is **exposure time**, i.e. the length of time for which a witness is exposed to an event. It was shown as long ago as 1885, in a study by Ebbinghaus, that the longer we are exposed to something, the better our perception of it is. However, people are often very poor at estimating exposure time:

Box W: Loftus et al. (1987a)

Procedure: Participants were shown a 30-second video of a simulated bank robbery and asked to estimate how long it had lasted.
Results: On average, the robbery was estimated to have lasted two and a half minutes. Very few participants correctly estimated the time, or underestimated it.
Conclusion: People tend to overestimate the length of time of an event which they have witnessed.

Activity 11: overestimation of time

Why might this tendency to overestimate time be important in a legal context?
When you have finished, see page 50.

A further event factor is what is known as **detail salience**. In an armed robbery, for instance, the presence of a gun may be a salient feature for witnesses. They may focus on the gun and so have their attention distracted from other important features of the situation, such as the characteristics of the robbers. This is known as **weapon focus**, and has been shown experimentally:

Box X: Loftus et al. (1987b)

Procedure: Participants were shown one of two versions of a restaurant scene on video. In one version, a man pointed a gun at the cashier and she gave him money. In the other version, he gave her a cheque, and she gave him money. The eye movements of participants were monitored, and their recall for the event tested.
Results: Participants in the 'weapon' version fixated more on the gun than those seeing the 'non-weapon' version. Their recall for other details was also poorer, and they were less able to identify the man from a set of photographs.
Conclusion: A salient detail can focus attention, and so lead to poorer recall for other details of the event.

The violence of the event witnessed can also affect recall:

Box Y: Loftus and Burns (1982)

Procedure: Participants were shown one of two versions of a simulated armed robbery on video. One version included a scene of a boy being shot in the face while the robbers were making their getaway.
Results: Recall of details of the event was much higher for participants who had seen the 'non-violent' version of the event. Those who had seen the 'violent' version had less accurate and less complete recall, not only for events immediately before the shooting, but also for events up to 2 minutes earlier.
Conclusion: The shock associated with the 'violent' event disrupted the processing of information into memory, and its consolidation.

● Eye-witness memory for details of an event can be affected at the **registration** stage by **witness factors** and **event factors**.

● **Witness factors** include age, stress and expectations.

● **Event factors** include detail salience, in particular weapon focus, and the violence of the event.

Storage

Information is lost with the passage of time, which can be explained by the **trace decay** theory of forgetting, covered in an earlier section. As with the influence of exposure time on memory, this too was demonstrated by Ebbinghaus (1885). It has also been shown in a naturalistic study of long-term forgetting:

Box Z: Wagenaar and Groeneweg (1990)

Procedure: Seventy-eight survivors of Camp Erika (a second world war Dutch concentration camp) were interviewed between 1984 and 1987 about their camp experiences. The information they gave was compared with earlier evidence they had given just after the end of the war.

Results: There was general agreement in the later interviews on basic information. All but three of 38 people who had been tortured by the camp commandant, for example, remembered his name. However, much of the detail had been lost. The names of guards, for instance, given at the earlier interviews, were largely forgotten.

Conclusion: While basic information may be well remembered over time, details tend to be lost.

The studies by Loftus and Palmer, described in Box S and Box T, have shown that memory can also be distorted once it has been stored; memories of an event can be reconstructed as a result of the way in which questions are asked, i.e. depending on the choice of words and the use of leading questions.

Studies (e.g. Bekerian and Bowers, 1983) have also shown that mentioning details of an event to a witness after they have witnessed it can lead to

these details being 'recalled' later; new information has been incorporated into what is remembered. Sometimes this effect is only partial:

Box AA: Loftus (1975)

Procedure: Participants were shown a 3-minute video of a lecture being disrupted by eight demonstrators. They were later given a 20-item questionnaire. For some participants, this included the question: 'Was the leader of the 12 demonstrators a male?' For the others the question was: ' Was the leader of the 4 demonstrators a male?' A week later, they were asked how many demonstrators there had been.

Results: Those who had earlier been given the '12 demonstrators' question reported on average that there had been 8.9 demonstrators; those who had been given the '4 demonstrators' question reported on average that there had been 6.4 demonstrators.

Conclusion: Participants' memory had been distorted by the misleading information they had been given. Most participants compromised between the actual number of demonstrators they had seen and the misleading number.

However, as shown in the study carried out by Loftus (1979), described below Box T, this is less likely to happen when people are asked about something which is central to the event they have witnessed.

It has also been argued by McCloskey and Zaragoza (1985) that the influence of misleading information – the **misinformation effect** – has little to do with memory impairment, but more to do with two sources of bias in the testing procedure. The first of these they call **misinformation acceptance**. They suggest that one reason that participants can be misled is that they have failed to register relevant information when witnessing an event, and this is why they accept misleading information as being accurate. The second source of bias is **demand characteristics**, i.e. features of the testing situation which may lead participants to (mis)interpret the task. In this case, participants might accept the misinformation as accurate because it was provided by the researcher, or because they wanted to 'do well' on the test.

- Storage factors can affect recall. Basic information is often retained, but detailed information is lost over time.
- Memory can be **supplemented** by later information. It can be **distorted** by misleading information, known as the **misinformation effect**. This can also lead to completely **inaccurate information** being given.
- The misinformation effect has been challenged in terms of whether it is the result of **memory impairment** or the effects of **bias** in the testing situation.

Retrieval

As we have seen, techniques to collect information may affect the detail and accuracy of EWT. This is of particular importance in the light of the work of Loftus and others, which suggests that the way in which questions are asked can distort memory. This has important implications for people like the police and solicitors, who have to consider the phrasing of their questions very carefully.

Recently, psychologists have begun to evaluate police interview techniques, and have found that British police officers have little formal training in the interviewing of witnesses, and that they are often unaware of the shortcomings in their interview technique.

Officers typically aim to elicit descriptions of gender, height, age, dress, and so on. They ask for information which seems immediately useful, rather than accessing information which may be useful later on. Standard police interviewing techniques may not be the best way to get the maximum amount of useful information from the witness.

It is widely believed that **hypnosis** may be a way of improving recall, but this is somewhat controversial. A comprehensive review of hypnosis research led Orne *et al.* (1984) to claim that testimony produced under hypnosis was not reliable, and that it should not be accepted unless it was confirmed by independent evidence. People who have been hypnotised are very susceptible to suggestions made by the interviewer, and for this reason alone, testimony produced under hypnosis needs to be treated with caution.

However, a technique called the **cognitive interview** has been developed as a way of trying to ensure that police interviews are carried out in such a way as to get maximum accurate recall from witnesses. This technique is now widely used by police forces in the UK and the USA.

The cognitive interview

Geiselman *et al* (1984) developed a procedure called the **basic cognitive interview**, based on two principles of memory research: firstly, that there may be a number of retrieval paths to a memory, and that a memory may be accessible if a different retrieval cue is used; secondly, that a memory trace is made up of several features and the effectiveness of a retrieval cue depends on how much of it overlaps with the memory trace.

From these principles, a **memory retrieval procedure** was derived. Incorporating all these ideas reflects the common view of memory as a complex group of features. It may remind you of research you read earlier in the chapter on what affects the accuracy of remembering:

Figure 9: the basic cognitive interview

This technique involves:
- an eye-witness mentally reinstating the environmental and personal context of the crime. This includes reporting what was going on at the time, both in terms of the event witnessed and the witness's own thoughts and feelings
- the eye-witness being asked to report everything they can recall about the event, regardless of how unimportant it might seem
- encouraging an eye-witness to recount what happened in a variety of orders
- asking them to report from a variety of perspectives and points of view

Witness being encouraged to recall every detail

▷ Activity 12: linking the cognitive interview to memory research

Look back at the previous sections in this chapter. Can you make links between some of this material and the principles of the cognitive interview? When you have finished, see page 50.

The cognitive interview can also be linked with the **spreading activation model** of organisation in memory, proposed by Collins and Loftus (1975). This suggests that concepts in LTM are interlinked. Closely related concepts have short links between them, and links that are often used become stronger (shown as thicker lines in Figure 10) than links that are rarely used. When one concept is activated, this activation spreads out to related concepts, so activating the word 'robin' would also activate the related concepts of 'red', 'bird' and 'Christmas'. In turn, these could lead on to apparently unrelated concepts.

This model suggests that there is a complex interrelationship of links in memory, so asking a witness to recall information in different orders and from different perspectives increases the probability of a seemingly irrelevant piece of information triggering off something which may be useful.

When the basic cognitive interview was used, Fisher *et al.* (1987a) found it to be significantly superior to the standard police interview, in terms of the amount of information accurately recalled. Geiselman *et al.* (1986) found that this technique also seemed to strengthen resistance of witnesses to misleading information.

The technique has now been refined further through an analysis of real, taped police interviews, which has the advantage of high **ecological validity**. On the basis of this research Fisher *et al.* (1987b) recommended additional techniques for interviewing eye-witnesses. This is known as the **enhanced cognitive interview** technique.

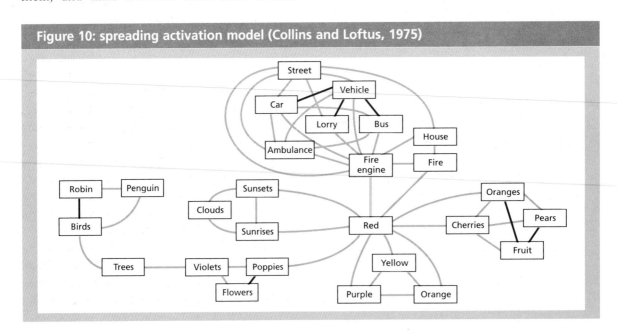

Figure 10: spreading activation model (Collins and Loftus, 1975)

Figure 11: enhanced cognitive interview

This technique includes:
- minimising distractions
- getting the eye-witness to speak slowly
- tailoring language to suit the individual eye-witness
- reducing anxiety
- avoiding judgmental and personal comments

Let me take you back to the previous incident

Tailoring language to suit the individual

All these techniques are designed to help the witness to focus on the task and to reduce anxiety. Fisher *et al.* (1990) found that these techniques elicited 45% more correct statements than even the basic cognitive interview. A field test with detectives of the Police Department in Miami showed that detectives trained in this enhanced cognitive interview technique collected 63% more information than a control group of untrained detectives. Wilkinson (1988) found that such techniques could raise the EWT of children to adult level.

The cognitive interview seems to be a way that really can make a difference both to the amount of potentially useful information obtained from witnesses, and to the accuracy of that information.

- **Hypnosis** as a way of improving recall is controversial.
- The **cognitive interview** has shown itself to be an effective way of increasing the completeness and accuracy of EWT.
- The **enhanced cognitive interview** can produce even more relevant information.

Face recognition

An important aspect of EWT can be identifying people suspected of carrying out a crime, so we will turn now to the topic of face recognition.

Having a memory for faces, which enables us to recognise other people, is of great significance in our lives. You can imagine how difficult life would be if you didn't recognise your mother, brother, best friend or partner. Human beings seem to have an amazing ability to recognise faces. Standing (1973) showed participants 10,000 faces over 5 days. When they were shown pairs of faces, one of which they had previously been shown, together with a new one, they were able to identify the face they had seen 98% of the time. This ability is also impressive when people are asked to identify faces which they have not seen for some time:

Box BB: Bahrick *et al.* (1975)

Procedure: Fifteen years after their graduation, participants were shown five pictures from year books. One picture of the five was a person with whom they had graduated from high school.
Results: The participants were accurate in identifying 90% of their classmates. It was found that even those participants who had graduated more than 40 years previously could identify 75% of their classmates correctly.
Conclusion: People have a well-developed ability to recognise faces.

Just as psychologists have learned a lot about memory from clinical cases of patients with disorders such as amnesia or the Korsakov syndrome, so they have learned about the processes of face recognition from people suffering from **prosopagnosia**. People with this disorder can't recognise the faces of people they know well – sometimes they cannot even recognise their own face in a mirror. They can, however, recognise friends and family from their voices, so the problem is not due to people having been forgotten.

There are two types of theory that try to explain this disorder. One suggests that it takes more precise discrimination to tell the difference between two faces than it does to tell the difference between a book and a pencil, for example, so failure to discriminate faces may lie in the lack of the ability to make this kind of fine distinction. The other type of theory suggests that there are specific processes that are needed if we are to recognise a face, and that these are lacking in prosopagnosics.

The idea that an inability to recognise faces is due to a lack of fine discrimination is not widely accepted. De Renzi (1986) worked with a prosopagnosic man who could make very good fine discrimination between different people's handwriting, for example, and between Italian coins, but could not recognise relatives' and friends' faces. Similarly, McNeil and Warrington (1991) reported the case of a farmer with prosopagnosia, who was nonetheless able to identify each of his 36 sheep without hesitation. It therefore does not seem likely that prosopagnosia is due to an inability to make fine discriminations.

The alternative theory, relating to processes specific to face recognition, is more likely. It is supported by the finding that there are areas of the brain which deal specifically with face recognition. Hay and Young (1982) suggested that familiar faces are stored in the brain in neural circuits known as **Face Recognition Units (FRUs)**. When we see a face, we scan our FRUs for a match, to decide whether or not the face is familiar. If a match is found, we can then access information about the person, such as their job and biographical information, which in turn may generate their name.

Ellis *et al.* (1979) investigated what information is most important when recognising familiar and unfamiliar faces. They found that recognition of unfamiliar faces depends more on external features,

such as the shape of the face and the hairline. For familiar faces, internal features are more important. According to Roberts and Bruce (1988), the area round the eyes is the most important, while the area round the nose is of least importance.

While people are usually extremely good at recognising faces, especially familiar faces, Shapiro and Penrod (1986) found that in eyewitness identification, people show inferior recall compared with traditional studies of face recognition. One reason for this may be that, unlike laboratory studies, the circumstances in which a face is first seen and when identification needs to be made may be quite different.

Quite often an identification may need to be made from footage supplied by security cameras:

▷ Activity 13: identification of faces from video

video picture

The man in the CCTV picture?

Are these pictures of the same man or of different people? How sure are you? Why is it difficult to make a judgment using this kind of material? Why might it be easier if the images were of someone you knew?

When you have finished, see page 50.

Other characteristics of face recognition also make identification problematic. Shepherd *et al* (1974), for instance, found that people have more difficulty in recognising faces of people from another race. Older people also have more difficulty than younger people in recognising faces they have only seen once (Farramond, 1968).

In many cases, people need to describe to the police the faces of people whom they have seen carrying out a crime. For many years, police forces have been using aids to help witnesses, one of the earliest of which was the **PhotoFIT** system, developed by Penry (1971). This consisted of sets of photographed features – hair, eyes, nose, mouth and chin – from which the witness could select elements to build a representation of the face they had seen. This system could produce a general likeness, but was found to be poor in terms of creating a close likeness.

More recently, **E-FIT** (Electronic Facial Identification Technique) has been developed, using computer graphics. Again, faces are built from a library of features, selected on the basis of a verbal description by the witness. As well as giving a picture which is of similar quality to a photograph, this system has the advantage of being much more flexible in terms of the modifications which are possible.

Sergent (1984) has shown that configural information, i.e. the way in which different facial features relate to each other, is important in the representation of faces in memory. The E-FIT system takes this into account, in that it allows very subtle adjustments to be made to the configuration of features making up the face.

A system called **FRAME** (Facial Retrieval And Matching Equipment), described by Shepherd (1986), uses verbal descriptions of faces given by witnesses to retrieve possible matches from mugshots. The advantage of this system is that it uses the information which witnesses can give, while making use of our well-developed capacity to recognise faces. It also saves witnesses the time-consuming task of searching through albums of mugshots. Its effectiveness has been tested experimentally:

> **Box CC: Ellis *et al.* (1989)**
>
> **Procedure:** Each participant saw a target face for 10 seconds, which they were later asked to identify. Using a database of 1000 male faces, a comparison was made between the effectiveness of the FRAME system and a mugshot album search.
>
> **Results:** The FRAME system produced 69% correct matches, compared to only 44% for the album search. There was also a much higher percentage of false alarms when mugshot albums were used.
>
> **Conclusion:** The use of verbal descriptions together with mugshot albums is more effective in leading to face recognition than the use of mugshot albums alone.

- EWT can require witnesses to identify people whom they have seen committing a crime. While people are in general very good at face recognition, particularly of familiar faces, they tend to be less good at eyewitness identification.
- Several systems have been developed to aid this process. FRAME, which combines verbal descriptions with possible matches from a database of mugshots, has a high success rate.

Notes on activities are on page 50.

Notes on activities

1. Testing only one person is not really the best way to establish the general rules of psychological functioning. It is impossible to generalise to the rest of the population, as you can't guarantee that one person is representative of everyone.

   It is also possible that experimenters carrying out research on themselves might be tempted to influence the results to fit their expectations, or do so unconsciously.

   The research also has **low ecological validity** – it is arguable whether nonsense syllables adequately represent the richness of information we hold in our memories. It is not something we generally spend time doing! Using nonsense syllables does, however, ensure that the material is not distinctive, and hence avoids the problem that some information may be more memorable to some participants than others.

5. The shape of the curve implies that the first few words on the list are recalled well because they have been stored in LTM, whereas the last few words are recalled from STM. The first few words go into LTM because time has elapsed and they have been processed semantically, whereas the last few words have not had time to be transferred into LTM so are still in STM. The shape of the graph therefore gives evidence for the fact that we have two distinct stores in memory, as Atkinson and Shiffrin suggested. This should also remind you of Ebbinghaus' explanation of forgetting which you read about earlier in this chapter (Box A).

11: How long events lasted can be crucial in a criminal trial. When people overestimate the length of time they were exposed to an event, they create the impression that they had longer to look at something than they actually did, and this may falsely increase their credibility as witnesses.

12: Many of the ideas of the cognitive interview are based on **cue-dependent forgetting**. Talking about how the witness and other people present at the time might have felt is linked to state-dependent forgetting, so that reinstating the emotional state will provide cues which may trigger off additional information. Mentally reinstating the context may have a similar effect.

13. Burton *et al.* (1999) found that people had great difficulty in making the kind of identification required in Activity 18. The video images are of poor quality, and there are differences in the lighting of the pictures and the angle at which the faces are seen. However, people do not find the task is so difficult if the person is known to them, presumably because they are familiar with what a known person looks like from different angles, and there may be additional information from the way in which the body moves.

Attachments in development

3.1 INVESTIGATING ATTACHMENT

Attachment can be defined as a strong emotional bond with another person; in babies attachment to their mother or major carer is particularly evident. They become distressed when their mother leaves the room and are often unwilling to be comforted by someone else. They seek her out when they are stressed, and are generally oriented towards her: looking at her, moving to stay close to her and making sounds directed at her.

Schaffer and Emerson (1964) described the stages of attachment which take place during the first 18 months of a child's life. They used two measures of attachment. The first was **fear of strangers**, the response of an infant to the arrival of a stranger, whether or not the mother is there. The second was **separation anxiety**, the amount of distress shown by a child when separated from the mother, and the degree of comfort and happiness shown when they are reunited. They found that attachment could be described in terms of three stages (Figure 1).

There is, however, a lot of individual variation in the development of attachment. For example, Schaffer and Emerson found that the second stage of specific attachment could start at any time between six months and a year, and was not necessarily formed with the mother. There was also variation in the number of multiple attachments formed, and when they were formed (see Box A).

Figure 1: stages of attachment (Schaffer and Emerson, 1964)		
stage	**approximate age range**	**characteristics**
indiscriminate attachment	up to about 6 months	It does not matter who is holding the baby. The baby smiles at anyone, and protests when put down, whoever is holding them.
specific attachment	from about 7 months to a year	One specific attachment, usually to the mother. Fear of strangers and separation anxiety are intense for 3-4 months.
multiple attachments	from about one year onwards	Shows attachment to one other person, then to a number of other people important in their life.

Box A: Schaffer and Emerson (1964)

Procedure: Sixty babies were observed during monthly visits to the family home during the child's first year, and a follow-up visit was made at 18 months. Patterns of attachment were noted. Mothers were interviewed about how the babies behaved with people they were brought into contact with.

Results: In the first six weeks, babies showed no preference for a particular person. During the first six months, they became more sociable towards anyone who wanted to interact with them. By seven months, nearly a third had formed several attachments; 10% had 5 attachments by this time. Most, however, showed a preference for their major carer at seven months, and were wary of strangers. By ten months, however, nearly 60% had more than one attachment, rising to 87% at 18 months. Only a half were mainly attached to their mothers, with a third showing a preference for their fathers. Others had formed a major attachment to a grandparent, or to a brother or sister.

Conclusion: While there was a general pattern of attachment development, there was wide individual variation.

The **indiscriminate attachment** phase is a period of preparation for the intense carer-child relationship which follows. During this time, the infant's experience of responding to others establishes a pattern which later will be directed away from numerous people to focus on just one person. As we shall see, the **specific attachment** phase may set a pattern for future relationships. It also provides the child with emotional security, a secure base from which to explore and to which they can return for emotional support. Attachments formed when the child enters the **multiple attachment** phase are usually less intense than the one formed during the specific attachment phase.

This pattern of the development of attachment behaviours has also been found in cross-cultural studies. For example, Figure 2 shows a similarity in the development of separation anxiety in four very different cultures:

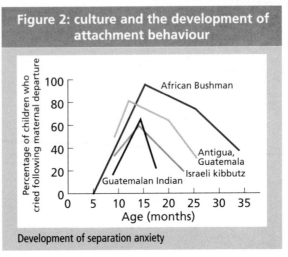

Figure 2: culture and the development of attachment behaviour

Development of separation anxiety

Bowlby (1969) suggested that as a result of their experience of the stages of attachment, children develop an inner representation of the mother-child bond, which serves as an **internal working model** of the relationship they have with their primary carer. By this he meant a cognitive representation, or schema, based on day-to-day interactions with the carer. (See chapter 2 for a fuller account of schemas.) He believed that this internal working model persists, relatively unchanged, throughout life, and becomes a model or guide for all future close relationships.

The effects of attachment can be seen when infant and attachment figure are separated. In the 1950s and 1960s, mother and child were separated when either needed to spend time in hospital. Visiting was not encouraged, as it was thought likely to be too upsetting. Robertson and Robertson (1953) made a series of films to demonstrate the effect of this practice, which they believed caused unnecessary distress to young children. Their findings were brought together in a book, *Young Children in Hospital*. One example is given in Box B:

Box B: Robertson and Robertson (1953)

Procedure: John (17 months) spent time in a residential nursery while his mother was in hospital. His behaviour during this time was observed.

Results: For the first few days, John's response was one of protest. He tried to gain attention and form attachments with the nurses, but they had other demands on their time. He showed considerable distress. After a few days, John showed despair. He cried a lot, refused food and had difficulty sleeping. Finally he seemed to give up altogether. His behaviour showed detachment. He stopped trying to attract attention and showed little interest in other people. When his mother came to pick him up, he ignored her and wouldn't allow her to comfort him.

Conclusion: Children who have formed an attachment to a carer go through three stages when they experience separation: protest, despair and detachment.

This attachment of young babies, and what happens when there is a separation between a child and the main carer has been a major focus of interest to developmental psychologists.

Patterns of attachment

One major method of carrying out research investigating mother-infant attachment has been the use of the **Strange Situation** technique, developed by Ainsworth *et al.* (1978). This is described in Figure 3.

Using this technique, Ainsworth et al. identified three contrasting patterns of attachment (Types A, B and C). Further studies using this technique, e.g. Main and Solomon (1990), have added a fourth pattern (Type D). These are shown in Figure 4.

Figure 3: Strange Situation

(a) A mother and child in a playroom. The child is exploring a new environment

(b) A second female adult who is stranger to the child comes in and talks, first to the mother and then to the child

(c) The mother leaves the room at some point while the stranger is talking to the child

(d) The stranger interacts with the child

(e) The mother returns and the stranger leaves

(f) The mother leaves the room, so the child is alone

(g) The stranger returns to be with the child

(h) The mother returns to the room again

Each episode (a) – (h) lasts three minutes (or less if the child becomes distressed). A video measures the child's behaviour in terms of seeking, maintaining, avoiding, and resisting contact.

Figure 4: types of attachment

Type A: anxious-avoidant – the child ignores the mother when she returns, or mixes welcome with avoidance behaviour, such as turning away. The child treats the mother and the stranger in very similar ways.

Type B: secure – the child cries during separation from the mother, but is easily comforted when she returns. The child tries to stay close to the mother, and prefers her to the stranger.

Type C: anxious-ambivalent – the child is very upset when the mother leaves the room, but is not easily comforted when she returns. The child is angry and tries to avoid contact when she comes back, but this is combined with attempts to be close to her.

Type D: disorganised – the child seems dazed and confused, without any coherent way of dealing with separation and reunion.

Figure 5: cultural variation in the Strange Situation

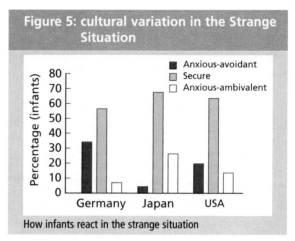

How infants react in the strange situation

Ainsworth found most children showed Type B behaviour. Types A, C and D all show insecure attachment. Typically, research using this classification method has found that approximately 20% of children show a Type A response, 70% Type B and 10% Type C. Type D behaviour is extremely rare and is associated with children who have been abused, or where there is parental pathology. However, cross-cultural research suggests that culture may be important in patterns of attachment and how they are shown. Van Ijzendoorn and Kroonenberg (1988) collected data from 32 studies using this technique, and in all the samples, secure attachment (Type B) was the most common response. However, they also found quite wide cultural variations. For example, in a Chinese sample only 50% showed secure attachment (Type B), and in a German sample, 35% showed anxious-avoidant behaviour (Type A). Takahashi (1990) found high proportion of anxious-ambivalent behaviour (Type C) in Japanese babies.

It seems improbable that babies in China, Germany and Japan are less likely to form secure attachments than the British babies studied by Ainsworth and others. A more convincing conclusion is that different patterns of mother-child relationships in different cultures can lead to a different pattern of responses to the Strange Situation. Takahashi (1990), for example, reports that Japanese infants are normally never left alone at this age, which could account for their extreme distress in the Strange Situation. When observed outside the Strange Situation, they did not appear to be insecurely attached. Similarly, according to Grossmann *et al.* (1985), German parents encourage their infants to be non-clingy and independent. The pattern of response of German children to the Strange Situation may therefore be the intended result of cultural beliefs and practices.

We therefore need to be aware that there may be a cultural bias in methods of assessing attachment such as the Strange Situation, and be careful of the conclusions we draw from this kind of research. There are common factors in the mother-child relationship across cultures which contribute to a secure attachment. At the same time, different cultures place different values on particular behaviours and characteristics, so there are likely to be wide cultural differences in the way these patterns are expressed.

Why is an infant–mother attachment formed?

Several theories have been put forward to provide an explanation of why the infant becomes attached to the mother.

An influential early theory was the **secondary drive hypothesis**, proposed by Dollard and Miller (1950). This theory, taking a behaviourist approach, suggested that attachment is a learned response. Feeding plays a central role in the infant–carer relationship. The baby's hunger is a **primary drive**, a motivational state arising from a basic physiological need. Since this need is repeatedly satisfied by the mother, her presence is associated with the satisfaction of this need, and so becomes a **secondary (or learned) drive**. The child is therefore motivated to seek the mother's presence and is distressed when she is not there.

More generally, **operant conditioning** suggests that if there is a positive outcome to a behaviour, it is likely to be repeated. Since the child is close to the mother during feeding, feeding positively reinforces attachment.

Feeding is also central to a **psychodynamic** explanation of attachment. You will remember from chapter 1 that for Freud, sucking provides oral gratification, so attachment behaviours are related to feeding.

There are some problems with theories which explain attachment in terms of feeding. You will remember from the Schaffer and Emerson study (Box A) that human infants can form a main attachment to family members who seldom if ever feed them. Feeding alone may therefore not be an adequate explanation. This has been demonstrated further in animal research:

Box C: Harlow and Zimmerman (1959)

Procedure: Rhesus monkeys were separated from their mothers shortly after birth. They were raised individually with two surrogate mothers.

These were models bearing some resemblance to adult monkeys, one consisting of a wire frame, and the other covered in soft cloth. Milk could be obtained through a teat on the wire mother. The monkeys were deliberately frightened by introducing into the cage a clockwork teddy bear, beating a drum.

Results: The infant monkeys showed their extreme distress in behaviours such as screaming, crouching, rocking and thumb-sucking. They spent most of their time clinging to the cloth 'mother', even though it did not give milk. They also clung to her when frightened by the teddy bear. They made no attempt, however, to cling to the wire mother.

Conclusion: Mothering is not only about the basic routine care involved in feeding. Primates also need a source of psychological warmth. What Harlow called the **contact comfort** provided by the cloth mother was important.

A rather more convincing theory has been put forward by Bowlby (1969). He proposed that the attachment of infants to their carers is the result of evolution, in that it is a behaviour which has developed because it is adaptive. The human infant is extremely helpless at birth, and could not survive without adult care. Behaviours which lead to the infant staying close to the mother mean that the baby is protected, and thus more likely to survive. Social behaviours such as smiling attract the mother to the baby, creating a relationship between mother and baby which will motivate the mother to care for the infant. We will look at Bowlby's work in more detail in the next section.

● An infant who is securely attached shows distress at separation from the mother, and seeks her out when stressed. Gazing, following and vocalising are examples of attachment behaviour.
● Attachment has been investigated using the **Strange Situation** technique developed by Ainsworth *et al*. They identified different kinds of attachment. Different patterns of attachment behaviour may be expressed in different cultures.
● Attachment has been explained as a learned behaviour related to **feeding**. More convincingly, it may have developed as an **adaptive behaviour** contributing to survival.

The maternal deprivation hypothesis

The British psychiatrist, John Bowlby, was the first major theorist to become interested in attachment. He was asked by the World Health Organisation to study the effects of being without their mother on children made homeless in the second world war. Bowlby's report for WHO was later published as a book: *Child Care and the Growth of Love* (1953). In it he proposed the **maternal deprivation hypothesis:**

> What is believed to be essential for mental health is that an infant and young child should experience a warm, intimate and continuous relationship with his mother (or permanent mother-substitute – one person who steadily 'mothers' him) in which both find satisfaction and enjoyment. (Bowlby, 1953, p.13)

▶ Activity 1: the maternal deprivation hypothesis

Read carefully through the quotation. What do you think Bowlby means by the terms 'warm', 'intimate' and 'continuous'? What do you think he means by 'mental health'? What kinds of problems does this term imply? How is the idea of unsatisfactory parenting used now to explain the emotional and behavioural problems of older children? Are Bowlby's beliefs about what makes satisfactory parenting still current today?
When you have finished, see page 71.

The origins of Bowlby's theory

According to Bowlby, if children do not form a close bond with one main carer, which is unbroken in the early years, emotional, social and cognitive problems will be the result. What led Bowlby to propose the maternal deprivation hypothesis?

His ideas drew on a number of sources. In his work with children, Bowlby had noticed that at around the age of 9 months, children start to protest and show distress when separated from their mother. As we saw earlier in Schaffer's stage description of attachment, this kind of behaviour is rare before 5 or 6 months, reaches a peak at

around the age of 12–16 months and then decreases. Bowlby suggested this distress showed that a bond had been formed with the mother. The fear of strangers served the purpose of preventing other attachments being formed. Bowlby used the term **monotropism** to describe a child's need to become attached to only one particular person if the child is to be mentally healthy. It is perhaps worth noting that Bowlby was a trained psychoanalyst, so Freud's emphasis on the importance of childhood experience was also an influence. Bowlby, too, believed that the first five years were crucial.

Two research studies were also influential in shaping Bowlby's ideas. One of them Bowlby carried out himself:

Box D: Bowlby (1944)

Procedure: Forty-four juvenile thieves in a child guidance unit were compared to 44 juveniles who had emotional problems, but had not committed a criminal offence.
Results: Seventeen of the thieves but only two of the other group of juveniles had been separated from their mothers for a period of at least a week in the first five years of their lives. The group of thieves showed what Bowlby called **'affectionless psychopathy',** an inability to feel affection or care about other people.
Conclusion: Maternal deprivation was the cause of the thieves' delinquency and their serious emotional problems.

▶ Activity 2: criticisms of the 'juvenile thieves' study

Can you think of any flaws in this study? You will need to think about the methodology and the conclusions Bowlby drew from his findings.
When you have finished, see page 71.

Another study which influenced the maternal deprivation hypothesis looked at the effects on children of being raised in an institution:

Box E: Goldfarb (1943)

Procedure: Two groups, each of 15 children, were compared. The 'institution' group were raised in a children's home until they were about 3½. They were then placed in foster homes. The 'fostered' group went straight from their birth mothers to foster homes.

Results: At 3, the institution group were behind in language development, they showed an inability to form relationships, a lack of guilt and a craving for affection. When tested later between the ages of 10 and 14, the institution group compared very poorly to the fostered group. Their average IQ was 72 (95 for the fostered group). They were restless, had problems concentrating and were unpopular with other children.

Conclusions: The inability of the 'institution' group to form an attachment with one person during the first three years led to social and intellectual retardation.

Activity 3: criticisms of Goldfarb's study

Are there any other factors, which Goldfarb did not take into account in drawing his conclusions, which could have brought about the differences between the institutional and fostered groups? When you have finished, see page 71.

In his later book *Attachment and Loss* (1969), Bowlby reinterpreted many of his original ideas on the basis of animal studies. We will look at these in the next section.

- **Bowlby** proposed the **maternal deprivation hypothesis**. This states that a warm, continuous relationship in the early years between an infant and one, permanent carer is necessary for mental health.

- In his work as a psychiatrist, Bowlby noticed a pattern of distress shown by young babies when separated from their main care-giver. On the basis of his observations, he proposed that infants show **monotropism**, i.e. an exclusive attachment, which Bowlby believed necessary for mental health.

- His own research on **juvenile thieves** found that they were more likely than a comparison group to have experienced separation from their mothers in their early years. There are, however, flaws in this research.

- Additional evidence came from research into children living in **institutions**. These children showed long-term social, emotional and intellectual damage, though again the research can be criticised.

Attachment in animals

Bowlby's belief in the importance of a close and permanent bond with a mother or other carer also received support from animal research. An important theoretical area was the work of Lorenz on imprinting. In the period immediately following birth or hatching, young birds and mammals show a following response to a moving object. Usually the moving object will be the mother. The process of learning which object to follow is known as **imprinting**.

This behaviour has obvious survival value. The mother will protect her young from predators, feed them and generally cater for their needs. It was initially thought that imprinting had a **critical period**, i.e. a restricted period of time in which it had to take place. If it did not happen then, it could not happen, and once the bond was formed, it was irreversible. Although the principles of imprinting have since been modified, and it has been found to be rather more flexible than initial research suggested, the notion of a critical period was still current as Bowlby was developing his ideas.

Goslings imprinted on Lorenz

Lorenz demonstrated that goslings would imprint on him. He found in the course of his studies that these goslings, and other animals which had failed to imprint on an appropriate carer, had serious social and sexual problems as adults. His researches led him to believe that this abnormal behaviour was irreversible.

Bowlby extended these ideas to attachment in infants. In evolutionary terms, those infants genetically predisposed to form strong attachments would be more likely to survive to sexual maturity in a sometimes harsh environment, and so pass their genes on to their own offspring, demonstrating the Darwinian notion of **fitness**. Bowlby suggested that the critical period for children to form this bond is from around 6 months to 3 years. He believed that the social and emotional wellbeing of children would be seriously affected if they were unable to form a strong, stable attachment during this period, or were separated from their primary carer for any length of time.

It is of course necessary to be cautious when extrapolating from goslings to people. Imprinting is a reflex leading to following behaviour, whereas attachment involves the development of emotions. While imprinting is superficially similar to attachment, therefore, it may not be an adequate model for human attachment. However, other evidence from research on maternal deprivation in monkeys, carried out in a series of studies by Harlow and his associates, is perhaps more convincing. One of these studies has already been described in Box C.

Harlow and Harlow (1962) showed the long-term effects on monkeys of the early experience of being reared without a mother. When monkeys reared in this way were later put together with normally reared monkeys, they were unable to interact normally. Some were withdrawn, clasping their heads in their hands and rocking back and forth repetitively. Some were self-harming, chewing and biting their own bodies until they bled, or were aggressive to others. Males could not mate successfully. Females, if they did mate, were cruel and unsatisfactory mothers, rejecting their infants and refusing to let them nurse.

It seems, then, that infant monkeys do not develop normal behaviour without a live mother; social and sexual behaviour is much impaired. This suggests that the importance of attachment behaviours goes far beyond obtaining nourishment. Attachment may have far-reaching consequences for the later social development of infants.

You probably found reading about these studies rather upsetting. It is unlikely that they would meet the ethical standards required today when carrying out research on animals, although this is partly because we already have the information they provided; if this research had not already been done, it is possible that a case could be made for carrying it out. The studies do serve to show that not having an attachment figure has devastating consequences for infant monkeys. Given that monkeys and humans are closely related, these findings lent support to Bowlby's belief in the importance of attachment in human infants.

- Bowlby's ideas were partly influenced by animal research.
- Lorenz' work on **imprinting** suggested that young animals form an exclusive and permanent bond with a moving object soon after birth. This must happen within a **critical period**. Failure to imprint appropriately leads to later problems with mating. Imprinting may not, however, provide a close parallel to attachment.
- Harlow's work on monkeys lends more convincing support to Bowlby's ideas.

Critique of the maternal deprivation hypothesis

There would now be little agreement with Bowlby's maternal deprivation hypothesis in its original form, and Bowlby himself modified his ideas in his later writings. When his hypothesis was first proposed, however, what he had to say was extremely influential. To understand why this was so, we need to look briefly at the social and political climate of the time.

During the war while the men were away fighting, a lot of women had needed to join the workforce, and they were still working when the war had ended. Since one of the circumstances likely to damage children, listed in *Child Care and the Growth of*

Love, was 'mother working full time', Bowlby's ideas were a powerful argument for women not working. Large numbers of servicemen were now returning to Great Britain after the war and needed jobs.

It was thus in the interests of those in power to give Bowlby's ideas publicity, both to provide jobs and to save the expense of providing care for children who could be looked after at home. Since Bowlby's ideas meshed with public concerns, people were generally receptive to what he had to say.

A lot of research has since been carried out to evaluate the maternal deprivation hypothesis, and it has been questioned on several counts.

▷ Activity 4: assessing the maternal deprivation hypothesis

Look back to the quotation from *Child Care and the Growth of Love* on page 56 to remind yourself of Bowlby's original formulation of the maternal deprivation hypothesis. You should also look at your notes on Activity 1. What reservations do you have about Bowlby's claim? What aspects of it do you think need further investigation?

If you know any very young children, you might find it helpful to think of the patterns of care they experience. Are they different from what Bowlby is describing as essential? How? What do you think might be the effects of different kinds of care? When you have finished, see page 72.

As the discussion of Activity 4 suggests, several aspects of Bowlby's views have been questioned by later researchers. We will look at what this later research has to tell us in the next sections.

● Bowlby's **maternal deprivation hypothesis** has been very influential. The political climate of the time ensured that it received wide publicity.
● Many aspects of Bowlby's theory have been questioned. Bowlby himself modified his ideas in his later writings.

Can fathers be 'mothers'?

Up to now, we have been discussing maternal deprivation; fathers haven't been mentioned. Clearly children also form attachments to fathers, and the Schaffer and Emerson study (Box A) suggests that this can be an important influence in a child's life. Many children could indeed be said to suffer *paternal* deprivation. For example, their fathers may work long hours, or be in prison, or children may live in single-parent families, which usually means with their mother. This emphasis on the mother reflects the traditional attitudes of our culture, where men and women are seen as having different roles in society and the family. The anthropologist Margaret Mead goes so far as to claim that a father is a 'biological necessity, but a social accident'.

Although Bowlby recognised that children form more than one attachment, he claimed that the attachment to the mother or permanent mother substitute is the strongest and the most crucial. The question here is what Bowlby means by a 'permanent mother substitute'. Could this be the father? The evidence of the Schaffer and Emerson (Box A) study supports the idea that fathers can indeed be 'mothers'.

The Schaffer and Emerson study also suggests that the vast majority of young children form multiple attachments, and we shall now look at this in a little more detail.

One attachment or many?

Stacey *et al.* (1970) studied four-year-old children in Wales who went into hospital to have their tonsils removed. They stayed four days, and their parents were not able to stay overnight. Some coped very well, and it was found that they had experienced this kind of separation before, mostly staying overnight with their grandparents or a friend. Like the Schaffer and Emerson study, these findings suggest that children are indeed capable of forming more than one attachment, and that other attachments mean that they do not find temporary separation from the major carer as distressing as Bowlby was suggesting.

Attachments to grandparents can be very important to young children. For many of the children in Dunn and Kendrick's (1982) study of family relationships, a grandmother was a major presence in their lives. This is particularly likely to be the case when the mother is a single parent, and the grandmother can share childcare. We need also to look at patterns of attachment in cross-cultural research:

Box F: Werner (1991); Tyszkowa (1991)

Werner (1991): In black extended families in the USA, the maternal grandmother is seen both by her daughter and herself as actively involved in childcare. In cases where the mother works, the grandmother is often the primary carer. In Native American families, the role of grandparents in child-rearing is seen as crucial. When there is no biological grandparent, an unrelated older person is often adopted into the family to fulfil this role.

Tyszkowa (1991): Grandparents also have a central role in Poland. They are additional attachment figures, but are also valued for the ability their experience gives them to pass on family and social history to the child.

There is, however, a limit to the number of attachments which can be formed:

Box G: Tizard and Rees (1975); Tizard and Hodges (1978)

Procedure: Sixty-five babies in institutional care were studied. They had all entered an institution before 4 months, and remained until at least two. By the age of $4\frac{1}{2}$, 15 had returned to their mothers, 24 had been adopted and 26 had stayed in the institution. The institutions offered a far more stimulating environment than that described in the Goldfarb study (Box E). By the age of 2, the children who were to stay in the institution had had on average 24 carers. This had risen to 50 at $4\frac{1}{2}$.

Results: At $4\frac{1}{2}$ and 8, there were differences between those who stayed in the institution and the other two groups. More than two-thirds of the children staying in the institution were described at $4\frac{1}{2}$ as 'not to care deeply about anyone'. Many were said to be very attention-seeking. When followed up at 8, they were seen by teachers to have severe problems. They were attention-seeking, restless, unpopular and antisocial.

Conclusion: For normal social and emotional development, there are limits to the amount of shared care a child can tolerate.

● For many young children, their main attachment is to the **father**. For many children, the **grandmother** is an important attachment figure.
● Most also form multiple attachments in their first year. At the same time, there are limits to the number of attachments a child can make if that child is to develop normally.

3.2   ATTACHMENT DIFFICULTIES

We need to look now at whether the circumstances which lead to some young children failing to form or maintain secure attachments affect the outcome for the child.

Privation, disruption, and distortion

The three key terms here are:

privation: the child has never had the opportunity to form a close attachment
disruption: a bond has been formed which has later been broken
distortion: a bond exists between child and carer but there is conflict and unhappiness

Rutter (1972) pointed out that *de*privation implies the loss of maternal care, whereas the child may never have had the opportunity to form close bonds in the first place. He suggested that instead of deprivation, we need to make this distinction by using two new terms: **privation** and **disruption**.

▶ Activity 5: privation and disruption

What kinds of circumstances could lead to the disruption of early attachments? Do you think the circumstances you have described might lead to different long-term outcomes? Do you think privation and disruption might have different effects? Refer to your notes on this activity as you read this section.

Box H: Pringle and Bossio (1960)

Procedure: Children in long-term institutional care were studied. The aim was to find out why some of these children were much less maladjusted than others.

Results: Children who had stayed with their mother during the first year were generally better adjusted than those who had entered the institution soon after birth, and who had not formed a stable attachment. These children had difficulty in forming relationships.

Conclusion: There is a better outcome when a relationship has been disrupted than when a child has not had the opportunity to form an attachment.

Disruption of attachment can come about through the death of a parent, or a child being taken into care by the local authority, or when the parents separate or divorce. Bowlby emphasised the relationship between a broken home and later delinquency, and believed that it was lack of maternal care which led to later problems. There are other problems, however, associated with family break-up. There is likely to be tension and discord in the home in the time leading to the break-up, and this may well continue afterwards. This led Rutter to make a further distinction between disruption brought about by bereavement, and the **distortion** of relationships associated with divorce.

There has been a lot of research comparing the effects of disruption and distortion of attachments. Going back to Bowlby's notion of delinquency, Rutter (1972) reported that the delinquency rates for boys who had lost a parent (**disruption**) was very similar to that for boys in intact families. However, the rate for boys whose parents had divorced (**distortion**) was significantly higher. There was also a higher delinquency rate for boys who lived in intact but unhappy families (**distortion**), compared with those whose parents were divorced, but where relationships remained good (**disruption**). It seems that disruption is less of a problem than distortion.

The effects of divorce were confirmed in a study by Hetherington *et al.*, which also identified an additional factor:

Box I: Hetherington *et al.* (1979; 1982)

Procedure: This longitudinal study studied 4-year-old children of divorced parents living with the mother.

Results: Initially, when compared with a control group from intact families, these children showed less mature play, and tended to be negative, attention-seeking, dependent and aggressive. Two years after the divorce, there was no difference between the girls with divorced parents and controls. For boys, however, problems continued, though they had become less extreme. Four years later, the differences between boys and girls persisted. Boys were more aggressive and lacked social skills compared with controls.

Conclusion: There are gender differences in adjustment to disruption and distortion.

Long-term effects of insecure attachment

From research described in earlier sections, it is clear that the lack of a secure attachment can have short-term effects. You will remember that Bowlby's **maternal deprivation hypothesis** proposed that there would also be long-term effects.

His study of 44 juvenile thieves, described in Box D, and Goldfarb's longitudinal study, described in Box E, lend some support to this idea. In addition, we have looked briefly at other research findings, e.g. the Rutter study (mentioned in the previous section), the Tizard and Rees and Tizard and Hodges studies in Box G, the Pringle and Bossio study in Box H, and the Hetherington *et al.* study in Box I, which have all supported the idea that the effects may also be relatively long-term.

This links in with the suggestion made by Bowlby, mentioned earlier, that children develop an **internal working model** of the relationship they have with their primary carer which has long-term implications. We will look briefly at some further research in this area.

Box J: Main and Cassidy (1988)

Procedure: A variant of Ainsworth *et al*'s Strange Situation technique was used with children aged 3–6.

Results: There were considerable differences between children in terms of their behaviour and their self-image:

1. some children see themselves as lovable, and value close relationships with others.
2. some see themselves as unlovable, and act in ways which are likely to make others reject them; they are more interested in activities than people.
3. some children interact inappropriately, responding to parents with unnatural enthusiasm or hostility.
4. some are still upset by separation from the parent at this age, showing whiny, clinging behaviour.

   Main and Cassidy related these different patterns to the four types identified in Strange Situation studies of infants.

Conclusion: There are pronounced individual differences in relationship types at age 3–6 which can be related to attachment patterns seen in younger children.

▶ ## Activity 6: the Strange Situation revisited

Main and Cassidy found patterns of attachment in older children which they related to the distinctions made by Ainsworth *et al*. Can you match each of the kinds of relationship they describe in Box J with one of the four types of attachment found in infants? You will need to look back to the descriptions in Figure 3.

When you have finished, see page 72.

Moving on from this work, Main and her colleagues developed the **Adult Attachment Interview (AAI)**, to find out whether these patterns of attachment could influence adult relationships, as Bowlby suggested, and whether in particular they could be related to the quality of the adult's attachment to their own child. Four main patterns emerged from the AAI:

Figure 6: patterns of adult attachment based on the AAI (Main and Goldwyn, 1984)

1. autonomous-secure: even if their early attachment experiences were not entirely positive, these adults could recall them objectively, and valued relationships. They were likely to have securely attached children.
2. dismissing-detached: these adults had few childhood memories, or produced idealised recollections. They placed little value on relationships. Their children tended to be anxious/avoidant.
3. preoccupied-entangled: these adults were still preoccupied with their relationships with their parents, and still tried to please them. Conflicts with them were often unresolved. Their children were likely to be anxious/ambivalent.
4. unresolved-disorganised: these adults had suffered traumatic separation from the attachment figure, with which they had not come to terms. They had often been abused. Their children tended to show insecure disorganised behaviour patterns.

The findings of Main and Goldwyn suggest a link between early attachment experience and the quality of mothering that the adult provides. Hazan and Shaver have extended this idea by investigating a possible link, using Ainsworth *et al*'s categories, between the kind of mothering experienced and experience of adult romantic love:

Box K: Hazan and Shaver (1987)

Procedure: Using Ainsworth *et al*'s three basic attachment types (see Figure 3), the experimenters wrote descriptions of three types of corresponding adult attachment. They produced a 'Love Quiz' for a newspaper, and readers were invited to pick which description of adult relationships best applied to them, and were also asked to complete an adjective checklist to describe the kind of parenting they had received as children. ✎

🖋 Ainsworth *et al*'s categories and the linked descriptions of adult attachment and type of parenting received are shown in Figure 7.

Results: There was a significant relationship between the kind of parenting received as a child and the choice of description of participants' adult attachments.

Conclusion: There is a link between early attachment experience and the nature of relationships formed as an adult.

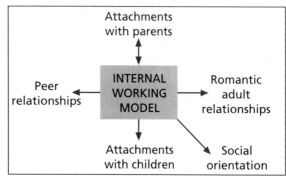

The internal working model through the life span

Figure 7: Hazan and Shaver (1987)

attachment style	type of parenting	adult relationships: self-description
securely attached	readily available attentive, responsive	I find it relatively easy to get close to others and am comfortable depending on them and having them depend on me. I don't often worry about being abandoned or about someone getting too close to me.
anxious-avoidant	unresponsive, rejecting, inattentive	I am somewhat uncomfortable being close to others; I find it difficult to trust them completely, difficult to allow myself to depend on them. I am nervous when anyone gets too close, and often, love partners want me to be more intimate than I feel comfortable being.
anxious-ambivalent	anxious, fussy, out of step with child's needs. Only available/responsive some of the time.	I find that others are reluctant to get as close as I would like. I often worry that my partner doesn't really love me or won't want to stay with me. I want to merge completely with another person, and this desire sometimes scares people away.

Both the Main and Goldwyn study and that of Hazan and Shaver give some support to Bowlby's idea of an internal working model which persists into adulthood. This relates both to the kind of parenting they themselves provide, and their experience of adult relationships.

There is also some evidence that the quality of early attachments is not only relevant to later relationships, but also to wider social orientation, for example the response to crises within society.

Box L: Mikulincer *et al.* (1993)

Procedure: The response of young Israeli adults to the Iraqi Scud missile attacks during the Gulf War was investigated, to find out whether there was a relationship between attachment style and responses to this threat to their society.

Results: Securely-attached individuals (Type B) coped with the trauma by seeking emotional support from others. Ambivalent types (Type C) showed a more extreme emotional response, while avoidant types (Type A) tried to distance themselves psychologically from these events. For people with patterns of insecure attachment, the psychological distress experienced was greater than for securely-attached people.

Conclusion: Early patterns of attachment are related to how people respond to crises.

- Rutter distinguished between **privation**, **disruption** and **distortion** of relationships. Privation and distortion seem to have more serious effects than disruption.
- **Distortion** may come about through divorce, and may also happen in intact but unhappy families.
- Bowlby believed that children develop an **internal working model** of relationships, which persists relatively unchanged into adult life.
- The **Adult Attachment Interview (AAI)** technique shows that early attachment experience can affect a carer's relationship with their own child, adult relationships, and then response to social crises.

3.3 ARE EARLY DIFFICULTIES REVERSIBLE?

The discussion in the previous section suggests that there may indeed be long-term effects from insecure early attachment. But are such effects inevitable? We will start by looking at some animal research in this area.

Look back now to Box C to remind yourself of Harlow's research on infant monkeys. This was followed up by a study to see if the extreme effects of maternal deprivation Harlow noted could be overcome:

Box M: Suomi and Harlow (1972)

Procedure: Monkeys were raised in isolation for 6 months. They were then placed with normally-reared 3-month-old monkeys.

Results: The isolated monkeys were withdrawn, and showed the stereotyped rocking behaviour observed in earlier studies. When placed with adults or peers, they were attacked, and could not respond appropriately to others. After a few weeks with the normally-reared younger monkeys, however, they started to explore their environment and take part in social play. Stereotyped behaviour decreased. After 6 months, their social behaviour was virtually normal.

Conclusion: Interaction with monkeys who were younger helped to reverse the effects of early deprivation.

There is of course the problem that this research was carried out on monkeys, and we need to be careful when extrapolating these findings to human infants. At the same time, it does present a fairly optimistic picture of the reversibility of early deprivation, which has been supported by research into the role of peers in human attachment:

Box N: Freud and Dann (1951)

Procedure: A case study was carried out of 6 Jewish war orphans whose parents had been killed in the genocide of the second world war. They had been brought up in a concentration camp by a succession of short-term carers. Though little is known about their early lives, it is likely that they had had traumatic experiences during this time. The study was carried out at the Bulldogs Bank children's home. The children were between 3 and 3 years 10 months at the start of the study. To begin with, they were aggressive and destructive, had very limited language, and poorly developed social skills. They were not potty trained, for example, and could not use a knife and fork. However, they were extremely attached to each other, did everything together and refused to be separated.

Results: They gradually started to make progress and were adopted. They went on to lead reasonably successful lives.

Conclusion: A close attachment to a primary carer early in life is not as crucial as Bowlby suggested. The outlook is positive if the child is able to form attachments with someone, not necessarily an adult carer.

In addition, adoption studies have indicated that the time during which secure attachments can be formed is not as limited as Bowlby's maternal deprivation hypothesis suggested. Kadushin (1970) studied 91 families who had adopted children over the age of 5. In over 4 out of 5 families, strong attachments had been formed between child and carer, and in only two cases had the child left the adoptive home.

Finally in this section we will look at some cases of severely deprived children:

Box O: Davis (1947)

Procedure: Davis described a case study of a child who had been kept in virtual isolation for the early part of her life. Isabelle was illegitimate, which at that time was considered extremely shameful, so she had been hidden away. She could not speak, since her mother was a deaf mute. She had been kept in a dark room with almost no social contact. After she was found at 6½, she was given a lot of loving care, as well as considerable attention, to help her development.
Results: Eighteen months later, the change in Isabelle was dramatic. She did well at school and made friends with other children. She was a happy and cheerful little girl.
Conclusion: The effects of early deprivation can be overcome later than Bowlby suggested.

The case of Genie is another example of an isolated child:

Box P: Curtiss (1977)

Genie spent the first years of her life alone, tied to a potty chair and fed on baby food. She had lived her life in virtual silence, not being spoken to and being punished for making any sound herself.
She was found at the age of 13½. She developed attachments to her foster carers, but after a settled period in their care, she was moved to a succession of short-term carers, some of whom mistreated her. Her mother eventually refused to allow anyone access to her, and it is not known what happened to her later in life. During the years when her whereabouts were known, Genie only acquired limited language skills.

Even in this extreme case, it seems that it is still possible for children to form attachments later in life. Genie's inability to develop language suggests that she suffered cognitive deficits as a result of deprivation. It is not possible to know, though, whether these deficits were the result of the lack of an early attachment figure or other aspects of the deprivation she experienced. It is also possible, of course, that Genie was hidden away because she was in some way not a normal infant.

In general, it seems that the outlook for children who suffer early deprivation, even if this is very severe, is not as bleak as Bowlby originally suggested.

● Animal research has suggested that the effects of early deprivation can be reversed by the company of **peers**. There is evidence that this is also true for humans.
● Studies of **late adoption** suggest that attachments can be formed and the effects of early deprivation reversed much later than Bowlby suggested.
● Even in cases of **severe deprivation**, normal intellectual and social development is possible.

3·4 OTHER FACTORS IN SOCIAL AND EMOTIONAL DEVELOPMENT

Activity 7: other factors in social and emotional development

Up to now we have concentrated on the effects of carer behaviour on the child. Can you think of any other factors which might affect how infants and children develop?
When you have finished, see page 72.

Buss and Plomin (1984) noted that very early on, infants show wide individual differences in **temperament**. This can be defined as the consistent ways in which children respond to their world, which is relatively stable across different situations. Buss and Plomin's **EAS** model believes distinctions can be made on three dimensions:

emotionality: some infants become upset very much more easily than others.

activity: infants have different preferred levels of activity.

sociability: they differ in their preferred amount of interaction with others.

It could be that temperamental differences affect early infant-carer interactions, which may in turn affect attachment and later development. For example, Waters (1978) found that infants who do not readily attend to people and objects are more likely to develop insecure attachments.

We need also to consider here what is known as **goodness-of-fit**. What this means is the extent to which the characteristics of child and carer are compatible. For example, it may be difficult for a mother who wants to spend a lot of time interacting with her child if the child is low on sociability.

This can be related to the **transactional model** of infant-carer interaction described by Sameroff (1991). This model emphasises the active role of a child in its own development. Both carer and child influence each other's behaviour. An example is shown in Figure 8:

> ### Figure 8: an example of the transactional model of mother-child interaction (from Sameroff, 1991)
>
> 1. After a difficult childbirth, a mother is anxious and behaves inconsistently to her child.
> 2. In response to this inconsistency, the child develops irregular patterns of feeding and sleeping.
> 3. As a result of this irregularity, the mother perceives the child as having a difficult temperament. She spends less time interacting with the child.
> 4. Due to the relative lack of interaction, the child is slow in developing language.

It is difficult here to pick out one particular cause for the mother-child problems. It would certainly be simplistic to see the outcome purely as the result of poor parenting. Both mother and child are involved in a complex developmental sequence.

We also need to look beyond children's relationship with their primary carer to explain later development. Rutter (1972) suggested that there are four factors associated with later behavioural problems: family discord, parents having psychiatric problems or a criminal record, social disadvantage (e.g. poor housing and poverty) and a poor school environment. He found that these factors were good predictors of problem behaviour in children.

It is necessary to look at wider family characteristics, then, and factors outside the family, in order to explain why children develop problems. It would be interesting to know how many of the factors Rutter identified applied to the 44 juvenile thieves studied by Bowlby (Box D).

- We need to look beyond maternal behaviour in order to explain developmental problems.
- Children's **temperament** may contribute to developmental difficulties. This can also be related to **goodness-of-fit** between the characteristics of child and mother, and Sameroff's **transactional model** of mother-child interaction.

● Wider social and economic factors may also influence development.

3.5 CRITICAL ISSUE: DAY CARE

You will remember that Bowlby believed that young children need continuous care from their mother or permanent mother-substitute. For children to enjoy good mental health, they should not be cared for by someone other than the major carer, so any form of day care would be damaging. In his 1951 report to the World Health Organisation, Bowlby claimed that the use of day care would lead to 'permanent damage to the emotional health of a future generation' (WHO, 1951, quoted in Tizard, 1991).

Bowlby's ideas continued to be extremely influential for many years. Penelope Leach, a popularly accepted authority for new mothers, was writing in 1979:

I believe that for children under three there should be no form of socially approved *group-care*. My ideal society has no day nurseries ....Babies and very small children each need a 'special' and continuous person or people and they need to have their daily lives based on somewhere they know as 'home'.

However, a child being continuously cared for by a mother is no longer the norm. Many young children spend at least part of their time at a nursery, with a childminder or being cared for by people other than their mothers in some more informal arrangement. In a survey carried out by the US Bureau of the Census (1994), for example, it was found that 60% of mothers with a child under two were employed, and their children were therefore experiencing day care.

There has been a good deal of research into the effects of the separation from the main carer which this entails, to find out whether it is harmful to children, as Bowlby and others have suggested, and in particular whether it weakens the bond with the mother.

As we will see, most studies have concluded that day care need not have an adverse effect on young children. Clarke-Stewart and Fein (1983), for example, found that children of mothers who work

still form attachments to their mother, and prefer them to other carers. There is one exception to these general findings, however:

Box Q: Belsky (1988)

Procedure: The quality of attachment shown by young children who spent time in day care was compared with the quality of attachment shown by children remaining at home with their mothers. Attachment was assessed using the Strange Situation technique.

Results: There was a greater risk of children forming insecure attachments if they had been in day care for at least 4 months before their first birthday, and if they spent more than 20 hours per week in care. While a large number of children in day care developed secure attachments, a larger proportion of children showing insecure attachments was found among those experiencing day care than those who did not.

Conclusion: In certain cases, children who spend time in day care are more likely to show insecure attachments than those kept at home with the mother.

Figure 9: security of attachment and extent of non-maternal care (Belsky, 1988)

	Extent of non-material care	
	More than 20 hours/week	Less than 20 hours/week
Secure attachment	59%	74%
Insecure attachment	41%	26%
N = 464		

Taken at face value, this conclusion seems rather worrying. It implies that day care may prevent a secure attachment being formed and that the child's future development may therefore be at risk. However, are there other ways of interpreting these findings?

◖ Activity 8: day care and insecure attachments

The Belsky study used the Strange Situation as a measure of attachment. Look back to the earlier section discussing this technique. In the light of this discussion, is there another way in which the findings of this study could be interpreted? In coming to a conclusion, you will need to consider the child's experience of separation and reunion. When you have finished, see page 72.

Given the problems of interpreting the results of the Strange Situation, it seems possible that day care may not be as harmful as Belsky's research suggests. There is also evidence that it may also have some very positive outcomes, and we will look now at research investigating this possibility.

The effects of day care on children has been investigated in the Thomas Coram Research Institute Study, described in Box R:

Box R: Melhuish *et al.* (1990a and 1990b)

Procedure: Eighteen-month-old children were observed in a day care environment and at home. About a third in day care were cared for by a relative, half by a childminder and the remainder attended a nursery. Further measures were taken when the children were three years old.

Results: Some behaviour was very similar in all the settings observed, e.g. the amount of individual play and crying. There were differences in attention and verbal interaction (highest in the home and least in nurseries). Affection shown to and by the child was highest in the home and lowest in nurseries. Aggression was highest in the nursery setting. The behaviour of children in the Strange Situation when reunited with the mother was comparable across all the settings.

At the age of 3, affectionate interactions were more frequent where mothers and relatives were caring for the child. Sharing

and empathy were more likely to be shown by the nursery children.

Conclusion: Different kinds of day care are associated with different patterns of behaviour. Day care may have some negative effects, but may also have some positive effects on social behaviour.

Melhuish *et al.* pointed out that we need to look not only at the nature of the care provided, but also at the quality of care. The nurseries they observed had a relatively high child to carer ratio, compared with the other settings, which meant that staff needed to become more involved in controlling the children, and had less time to interact with them. Many of the staff were young, without experience of children of their own, and staff turnover was high. All these factors might contribute to lower-quality care.

In poor daycare ...

The nurseries had a high child-care ratio

The staff were young

The staff had no experience of children of their own.

The staff turnover was high

The question of quality of care was also investigated by Kagan *et al.* (1980):

Box S: Kagan *et al.* (1980)

Procedure: This was a longitudinal study into the effects of day care. It looked at children who were in day care for seven hours a day, five days a week, over 5 years. Children were tested at intervals for cognitive development (e.g. language skills), social development (e.g. relationships with other children), and attachment to the mother.

Results: The day care group was compared with a control group of children being cared for at home. There were no differences, provided the day care facility was staffed by experienced carers, there was a good child-to-carer ratio, and there was appropriate equipment.

Conclusion: Good-quality day care has no serious negative effect on children's development.

There is also evidence that good-quality day care may have a very positive effect on children's development:

Box T: McCartney *et al.* (1985)

Procedure: The development of young children in Bermuda was investigated, where 85% of children enter day care before the age of two.

Results: Verbal stimulation by carers and overall rating of the quality of day care predicted enhanced cognitive, language and social skills in the pre-school years.

Conclusion: Good-quality day care can make a broad contribution to children's development.

There were similar findings in a Swedish study (Andersson, 1992) of children entering good-quality day care before the age of 12 months.

The key issue here is the quality of care provided. In America, guidelines have been produced which define the characteristics of good-quality care in a day care setting, many of which relate to aspects of good quality care noted by Kagan *et al.* (Box S).

Figure 10: appropriate infant and toddler day care (National Association for the Education of Young Children, 1991)

characteristic	signs of quality
physical setting	clean, well-lit, well-ventilated and uncrowded environment; fenced outdoor play space available
carer-to-child ratio	ratio of no more than 1:3 for infants and 1:6 for toddlers; consistent staffing so that relationships with particular carers can be formed
daily activities	schedule includes active play, quiet play, naps and meals; flexibility to meet children's individual needs
adult-child interaction	prompt carer response to distress; carers hold, talk to and read to children, and are responsive to the needs of the individual child
carer qualifications	training in child development, first aid, and safety
relationships with parents	parents are welcome at any time; carers discuss children's behaviour and development with them
toys and equipment	appropriate play materials, both for indoor and outdoor play, are available, and within reach of the children

◖ Activity 9: the quality of day care

If you can arrange to do so, visit a local day care centre. Make an assessment of the facilities it offers, using the signs of quality in Figure 9 to guide you. Talk to the children to find out what they enjoy about the centre. You could also talk to the staff (if they are not too busy with the children!)

In most of Europe, the provision of day care is regulated. In the USA, however, standards are set at state level and are very variable. Zigler and Gilman (1993) found that many young children attend unlicensed day care homes where there is no check on health and safety standards, and where one carer may be responsible for as many as 12 babies. Phillips *et al.* (1994) found that many children who attended poor-quality day care came from poor homes, suggesting that these children may be doubly disadvantaged, both at home and in the day care environment. So what are the effects of poor-quality day care?

Box U: Howes (1990)

Procedure: Children entering poor-quality day care before the age of 12 months, and who stayed there throughout the pre-school period, were assessed during their first year at school.

Results: Teachers rated these children as being very easily distracted, with difficulty focusing on an activity and becoming involved in it. They were also less considerate of others than children who had not experienced day care.

Conclusion: Poor-quality day care is associated with a lack of the skills necessary for cognitive development, and poor social relationships with other children.

Poor-quality day care can have serious effects on children's social, emotional and cognitive development, and it is children from already disadvantaged backgrounds who are more likely to experience such care. At the same time, however, good-quality day care can help to reduce the negative impact of a disadvantaged background for such children:

Box V: Campbell and Ramey (1991)

Procedure: In the Carolina Abecedarian project, over 100 children from disadvantaged homes, aged from 3 months to 3 years, were enrolled in a full-time year-round day care programme. They received stimulation aimed at developing motor, cognitive, language and social skills. Their development was compared with a group from a similar background who were not on the programme.

Results: On intelligence tests, scores for the group which had experienced day care were significantly higher than for the controls. This advantage was still apparent at 12 years old. The effects were greater for those who had entered the programme at a younger age.

Conclusion: For disadvantaged children, appropriate day care can help to develop cognitive skills.

It is encouraging, given that many mothers need to make day care arrangements for their children, that the effects of day care (provided it is of good quality) do not seem to be as negative as Bowlby suggested. However, just as Bowlby's ideas need to be seen in the social and political context in which they were put forward, it could be argued that findings that day care is not necessarily harmful to young children, and might even have positive effects, could have found ready acceptance in an industrial climate which welcomes women into the workplace as cheap and tractable labour.

Day care: the mother's perspective

In the quotation from *Child Care and the Growth of Love* given earlier, Bowlby pointed out that the relationship between mother and child should be one in which '*both* find satisfaction and enjoyment'. But is this always possible?

When a parent (usually the mother) gives up work outside the home, her life will change drastically. She may feel cut off from the adult company and conversation which she is used to in her work environment, and she may miss the challenges work has provided. If she has had a stimulating job, she may feel bored at the prospect of life at home, where one day is very much like the next. A study by Boulton (1983) found that women in this situation can experience depression and loss of identity. Over half the mothers interviewed found fulfilment in parenting, but a large minority did not.

Schaffer (1990) has also pointed out that the mother's perspective needs to be taken into account when considering what is best for the child. It is likely that a child will develop better with a mother who is happy and enjoys work than with one who is bored and frustrated as a full-time carer. In a review of 122 studies of working mothers, Hoffman (1974) found that dissatisfied mothers were more likely to be inadequate mothers. This was true whether or not the mother was working, and was also true across social class boundaries. In these circumstances, day care may be beneficial for both child and mother, and for the relationship between them.

● Research into **day care** suggests that it may have negative effects on a child. It may also have a positive effect.
● The **quality** of day care is important.
● Good quality day care can help to **reduce negative aspects of development** associated with children coming from a disadvantaged background.
● The **mother's perspective** also needs to be taken into account when considering day care.

Notes on activities

1 The terms 'warm' and 'intimate' indicate that in Bowlby's view, adequate routine care is not enough. He is concerned with the *quality* of the relationship between baby and carer. 'Continuous' implies that mothering in the early years should be full-time. 'Mental health' relates to how well a child is adjusted, both in early infancy and later as an older child and an adult. A child with good mental health is happy and emotionally secure. Poor mental health can be shown in a range of behaviours, such as clinging, aggression, social withdrawal and so on.

There is still a widespread belief that problems in childhood are associated with the child's early experience. Parents are often blamed when children show poor social skills, are aggressive or show other problem behaviours. The precise connection made, though, can vary: perhaps parents are thought not to have given their children enough attention, perhaps children may be seen as lacking discipline and so on.

2 In considering the methodology, you may have thought that this study would have been stronger if there had been a more adequate control group. Both groups had emotional problems; it would have been interesting to compare these samples with children who showed no such problems, since Bowlby was proposing that emotional problems would be the outcome of maternal deprivation.

In addition, this is a correlational study, looking for a relationship between two factors. This method has the drawback that it can't establish whether any relationship which is found is causal, i.e. that one factor (in this case, maternal deprivation) causes the other (affectionless psychopathy). It could be that a further factor, e.g. family problems, was responsible both for the lack of continuity of care and the serious emotional problems experienced.

In addition, since the study is retrospective, it is difficult to identify what other factors – physical, social, emotional and so on – might have been involved in bringing about these children's problems.

3 The children who were studied were matched to an extent on such factors as mothers' occupation and level of education, but there may well have been other important factors – for example, temperamental differences or general health –

on which the groups were not matched. Characteristics such as how alert or intelligent or outgoing they seemed to be may have been factors in deciding whether they found foster homes straight away, or spent their early years in the institution.

It is also possible that it is not the lack of a permanent carer so much as the general lack of stimulation which was at least in part responsible for the differences between the two groups. In the institution Goldfarb studied, babies under 9 months were kept isolated from each other, in order to prevent the spread of infections, and had little contact with adults except for routine changing and feeding. There was a high turnover of carers, and for this reason, carers were discouraged from forming bonds with the children in their care. Throughout the time before they were fostered, then, they experienced considerable social isolation.

4 You have probably come up with similar questions to those investigated by later researchers. You may know children who regularly spend time away from their major carer – for example, who go to a nursery. So how continuous does care need to be? Bowlby focused very much on infant and mother in the development of attachment, but what about the role of the father? Should we accept the concept of monotropism or can the child form attachments with more than one person? What about the reasons why the close bond Bowlby saw as vital cannot be established or maintained? Do the circumstances make a difference? Does what Bowlby sees as an inadequate start in life mean there will necessarily be later problems, as the idea of a critical period implies, or can the effects of early experience be reversed? Are there individual differences between children in terms of the effects of their early experience? Does continuous care such as Bowlby describes guarantee the development of mother-child attachment?

6 The first description relates to Type B, a secure attachment. The second relates to Type A, the third to Type D and the last one to Type C.

7 Two possible factors here are the characteristics the child brings to early relationships and the impact of wider social and economic conditions.

8 It could be argued that children in day care have learned that separation is only temporary and is always followed by reunion with the mother. For these children, separation would not be such a threatening experience as for those who have seldom or never experienced it. This might be reflected in their response to the Strange Situation; the patterns of behaviour they showed could reflect the pattern of care they had experienced, but would not necessarily mean that they had not formed a secure attachment. You might like to relate this to the response of Chinese, German and Japanese children to the Strange Situation discussed earlier.

It is possible also that there are reasons other than being in day care which lead to these children showing insecure attachment. For example, it could be that there are differences between those mothers who choose or need to work, and so put their children in day care, and those who do not.

Stress

4.1 WHAT IS STRESS?

Most people at one time or another have claimed to be suffering from stress. As with many other concepts, however, the use of the term 'stress' is rather more complex in the context of psychology than in everyday situations.

We tend to think of stress as unpleasant, and as something to be avoided. However, stress can broadly speaking be seen as a response to any kind of stimulation, so a complete lack of stress would relate to a complete lack of stimulation; in this sense, a certain amount of stress is beneficial. This can be related to the **Yerkes-Dodson law**, which links arousal and performance:

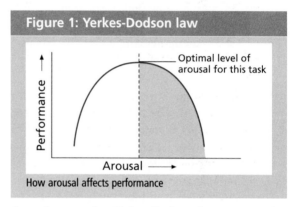

Figure 1: Yerkes-Dodson law

How arousal affects performance

According to the Yerkes-Dodson law, we need a certain amount of arousal in order to perform well. There is an optimal level of arousal, however, and if we move beyond that point (see the shaded part of the diagram in Figure 1), performance drops off, and we experience what we would generally refer to

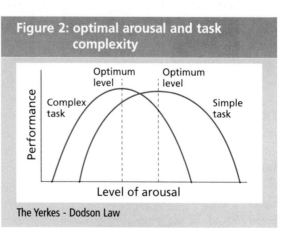

Figure 2: optimal arousal and task complexity

The Yerkes - Dodson Law

as stress. The more complex the task we are asked to perform, the lower the optimum level of arousal.

Selye (1974) distinguishes between **distress** and **eustress**. Distress refers to the kind of stress which is experienced as unpleasant, when we feel that we can't cope with what is being asked of us. Eustress, however, refers to pleasant stress, such as we experience when we take part in moderate exercise. Even though stress has its positive side, though, we will be concentrating here on its more negative aspects.

4.2 MODELS OF STRESS

Cox (1975) has proposed that there are three different models of stress. These different approaches vary in the emphasis they give to external and internal factors.

The first is the **engineering model**, and focuses on characteristics of the environment related to stress. In the same way that the metal from which a heavily-used bridge is constructed will become weakened and eventually suffer from metal fatigue, so people become stressed as the result of their experiences. This model looks at the kinds of factors which lead people to experience stress, and thus focuses on the *causes* of stress.

The **physiological model** is concerned with how our bodies respond to stress. Selye (1956) defines stress as 'the non-specific response of the body to any demands made upon it', and we will be looking at his work in more detail in the next section. This model is concerned with our *reactions* to a **stressor**, i.e. anything which causes stress.

The third model is the **transactional model**. As the name implies, this model sees stress in terms of the interaction between people and their environment. Stress can therefore be defined as an imbalance between a person's perception of the demands a situation makes of them and their estimation of their ability to meet those demands. Note that this model is concerned not with an objective appraisal of the demands a person is faced with, but an individual's *perception* of these demands in relation to their ability to cope with them. This model is therefore concerned with the relationship between external stressors, the physiological stress response and ways of coping with it.

Cox (1978) shows how these elements can be linked:

Figure 3: the transactional model of stress (Cox, 1978)

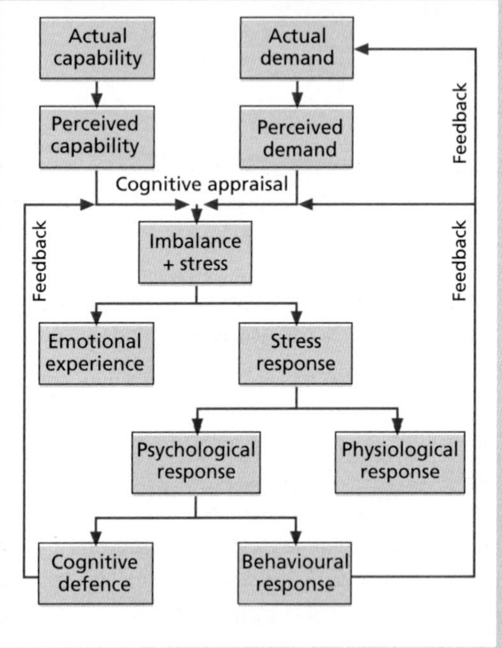

How arousal affects performance

There are individual differences in what is felt to be stressful, the precise physiological response to stressful situations, and in coping strategies:

▷ Activity 1: stress and individual differences

a What kinds of events do you find particularly stressful?
b How does your body react to this kind of event?
c What coping strategies do you use?
Ask a few other people the same questions and compare their answers with your own. Did everyone give similar answers, or were there differences?

In the next sections, we will look in more detail at the different elements of stress which have been outlined.

● Stress can be defined as the physiological state which prepares an organism for action. A **stressor** is something which causes stress.

● A certain amount of stress is beneficial, but most research has focused on the **negative effects** of stress.

● Researchers are interested in the **physiological response** to stress, the **causes** of stress, and **coping strategies** for dealing with stress.

4.3 THE PHYSIOLOGICAL RESPONSE TO STRESS

Selye (1956) proposed that there is a similar pattern of physiological response to stressors, irrespective of the nature of the particular stressor. He came to this conclusion on the basis of studies of rats. They were exposed to extreme cold, fatigue, electric shocks and surgical trauma, and in each case the physiological response was the same, which led him to believe that there was a non-specific reaction of the body to any kind of damage. He called this the **General Adaptation Syndrome (GAS)**. It is also known as the **pituitary-adrenal stress syndrome**, since the pituitary and adrenal glands are involved in the stress response. Selye described three stages of the stress response: the **alarm reaction**, the **resistance** stage and **exhaustion**.

The **alarm reaction** is concerned with the physiological changes associated with arousal. The first part of this reaction is the **shock phase**, an immediate reaction to a stressor. The person experiences tachycardia (an abnormally rapid heartbeat), and both temperature and blood pressure are lowered. This is followed by the **countershock phase**, as the body marshals defensive forces against the stressor. The mechanisms of the alarm reaction centre on the **autonomic nervous system (ANS)** and the **pituitary gland**.

The ANS regulates many aspects of our functioning over which we do not need to have conscious control, such as breathing and digestion. It controls a number of internal organs – for example, the heart muscle and the gut, and a number of glands, such as the salivary and adrenal glands. It has two branches, the **sympathetic nervous system (SNS)** and the **parasympathetic nervous system (PNS)**, which are generally in balance. When the SNS is dominant, there is a pattern of arousal, associated with situations which demand activity. When the PNS is dominant, there is a pattern of relaxation. It is the SNS which is involved in the alarm reaction. In a situation of possible threat, your body needs to prepare itself for action, so high levels of SNS activity help to cope with the demands of the situation by increasing your heart rate and the blood supply to your muscles.

The main system involved in the stress response is called the **hypothalamic-pituitary-adrenal axis**, and it is highly sensitive to environmental change. We will look briefly at the elements which go to make up this system.

The **hypothalamus** plays a central role in the stress reaction. It is a small structure in the forebrain, just above the pituitary gland, to which it is connected by a structure called the **infundibulum**. Through this connection, it controls the secretion of all the hormones released by the pituitary gland. It controls ANS centres in the brainstem, which in turn control the ANS. It is particularly involved in states of arousal, and for this reason is important in the stress response.

We have two **adrenal glands**, two small glands above the kidneys, each of which is made up of the **adrenal medulla** and the **adrenal cortex**. The **pituitary gland**, a gland at the base of the brain, controls the adrenal cortex. When the adrenal cortex is stimulated by the pituitary hormone **ACTH (adrenocorticotrophic hormone)**, it secretes **corticosteroids** into the bloodstream. Even very mild stimuli, if they are unexpected, can trigger the release of ACTH, and set this process in motion. There are many different corticosteroids, but those relevant to stress are the **glucocorticoids**, e.g. cortisone and hydrocortisone. These substances facilitate the conversion of stored fat and protein into energy. They also suppress the body's **immune system**.

The ANS controls the **adrenal medulla**. When it is stimulated, the adrenal medulla releases two hormones into the bloodstream, **adrenaline** and **noradrenaline**. They increase heart rate, blood pressure and sweat gland activity. They also mobilise fat reserves, in preparation for energy expenditure, so they prolong the effects of SNS arousal.

Activity 2: the stress reaction

Use the words from this list:
ACTH, adrenaline, blood pressure, cortex, corticosteroids, energy, heart rate, hypothalamus, immune, medulla, noradrenaline, stressor, sweat gland, activity, sympathetic to complete this diagram and show the processes involved in the stress response:

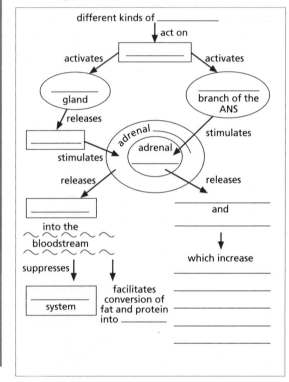

The alarm reaction makes the body more alert and active, and prepares it for what Cannon (1929) has termed **fight-or-flight**, i.e. a behavioural response to a stressful situation. This response can be understood in evolutionary terms. At the beginning of our evolutionary history, when a person was under extreme stress – such as being faced by a predator, or having a stranger encroaching on his territory – only two choices were available: to fight off the attack or to run away. The physiological boost provided by SNS activity would facilitate either of these responses. Although we have the same autonomic responses as our distant ancestors, most of the stressful events and situations which we encounter cannot easily be resolved by the physical response of fight or flight, but need to be responded to in a more rational way. The response of the ANS is therefore now maladaptive; there is no outlet for the physical responses caused by stressors, with the result that they can be detrimental to health.

The effects of the alarm reaction include **pupil dilation**, **deeper breathing**, a **faster heartbeat**, and **digestive changes** (where sugar metabolism is speeded up, but not the processing of foods like proteins and fats which take longer to work their way through the digestive system). The spleen releases stored red blood cells.

Activity 3: the alarm reaction and fight-or-flight

If you were exposed to physical threat, how would these elements of the alarm reaction help you to produce a fight-or-flight response?
a pupil dilation
b deeper breathing
c faster heartbeat
d conversion of stored fat and protein
e release of red blood cells
When you have finished, see page 99.

As well as these changes, additional **blood platelets** are produced. These help clotting, and so prepare the body to repair physical damage. The brain produces neurotransmitters called **endorphins**, which block out the immediate feelings of pain. **Sweating** helps to cool down the body. All these contribute to an effective fight-or-flight response. The physiological response to stress in the alarm reaction can be assessed by measuring the levels of corticosteroids and adrenaline in the urine.

The pattern of physiological activity in the fight-or-flight response cannot be maintained for long, and the body moves into the **resistance stage**. In this stage of the stress response, the body starts to recover from the alarm reaction. There is full adaptation to the stressor, during which symptoms improve or disappear altogether. There is a decrease in the activity of the SNS branch of the ANS, with a lower output of adrenaline and noradrenaline. However, there is an increase in output from the adrenal cortex. Blood sugar levels, which have been raised during the alarm reaction, return to normal. If the stressor is removed, the body reverts to normal functioning, though increased hormone levels persist for some time. However, there is little likelihood of there being any permanent physiological damage.

If the stressor is not removed, the PNS branch of the ANS acts to return the functioning of internal organs, such as the heart, to normal. However, while the body is attempting to defend itself against stressors, it is only partially successful. Cell repair is inhibited, and the immune system may be damaged, increasing the likelihood of infection and a lowered ability to cope with physical damage. If there is a second stressor, resistance is lower, and the final (exhaustion) stage is reached sooner (see Figure 4).

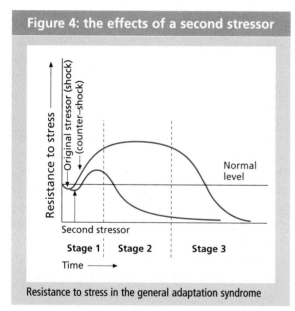

Figure 4: the effects of a second stressor

Resistance to stress in the general adaptation syndrome

If the stressor is severe, and experienced over a prolonged period of time, the final stage of **exhaustion** follows. Heart rate and blood pressure return to apparently normal levels, but the excessive levels of adrenaline and noradrenaline in the bloodstream cause the adrenal glands to stop functioning properly. Body tissue and internal organs are damaged. Even mild sources of

additional stress cause an immediate and strong reaction. Symptoms reappear, and if stress continues, death may be the result.

Solomon (1969) found that at this stage resistance to illness is lowered. People have a tendency to fatigue, and feel generally weak and unwell. These effects are linked to the suppression of the immune system, discussed earlier. It is in this stage that what Selye called **diseases of adaptation** occur, such as ulcers and coronary heart disease (CHD). In the long term, the individual will suffer from **burnout**, where they are no longer capable of functioning adequately.

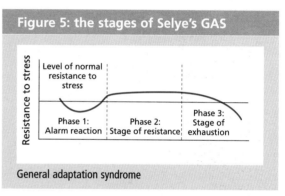

Figure 5: the stages of Selye's GAS

General adaptation syndrome

Selye's model is a useful guide to the physiological response to stressors. However, it was developed as the result of work with non-human animals, so it does not take into account psychological factors in the stress response. For example, people are likely to make a cognitive appraisal of a stressful situation – to what extent is this situation threatening? how able am I to cope? – which will affect their response.

● Selye proposed the **GAS** as a non-specific physiological response to stress of any kind. There are three stages: the **alarm reaction**, the **resistance stage** and the **exhaustion stage**.
● The **alarm reaction** involves the **hypothalamus**, the **pituitary gland** and the **adrenal glands**. It prepares the body for **fight-or-flight**.
● Long term exposure to a stressor leads to **physiological damage**, including a damaged **immune system**. This stage is associated with the development of diseases of **adaptation**. It can lead to **burnout**.

4.4 SOURCES OF STRESS

Three main factors influence whether or not something is experienced as stressful. The first is **predictability**. Stimuli which are either totally unpredictable (such as crashing your car) or totally predictable (such as the noise of a television from next door in the evening) have both been found to be stressful, though most of the time it is unpredictability which is more of a problem.

Something predictable or something unpredictable – both can be stressful.

The second factor is **controllability**. When things are out of our control, we feel more stressed by them. The neighbour's television may upset us, for example, but our own will not. Seligman (1975) showed the effects of lack of control in his work on **learned helplessness**. Rats were given shocks to their feet; there was nothing they could do to avoid being shocked. When they were later put in the same situation, they failed to take action to avoid being shocked, even though escape was possible: they had learned to be helpless. Hiroto and Seligman (1975) carried out a similar experiment with human participants. They were exposed to inescapable loud noise, and were later asked to carry out a task, again accompanied by loud noise. Although the noise was now controllable, the participants failed to control it.

We will be returning to the issues of predictability and control later in the chapter. These factors may be related to the development of stress-related illness, and are also important in stress management.

The final factor is **threat and loss**. These seem to be common to a wide range of stressful events; even pleasant events, such as holidays, can be threatening because we are in a new environment, and life events such as divorce clearly involve loss in many cases.

In all of these areas, it is important to note that it is not important that stimuli are objectively unpredictable, uncontrollable, or threatening, or that loss is likely; what matters is that we perceive them in this way – it is our cognitive appraisal of the situation that is important. We may be totally wrong!

A number of sources of stress have been identified and researched. These include environmental, physiological and psychological factors, and we will look at each of these in turn.

Environmental factors

One major source of environmental stress is **noise**, which can be defined as unwanted sound. Very loud noise will cause physical discomfort, but even fairly quiet noises will cause annoyance if they are not wanted in that situation. The classic example here is the dripping tap, or the buzzing fly which emerges just when you are trying to revise for an examination! Rosen (1970) has shown that noise leads to physiological responses associated with stress. In line with the Yerkes-Dodson law described earlier, it also affects task performance:

> ### Box A: Glass *et al.* (1969)
>
> **Procedure:** Participants were asked to carry out a simple clerical task in noisy conditions. The GSR (galvanic skin response, which measures the change in electrical resistance of the skin, and is an objective way of measuring arousal) was used as a measure of stress, together with the number of errors made. The researchers also looked at the effects of predictability and controllability.
>
> **Results:** The GSR showed a stress reaction when work was carried out in noisy conditions. Fewer errors were made when the noise was predictable, and even fewer when it was controllable.
>
> **Conclusion:** Noise is a source of stress, but predictability and controllability are factors which influence the extent to which it is experienced as stressful.

Stress resulting from noise can also have physical effects. Cohen (1980) found that there was a relationship between prolonged exposure to noise and the incidence of physical illness.

Another environmental factor is **temperature**. Baron and Ransberger (1978), for example, found that the occurrence of riots and civil disturbance in America was related to hot weather. The relationship peaked when temperatures were in the mid-80s, and then dropped off – presumably because it was too hot to make the necessary effort! It should be noted, however, that it is something of an assumption that rioting is necessarily a symptom of stress.

Pollution is also related to stress. Rotton *et al.* (1979) found that there was a correlation between the level of air pollution and mood. People reported feeling less happy when there were high levels of pollution. Again, though, this study rests on the assumption that negative mood can be seen as a straightforward symptom of stress.

Overcrowding can be another source of stress:

Box B: Calhoun (1962)

Procedure: Rats were provided with an environment with abundant food, water and nesting materials, and no predators. The behaviour of the rats was observed as the population of rats grew in size.
Results: Under crowded conditions, the rats were extremely aggressive. Male rats attacked pregnant females and often ate the new-born. Females often abandoned their young. The rats were more likely to become physically ill. Some animals became hyperactive, while some were withdrawn and appeared depressed. The population levelled off at about 150 animals, though the environment could theoretically have supported many more.
Conclusion: Stress induced by overcrowded conditions can lead to pathological behaviour in rats.

Activity 4: a critique of Calhoun's study

What criticisms could be made of this study? Can you think of any positive outcomes it might have had? When you have finished, see page 99.

Finally, living in an **urban environment** may be stressful. It is likely to contain all the elements we have discussed so far, and there will also be other factors which may lead to stress, such as the **invasion of personal space**.

Physiological factors

Selye (1956) listed several physiological sources of stress. These include infections, trauma, nervous strain, heat, cold, muscular strain and being X-rayed.

One important physiological source of stress is the disruption of circadian rhythms. Many of our physiological functions, such as heart rate, metabolic rate and body temperature, vary across a 24-hour period. They all have maximum values in the late afternoon and minimum values in the early hours of the morning. These patterns of variation are known as **circadian rhythms**. These rhythms persist even when our activity pattern is reversed, for example when we work at night and sleep during the day, and reversal can take some time.

What happens when a circadian rhythm is disrupted can be seen by looking at the effects of jetlag and shift work; in both cases, people have problems in adjusting to changes because they occur so rapidly.

In the case of **jetlag**, modern transport systems are capable of taking us across time zones so quickly that when we arrive at our destination, the local time (the **Zeitgeber**, or external cues which help to regulate circadian rhythms) tells us that the situation is different from that based on the information given by our own biological clock. The result is that we feel tired and disoriented; we are awake when others are asleep and vice-versa, hungry at the wrong times, and so on. It may take up to ten days for our system to adjust; some rhythms (e.g. body temperature) adjust more quickly than others (e.g. ACTH production). There are also individual differences, however, in how easy people find it to adapt; some may never do so completely.

What happens when circadian rhythms are disrupted has also been shown in the effects of **shift work**:

Box C: Blakemore (1988)

Procedure: Workers in a chemical company in Utah were studied. They worked a three-shift system, whereby they would work a day shift for a week, a night shift for the second week and an evening shift for the third week. The cycle would then start again. The effects of lengthening the period between shift changes and rotating the shifts in the opposite direction, in line with the body's preference for a longer rather than a shorter period of wakefulness, were investigated.
Results: As a result of the changes, productivity rose and workers were healthier.
Concusion: The constant shifts in circadian rhythms to which the workers had been forced to adapt had stressful effects in terms of productivity and health.

Similarly, Gold *et al.* (1992) found that nurses on rotating shifts made twice as many errors at work than those on permanent day or night shifts, again suggesting that the disruption of circadian rhythms causes stress, leading – as the Yerkes-Dodson law predicts – to poorer task performance.

- Environmental factors which can lead to stress include **noise, temperature, pollution, over-crowding** and the **urban environment**.
- It is also stressful when **bodily rhythms** have to be adjusted. These effects can be seen in **jetlag** and **shift working**.

Psychological and social factors

One basic psychological source of stress, mentioned earlier, is the **perception of threat**. We may assess a situation to which we are exposed as posing a threat to our physical well being, for example being asked to do something which we think is physically dangerous, or to make more physical effort than we feel capable of making. Similarly, we may feel that our psychological well being is threatened when we are asked to work very long hours, for example, or asked to provide more psychological support for someone with problems than we feel capable of giving.

Another psychological source of stress is **frustration**, which can be defined as: 'a negative emotional state which occurs when we are prevented from reaching a goal'. Frustration can come about through our own inadequacies – for example, wanting to be a ballet dancer but being too tall, or not being able to get to grips with a difficult concept in psychology – or from external factors beyond our control – for example, being late for an appointment because the bus was late, or the weather being stormy when we had planned a walk in the country. Many frustrations are relatively minor everyday events, and we shall return to this idea later in this section.

A further source of stress is **response conflict**. This can take three forms:

Figure 6: conflict and stress

type of conflict	examples
approach-approach conflict: choosing between two attractive options.	deciding between two university courses which both sound interesting.
	choosing which of two invitations for the same evening to accept.
avoidance-avoidance conflict: choosing between two unattractive options.	choosing to go to the dentist or put up with toothache.
approach-avoidance conflict: choices which have both pleasant and unpleasant characteristics.	wanting to go to a party that all your friends are going to, but knowing that someone you want to avoid is also likely to turn up.

In general, approach-approach conflict is the easiest to resolve, and therefore the least likely to cause stress, because there will be some positive outcome whatever choice is made. In contrast, avoidance-avoidance conflict is the most stressful, since the choice made inevitably leads to unpleasant results.

▷ Activity 5: resolving conflict

Identify a current example of a conflict you are facing. This can be an approach-approach, an avoidance-avoidance or an approach-avoidance conflict. Complete the chart below to help you to decide how to resolve it.

Firstly, identify the logical outcome or outcomes of each choice. Then on a scale of 1–5 rate the probability of each outcome occurring (from 0 = won't occur to 5 = certain to occur). Now rate the importance to you of each consequence, from 0 = not at all important to 5 = extremely important.

You may find it helpful to multiply the probability and significance ratings for each outcome, and compare the results for each alternative.

Another psychological approach to stress has been to look at the effect of **life changes**. Holmes and Rahe (1967) developed the **Social Readjustment Rating Scale (SRRS)** which linked life events to stress and illness. This scale ranked 43 events in terms of their stressfulness, using a numerical scale up to 100. The scale was developed using patients' records to identify events in patients' lives in the months before they became ill. One hundred independent people were then asked to think about each event and to rate it in terms of how much change it would bring about in a person's life. Figure 7 shows some of the events identified, together with the **LCUs (life change units)** of each.

type of conflict			
alternatives	logical outcome	probability	significance

Figure 7: sample items from the SRRS (from Holmes and Rahe, 1967)

life event	LCU
death of a spouse	100
divorce	73
marital separation	65
death of a close family member	63
gaol sentence	63
marriage	50
fired from work	47
marital reconciliation	45
gain of new family member	39
sex difficulties	39
change in financial state	38
change in number of arguments with spouse	35
son or daughter leaves home	29
outstanding personal achievement	28
trouble with the boss	23
change in residence	20
change in social activities	18
holiday	13
Christmas	12

Holmes and Rahe claimed that a score of 300+ LCUs in the preceding year were associated with a range of serious health problems, e.g. diabetes, heart disease, stroke and leukaemia, as well as less serious everyday problems such as headaches and stomach upsets. Rahe and Arthur (1977) found that people with high LCU scores were more likely to develop physical and psychological illnesses, were more susceptible to sports injuries and more likely to have traffic accidents.

▶ Activity 6: evaluating the SRRS

1. Bearing in mind that some of the life events here are pleasant, e.g. 'vacation' and 'marital reconciliation', what is it about a life event which leads to stress and increases vulnerability to illness?

2. Holmes and Rahe were suggesting that life experiences may lead to illness. Since the relationship they found was correlational, what alternative causal relationship would be possible? Use items from the list to illustrate this explanation.

3. How might individual differences between people having these life experiences make the relationship Holmes and Rahe were suggesting a complex one?

4. The SRRS looks at stressors in terms of single events. Why might this be a limited way of identifying sources of stress?

Compare your ideas with the discussion which follows.

You will have noticed that the crucial factor is not that the events are necessarily unpleasant (getting married or going on holiday are likely to be seen in quite a positive light), but the extent to which they bring change into our lives, to which we have to adapt.

Since the relationship Holmes and Rahe found was correlational, a cause-and-effect relationship such as they propose cannot be assumed. In some instances quite a good case could be made out for illness causing life events, rather than vice versa. For example, it might well be that stress and the early stages of illness could themselves cause such events as 'sex difficulties', or 'change in number of arguments with spouse'. Similarly, it is possible that illness could lead to inattention to work, which in turn would lead to mistakes being made and so 'trouble with the boss'.

Individual differences also mean that the pattern may be rather more complex than Holmes and Rahe suggest. Christmas, for example, can be very stressful for some people; if you are very short of money and have several children expecting expensive presents, for example, or if you have in-laws coming to stay who you don't get on with. But for others it could just be a few days away from work and not really anything very special. Even the most stressful event – 'death of spouse' – could vary in terms of the stress involved, depending on one's religious beliefs, whether the person died suddenly or at the end of a long and painful illness, and so on. In many cases, then, it is something of a generalisation to give overall numerical values to life events.

The detailed nature of these events, then, and how they are perceived by the individual are important. Lazarus and Folkman (1984) carried out many studies to look at these effects, and found that the central factor in the effects of life events was cognitive appraisal, or how we perceive and manage such events. This idea has also been linked to ways of coping with stressful events, and we will be looking at this later in the chapter.

A further problem is that the SRRS focuses very much on crisis events, which by definition don't happen very often. It does not take into account the gradual effects on the individual of, say, being in a job you don't like month after month, or the long-term care of a family member. Under these circumstances, people could become stressed who have not recently experienced any of the stressors on the SRRS.

Kanner *et al.* (1981) suggested that it may be not so much the impact of major events which leads to stress but the more minor everyday stressors which we all experience. To test this idea, they designed a **hassles and uplifts** scale, consisting of relatively minor experiences which have a negative or positive effect. The scale consisted of 117 hassle items, such as 'misplacing or losing things' and 'worries about weight' and 135 uplift items, such as 'feeling healthy' and 'relating well with spouse/lover':

Box D: Kanner *et al.* (1981)

Procedure: One hundred men and women aged 45-64 were studied over 12 months. The relationship between hassles and uplifts and psychological symptoms, both positive and negative, was investigated.

Results: Hassles were positively correlated with psychological symptoms associated with stress. There was a negative correlation between stress symptoms and uplifts. Hassles were a better predictor of stress symptoms than the SRRS.

Conclusion: Everyday stressors are a better predictor of stress (and therefore vulnerability to illness) than life events.

Activity 7: testing hassles and uplifts

Create your own hassles and uplifts scale. If you are working with other people, brainstorm possible items which could be included.

Set the scale out so that participants have a choice of responses, e.g:

I worry about my weight
often   sometimes   rarely   never

Work out a scoring system so that hassles score high (e.g. 3 for 'often', 2 for 'sometimes', 1 for 'rarely' and 0 for 'never'), with the scores reversed for uplift items.

Find participants who are willing to complete your scale (they should not know what the scoring system is). You will need to work out standardised instructions. Ask them also to rate how stressed in general they feel themselves to be on a scale of 0 – 10, where 0 = completely stress free and 10 = extremely stressed. Don't forget to thank them for taking part in your study and to debrief them when it is complete.

Draw a scattergram (see chapter 7) to show the relationship between the scores for the hassles and uplifts scale and the stress ratings. Do your findings support the idea of Kanner *et al*?

Work is also an important source of stress. Cox *et al.* (1981) asked a sample of people what they perceived to be the major source of stress in their lives. Fifty-four per cent identified work, while for a further 12% it was trying to balance the demands of work and home. Work seems to be an important source of stress, then, but what are the factors which may make it so?

One common source of stress at work is quantitative; people feel that they are overloaded and have too much to do, or are required to work too fast. Overload can also be qualitative, when people find their work too difficult or to require too much concentration. For example, Spector (1987) found that people who reported heavy workloads also experienced high levels of anxiety and frustration.

However, French *et al.* (1982) found that work underload can also be stressful. When people feel they do not have enough to do, or that their skills and abilities are not being fully used, they can become bored and frustrated.

A further source of stress in the workplace relates to **roles**. While the idea of roles is usually associated with the acting profession, we also adopt roles every day, including in the workplace, in the sense that at work we are expected to act in particular ways.

> ### Activity 8: work roles
>
> What does the role of a teacher involve? Make a list of the kinds of behaviours which are associated with being a teacher.
> When you have finished, see page 99.

The ways in which others expect a role occupant to behave are known as **role expectations**. However, there may be an element of **role ambiguity**, when an employee is not clear as to his or her precise role within the organisation. A person may be unclear as to their aims and objectives, and the expectations others have of them. They may also be unsure about the scope and responsibility of their job. Spector *et*

al. (1983) found an association between role ambiguity and frustration and anxiety.

A further source of stress in the context of work is **role strain**, also known as role stress, which refers in general to any situation in which a person has difficulty in meeting a role expectation. In many cases, role strain results from **role conflict**, where there is difficulty as a result of conflicting role expectations.

Nine possible sources of role strain are shown in Figure 8 below.

> ### Activity 9: identifying role strain
>
> Listed below are nine examples of possible role strain at work. Can you match each of them with one of the nine sources of role strain in Figure 8 which they might be likely to experience?
> a a working mother, with sick children at home
> b a general labourer
> c a sales person in a shop selling fur coats
> d a shy office clerk asked to take over a receptionist's duties
> e a vet asked to put down a healthy animal
> f a poorly-paid worker in a nuclear power plant

Figure 8: sources of role strain

source	example
1. role ambiguity	the job description may be unclear
2. intra-role conflict (conflict within a role)	librarians are expected both to lend books out and to keep them safe
3. inter-role conflict (conflict between different roles)	a doctor treats members of his own family
4. costs of fulfilling the role outweigh the rewards	a worker is poorly paid for a job which involves exposure to radiation
5. personality, self-concept or attitudes are incompatible with the role	a vegetarian is working in a meat packing factory
6. cultural ideology conflicts with role expectations	a man works as a lumberjack in a society where environmentalists are concerned with preventing the logging of forests
7. role overload (the job is demanding more than the individual can possibly do)	a doctor works in a war zone
8. role underload (the job is felt not to be demanding enough)	an overqualified new member of staff
9. the perceived role differs from the expected role	an office cleaner who thinks that she has to tidy everyone's desk as well

g a college graduate who takes a job stacking supermarket shelves

h a bricklayer who is proud of how quickly he can work, but is told that he must concentrate on making neater joints

i a salesman whose territory has been doubled in size in the last year

When you have finished, see page 99.

Role strain can lead to severe problems at work, as a result of the stress it causes. In a study of the American restaurant industry, Whyte (1948) found that waitresses were under a lot of strain (and were frequently reduced to tears) because they were caught between the customers on the one hand, who wanted their food quickly, and the chefs on the other, who felt they needed time to produce the food properly.

◖ Activity 10: dealing with role strain

Make a list of ways which could help to deal with the role strain Whyte's waitresses were experiencing. When you have completed your list, see page 99 and compare your ideas with the suggestions put forward by Hall and Savery in Figure 9.

Hall and Savery (1987) have put forward some suggestions for ways of reducing the effects of role strain. These are shown in figure 9.

The extent to which work may be stressful depends in part on the nature of the work, since some occupations seem to be more stressful than others. A study by Wolfgang (1988), using self-report questionnaires, found the highest levels of stress to be among nurses. People in positions of middle management are also particularly liable to suffer from stress, which Ivancevich *et al.* (1982) relate to work overload and role conflict.

- Psychological causes of stress include the **perception of threat**, **frustration** and **conflict**.
- Holmes and Rahe used the **SRRS** to show that major **life events** are associated with vulnerability to illness. This idea has been criticised since the research is **correlational**. In some cases, any causal connection could be in the opposite direction to that suggested. Individuals' **perceptions** of these events are likely to be a factor. The theory cannot account for stress symptoms in people who have not experienced any of these events.
- The hassles of daily life may be a better predictor of stress than major life events. This idea has been supported by research using the **hassles and uplifts** scale.
- **Work** can be a major source of stress. Both **overload** and **underload** can be stressful. **Role ambiguity** and **role strain**, particularly where there is **role conflict**, are associated with stress. The extent to which workers are vulnerable to stress is related to the nature of their occupation.

Figure 9: reducing role strain (Hall and Savery, 1987)

1. restructure the organisation to clarify roles, and priorities within roles, and to improve communications
2. select staff who are carefully matched to roles in terms of their abilities, personality, motivation and interests
3. make role expectations clearer, e.g. by providing a detailed job description
4. devise carefully planned, progressive programmes for staff induction, training and development
5. change to a more participative management style, so that workers have more say in what goes on
6. improve relationships between and within groups
7. screen staff for signs of stress
8. give staff advance warning of any changes, especially if these changes mean that there will be extra demands on them

4.5 PERSONALITY DIFFERENCES AND STRESS

It has been suggested that personality differences affect stress levels. Friedman and Rosenman (1974) believed that people could be divided into Type A and Type B, each type showing different behaviour patterns. Before reading on, try this test to find out which type you are:

▶ Activity 11: Type A or Type B personality?

Work through the following statements, each time circling the box which you feel most applies to you. Do not think too long about the statements – it is usually best to give your immediate response. If possible, try to avoid the 'cannot say' option.

1 I never seem to have enough time to finish everything I need to do.

    disagree   cannot say   agree

2 It doesn't really bother me if I have to wait in a queue.

    disagree   cannot say   agree

3 When I play games, I play to win. I get angry with myself when I lose.

    disagree   cannot say   agree

4 My life would be much easier if other people did their job properly.

    disagree   cannot say   agree

5 I find it helps to confide in someone when I have problems.

    disagree   cannot say   agree

6 It is important to me to be best at everything I do.

    disagree   cannot say   agree

7 I enjoy just sitting and watching the world go by.

    disagree   cannot say   agree

8 At the end of a meal, I like to sit and chat for a while.

    disagree   cannot say   agree

9 I usually try to do only one thing at a time.

    disagree   cannot say   agree

10 I tend to fidget when I am just sitting and listening to somebody.

    disagree   cannot say   agree

11 I don't really mind if I don't finish what I had planned for the day.

    disagree   cannot say   agree

12 I function best under pressure.

    disagree   cannot say   agree

When you have finished, see page 99.

People with a **Type A** personality are extremely competitive, and are highly motivated to achieve. They are restless, more than usually alert, and continually feel that they do not have enough time to fit in everything they need to do. They can't bear to wait their turn, have to do several things at once, and need to be admired by peers to sustain their self-esteem. They are hostile, cynical, angry and speak vigorously.

People with a **Type B** personality, on the other hand, may be equally ambitious, but this does not dominate their whole lives. They make time in their lives for family and friends, and their leisure pursuits tend to be less competitive than those chosen by Type A personalities.

It has been suggested that people with Type A personality are more likely to suffer from high blood pressure and CHD than people who do not have these characteristics, and we will be looking at this link more closely in the next section.

A further link between stress and personality has been suggested by Kobasa's concept of the **hardy personality**. Some people appear to cope very well with stressful situations, while others break down under very little pressure. Kobasa (1979) carried out a study to investigate the role of personality in these differences (Box E).

Since this was a correlational study, it has been criticised on the grounds that the personality characteristics Kobasa identified could be the result rather than the cause of illness. For example, it would be difficult for a person to become involved in work and social life if they were ill. However, this criticism was countered by the findings of a longitudinal study (Kobasa *et al.*, 1982), which monitored executives over a two-year period. This study found that those who had a more positive attitude were less likely to become ill.

Box E: Kobasa (1979)

Procedure: Six hundred executives and managers were asked to complete two questionnaires, a personality questionnaire and one listing the illnesses and stressful events which they had experienced in the previous three years.

Results: The responses could be put into two groups, those who had scored above average and below average on illnesses. For both groups, the scores for stressful events were high. However, in contrast to the high stress/high illness group, the high stress/low illness group were likely to:

- feel more in control of their lives.
- have a sense of commitment and purpose in their work and social lives.
- welcome change as a challenge.

Conclusion: A person with these personality characteristics can be described as a 'hardy' personality, i.e. one who is better able to cope with stress.

Kobasa's concept of the hardy personality raises the question: to what extent is it possible to develop the kinds of characteristics which she identified as important in combating stress? Her participants had the kinds of work which would provide challenge and change, and which was stimulating enough to encourage commitment. Her conclusions might not apply so easily to someone in a monotonous and routine job, or one leaving them too tired to make a commitment to outside interests.

◆ A link between **Type A** personality and stress-related illness has been suggested.
◆ People with a **hardy personality** are better able to cope with stressful experiences.

4.6 STRESS AND ILLNESS

Selye's GAS, discussed earlier, predicts that the experience of stress, particularly if it is prolonged, has long-term effects on physiological functioning. This includes damage to the immune system, leading to an increased probability of illness. Before looking at evidence for the link between stress and illness, we need to look briefly at how the immune system works.

The immune system

When **antigens** (dangerous foreign bodies such as bacteria or viruses) are detected, the immune system stimulates **leucocytes** (white blood cells) to destroy them. It also produces **antibodies** which bind to antigens, and identify them as targets to be destroyed. Antibodies remain in the bloodstream and continue to be effective if the same antigens are later present again.

The immune system also plays a role in **inflammation**. If you cut yourself, the blood vessels first of all contract to stop the bleeding. They then dilate, so more blood can flow to the damaged area. The blood carries leucocytes to combat any foreign bodies which might gain access through the wound. It follows that if the immune system is damaged, we become more vulnerable to the effects of foreign bodies, such as infection.

The persistent secretion of steroids (described in the GAS) interferes with the production of antibodies. Inflammation is therefore decreased, reducing the activity of leucocytes. As well as affecting the response to infection, it also seems to be the case that stress impairs the healing process. Sweeney (1995) found that for people who were highly stressed as the result of looking after relatives with dementia, a small cut took significantly longer to heal than for a non-stressed control group.

Animal research

The link between stress and illness has been investigated in animal studies, one of the most famous of which is called Stress in Executive Monkeys (see Box F over the page).

Box F: Brady (1958)

Procedure: Pairs of monkeys were linked up to an apparatus which gave electric shocks. Shocks were delivered over a period of 6 hours at 20-second intervals, continuing over several weeks. One monkey of the pair (the **executive**) could prevent shock to both monkeys by pressing a lever; the other (**yoked**) monkey also had a lever, but pressing it did not stop the shock.
Results: The executive monkeys developed ulcers, while the yoked monkeys did not.
Conclusion: The executive monkeys had to remain constantly vigilant to avoid being shocked, while their partners could do nothing to influence the situation. Constant vigilance is highly stressful, and this stress led to physical ill-effects.

While this study seems to support the link between stress and physical illness predicted by the GAS model, there have been some criticisms of it. Seligman *et al.* (1971) pointed out that the monkeys had not been randomly allocated to the executive and yoked conditions. The animals had to learn that pressing the lever was the required response to avoid shock; those who were able to learn this became executives, while the others were in the yoked condition. There were therefore individual differences between the monkeys in the two conditions, which may have had a part to play in the outcome.

Brady's study was later repeated in rather better controlled studies using rats:

Box G: Weiss (1972)

Experiment 1:
Procedure: A yoked design similar to that of Brady was used, with rats as participants. Shocks were delivered through tail electrodes so that the rats could not avoid shocks by adopting particular postures. Rats took part as triplets:

rat 1 – had control; could avoid shock by pressing a lever.
rat 2 – yoked to rat 1, no control; received shock when rat 1 failed to avoid shock.
rat 3 – control rats; put into apparatus but received no shock.
Results: The amount of ulceration was most for rat 1, less for rat 2 and least for rat 3.
Conclusion: The psychological factor of lack of **control** can affect ulceration.

Experiment 2:
Procedure: A similar method was used:
rat 1 – received a shock preceded by a warning signal, but avoiding the shock was not possible.
rat 2 – received the same shocks but with no warning.
rat 3 – a control who received no shocks.
Results: The amount of ulceration was most for rat 1, less for rat 2 and least for rat 3.
Conclusion: The effect of the shocks was related to **predictability**.

A link can be made between this study by Weiss and the relationship between stress, predictability and control at the start of the section on sources of stress; stress is more likely to be experienced where the stressor is either predictable, or highly unpredictable, and there is no control.

Using data from these studies, Weiss found that **response rate** affected ulceration. Those rats who produced a lot of responses suffered worse ulceration than those who made few responses. By pairing data from high-responding rats with control and yoked rats making few responses, he found the same effect as Brady had shown.

- The effect of stress on the **immune system** suggests that there should be a link between stress and **vulnerability to illness**.
- Stress leads to ulceration in monkeys, supporting a link between stress and **physical illness**.
- Similar studies using rats have demonstrated a link between **control**, **predictability** and stress.

Stress and illness in humans

A link between stress and illness in humans has also been investigated. Since stress affects the functioning of the immune system, people are more likely to catch colds after a stressful experience, because the body has a lowered resistance to cold viruses:

Box H: Cohen *et al.* (1991)

Procedure: Healthy volunteers were injected either with a common cold virus or a harmless salt solution. They were also given a stress index, based on the number of stressful events they had experienced in the past year, the extent to which they felt able to cope, and the incidence of negative feelings such as anger and depression.

Results: Almost all of those injected with the cold virus showed signs of infection, but only about a third developed colds. Even when other factors were taken into account (i.e. age, exercise, diet, use of nicotine and alcohol), there was a positive relationship between the stress index and cold symptoms (see Figure 10).

Conclusion: There is a positive relationship between stress and vulnerability to infection.

Figure 10: Cohen *et al.* (1991)

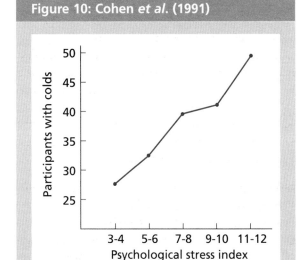

It has been suggested that stress is linked with headaches and asthma. It has also been related to more serious illnesses – cancer, CHD and hypertension – and we will look now at research in these areas.

Cancer

Since stress depresses the immune system, it reduces the body's ability to fight off attacks in the form of infections and viruses. A weakened immune system may also lower resistance to cancer cells.

Cancer occurs when a body cell begins to replicate out of control, so that there are many more of this type of cell than there should be. These cells then begin to invade areas of healthy cells, and unless they are destroyed or removed, they eventually cause damage to tissues and organs, and ultimately death. Cancers appear to be caused by an interaction between a hereditary predisposition, environmental factors such as cigarette smoke or asbestos fibres, and changes in the body's immune system.

Whenever cancer cells start to multiply, the immune system acts to check their uncontrolled growth. In a normal healthy person, the immune system manages to keep cancer cells in check. However, if the immune system has been weakened by exposure to stress, cancer is more likely to develop.

This has been demonstrated in animal research. Visintainer *et al.* (1983) injected animals with cancer cells and then exposed them to an uncontrollable stressor. The cancer cells developed more rapidly in animals who had been stressed than in controls.

The link between stress and cancer in people has also been investigated:

Box I: Jacobs and Charles (1980)

Procedure: Cancer patients were asked about stress in their lives before cancer was diagnosed.

Results: Patients often reported higher than normal levels of stress at this time.

Conclusion: The experience of stress may be linked to the development of cancer.

Activity 12: stress and cancer

Read through the study in Box I. Why might it be unwise to draw the conclusion from these findings that stress leads to cancer?

You will need to think about the possible ways in which the link established by Jacobs and Charles could be interpreted, and the method used in collecting the data.

When you have finished, see page 99.

Coronary heart disease

CHD results from **atherosclerosis**, a thickening of the walls of the coronary arteries which reduces or blocks the blood supply to the heart. There are several risk factors which affect the probability of a person developing CHD, including smoking, heavy drinking, obesity, poor diet and lack of exercise.

In the late 1950s, two cardiologists, Friedman and Rosenman, found that men were far more likely than women to develop CHD, although there were no real gender differences in such factors as diet. It was therefore clear that some other factor was also implicated. Since at this time most men worked, while most women did not, they suggested that work-related stress could also be a contributory factor. They investigated this possibility in a classic study, where stress was defined in terms of the behaviour shown by those with **Type A** personality traits:

Box J: Rosenman *et al.* (1975)

Procedure: A longitudinal study in the USA, starting in 1960, followed 3000 men, aged 39-59, for a period of $8\frac{1}{2}$ years. All were healthy at the start of the study. Participants fell into two approximately equal groups classified as Type A or Type B.

Results: Of the 257 men who died in the course of the study, 70% were Type A. Men who were Type A were almost two and a half times as likely to develop CHD than those who were Type B. Even when risk factors for CHD (like smoking and heart disease in the

family) were taken into account, they were still twice as likely to develop the illness.

Conclusion: Type A individuals are significantly more likely to develop stress-related illness than Type B.

These findings have been replicated in a number of countries, including England, Canada, Belgium, Sweden and New Zealand. Some studies, however, have not found such a strong relationship (e.g. Mathews, 1984). Ragland and Brand (1988) found that there was no difference between Type A and Type B men in the likelihood of developing CHD, and their findings gave some indication that Type A men might actually be at less risk.

So how can we make sense of these contradictory findings? It is possible that not all the personality characteristics associated with Type A contribute to the link with heart disease. Dembroski and Costa (1988) suggest that the key factors are hostility, anger and vigorous speech. Williams (1984) found that Type A people with a cynical, hostile outlook on life have an increased risk of heart disease, while Type A people with a positive outlook actually have a lowered risk.

So how does stress contribute to heart disease? You will remember that the fight-or-flight response releases noradrenaline and cortisol into the bloodstream, with the result that heart rate is increased and stores of fat are released to give muscles a quickly available source of energy. If some physical action is taken, this fat is used as energy, but if not, the fat may be deposited on the walls of blood vessels. These fatty deposits then create the blockages which restrict the blood supply to the heart, leading to CHD.

Hypertension

Hypertension is a state of chronically high blood pressure. In a small percentage of cases, there is a physical cause, such as kidney disease, but in the vast majority of cases, there is no medical cause. Hypertension, which carries an increased risk of stroke and can lead to CHD, has also been linked to stress:

Box K: Harburg *et al.* (1973)

Procedure: Participants living in Detroit were divided into 'high stress' and 'low stress' groups on the basis of the area of the city in which they lived. 'High stress' areas were defined as those with a high crime rate, high population density and high poverty.

Results: Those in the 'high stress' group were more likely to suffer from hypertension than those in the 'low stress' group.

Conclusion: There is some evidence of a link between environmental stress and hypertension.

Care must be taken in interpreting this kind of evidence, of course, since many factors in this kind of study cannot be controlled. At the same time, these findings do offer some indication that stress may be a factor in the development of hypertension.

There is also a lot of evidence (e.g. Goldstein, 1981) that people with high blood pressure tend to react to stressful situations with a more exaggerated and prolonged increase in blood pressure.

- A link has been established between stress and a vulnerability to **viral infection**. There is also a link with **headaches** and **asthma**.
- Damage to the immune system caused by stress reduces the ability of the body to destroy cancerous cells. Being highly stressed is one factor which may therefore make a person more likely to develop **cancer**.
- There is also a relationship between stress and **CHD**. This has sometimes been shown using **Type A** personality characteristics as an indicator of stress. However, it may be that only certain aspects of the Type A personality are linked with heart disease.
- **Hypertension** may also be caused by stress.

4.7 CRITICAL ISSUE: STRESS MANAGEMENT

As we have seen, stress is not only psychologically damaging but is also associated with a risk of developing illnesses such as cancer and CHD. It is therefore important to think about ways in which stress can be handled and reduced. We will look in this section at some of the ideas which have been put forward: biological and behavioural treatments, cognitive and psychodynamic approaches, together with the importance of social support and reducing stressors.

Biological approaches

Stress is often experienced as **anxiety**. **Anxiolytic drugs**, also known as **minor tranquillisers**, are frequently used to help people with anxiety disorders. Until recently, barbiturates were used, but their use has now been largely discontinued. This is because they are extremely dangerous in overdose, are highly addictive, and there are often unwanted interactions with other medicines a patient may be taking.

The most common drugs in current use are the **benzodiazepines**, for example **diazepam**, e.g. Librium or Valium. These drugs regulate the neurotransmitter **GABA** (see chapter 1 for more information on neurotransmitters). Diazepam is prescribed for short-term use (no longer than 2–4 weeks is recommended) where anxiety is severe and disabling, and the patient is suffering extreme distress.

One of the problems with these (or any) drugs is possible side effects. Possible side effects of diazepam include drowsiness, confusion, amnesia, headache, low blood pressure and occasionally apnoea (i.e. the patient stops breathing). Diazepam is also addictive, leading to psychological and physical dependence, so withdrawal has to be gradual.

An alternative anxiolytic drug is **buspirone**, which acts on **serotonin** receptors. While buspirone also has possible side effects, it does not lead to dependency, so withdrawal is not a problem. **Beta blockers** may also be used. They treat the physical symptoms of stress, reducing ANS symptoms such as palpitations and tremor. The reduction of physical symptoms may in turn lead to an improvement in the psychological symptoms of anxiety.

A major criticism of the use of drugs to reduce anxiety is that they do not deal with possible environmental factors contributing to the problem – such as having several young children or an elderly relative to look after, or having serious money worries – but only the physical symptoms. They may best be seen as short-term ways of dealing with stress, and may need to be used in combination with other therapies, such as counselling, if the problem is to be dealt with more radically.

Sometimes **alcohol** is used to reduce stress. It has a sedative effect, slows down neural function and loosens inhibitions. The same criticisms which can be made of other drugs, however, also apply to alcohol. Additionally, there is a positive relationship between alcohol consumption and stroke, so the use of alcohol to reduce stress can be counter-productive.

Behavioural approaches

Biofeedback is a behavioural approach to dealing with stress symptoms, using the principles of **operant conditioning**, outlined in chapter 1. The principle of biofeedback is simple: people's physiological functions, such as heart rate and blood pressure, are monitored and then this information is made known to them. They are trained in methods – usually involving relaxation – to bring these biological processes under voluntary control. Feedback can be visual (e.g. by a changing line on a TV screen) or auditory (e.g. a tone which changes in pitch). It requires specialist equipment, but this is relatively cheap and readily available. Erbeck *et al.* (1983) found that people could lower their blood pressure using biofeedback.

One problem with this method, however, is that some people find the necessary control quite difficult to acquire. Very often it may take many months for appropriate techniques to be acquired and beneficial effects to be seen. For these reasons,

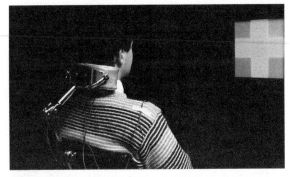

A biofeedback machine

alternative ways of changing these functions could be preferable, for example meditation, in which relaxation plays an important part.

The principle behind **meditation** is the focusing of consciousness, using rituals and exercises designed to empty the mind. The process includes physical exercises – such as regulating breathing and practising yoga positions – and mental exercises – such as focusing on a symbol or chant which is repeated over and over again. The result is a mild change in consciousness, in which the individual feels in a pleasant state of physical and mental relaxation. With practice, this may lead to mystical experiences in which there is a loss of awareness of individual identity, and a feeling of being at one with a wider consciousness.

▶ Activity 13: meditation

Try this exercise, using meditation techniques:

a Sit quietly in a comfortable position with your eyes closed.

b Deeply relax all your muscles. Start with your feet, and work your way up to your face. Keep your muscles relaxed.

c Breathe through your nose and concentrate on your breathing. As you breathe out, silently say the word 'one' to yourself.

d Continue this exercise for 20 minutes. (You can open your eyes to check the time but do not use an alarm).

e When the 20 minutes are up, sit quietly for a few minutes, first with your eyes closed and then with them open.

Did you feel relaxed, both physically and mentally, after this exercise?

As well as psychological effects, you may also have noticed physiological changes. The feeling of relaxation leads to a decrease in arousal. The parasympathetic branch of the ANS comes into action, leading to a reduced breathing rate, reduced oxygen consumption, a slower heart rate and lower blood pressure. There may also be release of endorphins, the body's natural pain-killers, leading to reduced sensitivity to pain.

Cases have been reported of people who have been able to control their metabolic processes to an incredible extent through meditation. In 1970, for example, Ramanand Yogi survived for over 5 hours in a sealed box, using only half the amount of oxygen which would normally be necessary to stay alive.

Meditation has been found to help in reducing anxiety, and has been used in sport psychology to help with relaxation and stress reduction (e.g. Syer and Connolly, 1988).

A broader approach involves encouraging the person to use appropriate behaviours to combat the effects of stress. One example is **exercise**. For example, Blumenthal *et al*. (1987) found that people who exercised were less likely to experience anxiety, depression and tension than those who did not.

Physiological changes during stress prepare the person for action, so exercise is an appropriate response to these changes; it uses up the blood sugars released by the hormones secreted into the bloodstream during stress. It also helps to work out tension that has built up in the muscles, and increases strength, flexibility and stamina, so making the person more able to combat future stressors. Aerobic exercise, such as brisk walking or swimming, also improves the efficiency of the cardiovascular system. Exercise also has the advantage of removing the person, albeit temporarily, from the situation which is causing stress.

Behavioural methods have also been used effectively to modify **Type A** behaviour. There have been two basic approaches here.

The aim of the **shotgun approach** is to change all the behaviours associated with the Type A personality. Friedman *et al*. (1986) in their Recurrent Coronary Prevention Program used a combination of behavioural methods, including advice on changing behaviour in terms of diet and exercise, and encouraging people to carry out behaviours which are incompatible with their personalities. They were asked, for example, to listen to people without interrupting, or deliberately to stand in the longest queue at the supermarket.

The **target behaviour approach** focuses only on those Type A behaviours which are likely to lead to heart disease. You will remember from the section on heart disease that Williams (1984) suggested that cynicism and hostility were the crucial factors.

It is argued that if behaviours associated with these characteristics can be modified, the risk of heart disease will be lowered.

While these are good ways of coping with stress, they still largely only deal with symptoms rather than causes. Behavioural programmes can also help to combat the underlying problem, however, e.g. help with time-management planning if a person feels overwhelmed by the demands made on them.

Social situations, e.g. meeting new people, taking part in meetings, and so on, can be experienced as very stressful. Cohen and Williamson (1991) found that people lacking the necessary social skills to deal with these kinds of situation were more likely to become ill. Stress can therefore be reduced if people learn to develop the necessary social skills through observation and role-play practice, before using them in real-life social situations.

- Stress can be treated in the short term with **drugs**. There may be problems with **side effects**, and they do not deal with environmental factors contributing to stress.
- **Biofeedback** can be used to control physiological stress responses. **Meditation** and **exercise** can also be effective.
- Behavioural methods have been used to modify the behaviour of those with a **Type A personality**, and to help people acquire relevant **social skills**.

Cognitive approaches

It has been suggested that people adapt best to stressful events by changing the way they think about them, and consciously taking control of their situation.

▷ Activity 14: the perception of stressful events

Do a small survey among your friends to find out what they think are the five or six most stressful things that have happened to them in the last few months.

Where there are events in common, ask your friends how they coped with these events. Did people who found them less stressful perceive them differently, or use different coping strategies? Think of a current stressor in your life. Can you think about it differently, in ways which may make it less stressful?

As we saw earlier, one factor which affects the extent to which stress is experienced is **control**. The **locus of control** theory put forward by Rotter (1966) is relevant here. 'Locus' means 'place', and the theory makes a distinction between people who have an **internal** locus of control, believing that they have some control over life events, and those who have an **external** locus of control, who feel that they are controlled by external forces and have little control themselves.

People with either an internal or an external locus of control can suffer from stress; people with an internal locus of control are likely to blame themselves when things go wrong, while people with an external locus of control may feel helpless in the face of what life throws at them. However, Johnson and Sarason (1978) found that people with an external locus of control were more likely to experience stress. Similarly, experiences over which we feel we have some control are usually less stressful than those over which we feel we have none. This idea has been used to help people cope with anxiety.

When I visit my dentist, he always tells me to raise my hand at any time if I want him to stop what he is doing. Visiting the dentist is now much less of a problem for me than it used to be. Brown (1986) discusses several studies using this system in a simulated dental surgery. The effect of the control this gives patients is usually less anxiety, and sometimes an increased tolerance for pain. It is perhaps worth noting that these findings contradict those of Brady (Box F); this contradiction is best explained by the constant vigilance over long periods required of Brady's monkeys if they were to avoid shocks.

One form of control is **information control**. Explaining to people undergoing a medical procedure what is going to happen and why is a good example of an effective way of reducing anxiety and stress.

The role of this kind of control has been shown in research:

Box L: Bourne (1971)

Procedure: Levels of stress hormones in US soldiers in Vietnam were tested before, during and after a Viet Cong attack.

Results: On the day when ordinary soldiers were preparing for the attack, their levels of stress hormones dropped; levels rose in the officers and radio operators.

Conclusion: The training the soldiers had received provided them with mechanisms which they could use in dangerous situations. Many of them believed that what they had been taught would protect them from harm. The preparations they made before an attack – e.g. checking weapons and filling sandbags – gave them a sense of control over the situation. The officers and radio operators did not have this protective routine.

Another study looked at this kind of control in a medical context:

Box M: Janis (1971)

Procedure: The relationship between pre-operative characteristics of patients waiting for abdominal surgery and their post-operative adjustment was investigated.

Results: Compared with patients with high or low levels of pre-operative fear, those with a moderate level of fear were more likely to ask for realistic information before the operation took place, and were the least likely to show emotional disturbance after the operation.

Conclusion: Information control can be beneficial to adjustment after an operation.

This study is interesting in finding that people with low levels of pre-operative fear were likely to experience more emotional disturbance than those with moderate levels. It is possible that very low-fear people were using ego defence strategies, such as denial, in the pre-operative situation, and did not ask for information about the operation for this reason. They were therefore not well equipped to cope with the effects of the operation.

Another kind of control is **cognitive control**. This involves encouraging people to think in different ways about an experience which they find stressful. These two kinds of control have been compared:

Box N: Langer *et al.* (1975)

Procedure: Participants were patients waiting for elective surgery, i.e. non-emergency surgery such as hysterectomies and hernia repairs. The 'cognitive control' group were asked to focus their attention on the positive aspects of their surgery, such as avoiding daily hassles, and the positive changes it would bring to their lives, and to avoid thinking about the negative aspects. The 'information control' group were told what was going to be done and how they would feel afterwards. Both groups were compared with a control group who were not prepared in this way.

'...asked to focus on the positive aspects of their surgery'

Results: Both information control and cognitive control helped patients to cope, compared with the control group. Cognitive control was more effective than information control in reducing anxiety.

Conclusion: Information control and cognitive control are both effective in stress reduction. Cognitive control, used together with information control, may be the most effective way of reducing stress.

A further cognitive approach to the control of stress has been developed by Meichenbaum (1965). This is a method of **cognitive restructuring** called **stress inoculation**. It is a three-stage procedure carried out with the help of a therapist, and aims to control the **catastrophising thoughts** which people often have in stressful situation. A person attending a job interview, for example, might think: 'I just know I'm not going to get this job'.

Figure 11: stress inoculation (Meichenbaum)

1. **conceptualisation:** the therapist helps the person to identify and talk about their feelings and fears, and how they have tried to cope with them.

2. **skill acquisition and rehearsal:** general techniques for coping with stress are taught and practised, such as relaxation and making a realistic appraisal of stressful situations. Specific skills, such as effective interpersonal communication, may also be taught.

3. **application and follow-through:** the therapist guides the person through a series of stressful situations. This helps the person to develop and practise the cognitive strategies necessary for coping with stressful situations.

Kobasa, whose concept of the 'hardy personality' was discussed earlier (see Box E) also takes a cognitive-behavioural approach to coping with stress in her suggestion as to how hardiness may be developed. Again, there are three elements:

Figure 12: coping with stress (Kobasa)

1. **focusing:** the person is trained to recognise the physiological signs of stress, such as increased heart rate or sweating. This helps them to recognise sources of stress.
2. **reconstructing stressful situations:** the person is helped to think about a recent stressful situation and consider ways in which it could have turned out better or worse. This aims to help the person make a realistic appraisal of the stresses they experience.
3. **compensation through self-improvement:** the person is encouraged to take on challenges they can cope with. Through this they learn that they are capable of coping with stressful situations.

The methods of reducing stress suggested by Meichenbaum and Kobasa can be linked with the **transactional model** of stress described at the start of this chapter. You will remember that this model suggests that stress can be defined in terms of a mismatch between the perceived demands a situation makes of us and our perceived ability to meet these demands. Both these methods aim to help us make a realistic assessment of the demands made of us, while at the same time improving our ability to cope with them. They also both involve the experience of coping successfully with stressful situations, so that we develop a feeling of control; as we have seen, control is an important element in successfully handling stress.

● Increasing a person's feeling of **control** in stressful situations can be useful in coping with stress. People with an **external locus of control** tend to experience higher levels of stress than those with an **internal locus of control**.
● Both **information control** and **cognitive control** can be effective.
● Meichenbaum and Kobasa have both suggested methods of reducing stress which aim to help people make **realistic assessments** of stressful situations, and develop **coping strategies.**

The psychodynamic approach

Freud has suggested that we deal with anxiety, which is the psychological manifestation of stress, by the use of unconscious **ego defence mechanisms** such as denial (mentioned in relation to Janis's study, Box M). You will remember from chapter 1 that Freud's theory proposes that anxiety arises as the result of unconscious conflict.

▷ Activity 15: ego defence mechanisms

Some of the mechanisms described by Freud which we use to deal with anxiety are:

repression	denial
reaction formation	sublimation
rationalisation	regression

What do each of these involve? Which is the only one which is effective in the long term? Check your answers with the information in chapter 1.

Because these mechanisms are unconscious, they involve self-deception: the whole point of them is that they prevent us becoming aware of unpleasant or threatening material. They rest on a distorted view of reality, both the reality of our own inner feelings and the reality of our social and physical world. They help us to cope effectively in the short term, but because they rely on self-deception and distortion, they are fundamentally unhealthy as long-term coping mechanisms. The only exception to this is sublimation, since it provides an acceptable outlet for unacceptable impulses.

Grasha (1983) has used Freud's suggestions about the nature of ego defence mechanisms to describe a range of **coping mechanisms**. In contrast to Freud's account, these are *conscious* ways of trying to cope with anxiety in a positive and constructive way. The coping mechanisms he describes involve looking for support from other people, thinking of ways to solve our problems, acknowledging our true feelings, and making decisions about what our aims are and how to achieve them. He redefines Freudian terms from this point of view:

Figure 13: coping mechanisms (Grasha, 1983)	
coping mechanism	**definition**
suppression	consciously putting something out of your mind until an appropriate time to deal with it.
substitution of thoughts	consciously substituting other thoughts and feelings for how we really think and feel to cope with the situation we are in.
playfulness	using past feelings and ideas to help solve problems in an enjoyable way.
concentration	deliberately putting aside thoughts and feelings unrelated to what we need to do.
logical analysis	analysing problems to help us make realistic plans to solve them.

Sublimation is both an ego defence mechanism and a coping mechanism, since it is a positive and constructive way of dealing with anxiety.

Activity 16: defence mechanisms and coping mechanisms

Match each of Grasha's coping mechanisms in figure 13 with the equivalent ego defence mechanism from Activity 15. Then match each with one of these scenarios:

a On Thursday, Martin is asked to work late by his boss, but this is also the day when he usually visits his mother in a nursing home. She will be disappointed if he doesn't go. There is no time to do both. He starts to think of various options: asking his boss if he can take work home, speaking to his mother on the phone and arranging to go the next day, and so on.

b Wendy has been asked to plan a Halloween party for the badminton club she belongs to. She is worried it will turn out to be a disaster. She remembers a similar party she went to a few years previously. She thoroughly enjoyed this party, and everyone else seemed to have a good time too. She starts to think about how some of the ideas from the previous party could be adapted for the Halloween party.

c It is Saturday evening. Viri is waiting to hear whether he has got a job he applied for. He is very keen to get the job, as his current job will be finishing in a few weeks. He decides to go to the pub with his friends, and ring up about the job on Monday morning.

d Helen is working hard on a report which needs to be handed to her boss the next day. She has a hospital appointment next week which she is worried about. She puts her worries to the back of her mind and focuses on getting the report finished.

e Anne is a head of department at a comprehensive school and has to work with other members of her department on the development plan for the coming year. She does not get on very well with David, and doesn't think he is very competent. When David arrives at the meeting, she greets him with a smile, and asks him what ideas he would like to include.

When you have finished, see page 99.

The effectiveness of both ego defence mechanisms and more cognitive coping mechanisms has been shown in a study by Greer *et al.* (1979). This study found that for women with breast cancer, who had had a mastectomy, the prognosis in terms of being free of cancer five years after treatment was much better for those who reacted with denial or who were determined to beat the disease. However, strategies such as denial can also be dangerous. For example, if a person with a heart problem does not follow his doctor's recommendations for lifestyle changes because to do so would mean acknowledging that he is ill, there could well be life-threatening consequences.

● Freud believed we use unconscious **ego defence mechanisms** to cope with anxiety. These are only effective in the short term.

● We may also use similar but conscious **coping mechanisms**.

Social support

Another way of dealing with stress is to draw on **social support**. Winnurst *et al.* (1988) found that the support of others – friends, family or social organisations – can be very helpful in reducing the stress experienced when undergoing a divorce or coping with a bereavement or the loss of a job. Similarly, Tache *et al.* (1979) found that adults who were widowed, divorced or separated were more likely to develop cancer than controls, a finding which could be interpreted in terms of the lack of social support.

The support of other people can help reduce stress

House *et al.* (1988) found that support groups can be a very useful resource for people faced with long-term stressful situations, such as illness or poverty. Support groups can help people to cope, not only because they provide other people to lean on, but also because people belonging to these groups can learn ways of coping from each other.

Reducing stressors

A final way of coping with stress is to look at the problem from a different angle. Instead of accepting that stress is inevitable, in some cases it may be possible to change the circumstances which lead to stress being experienced.

▶ Activity 17: reducing stressors

Amanda is 35 and has a daughter aged 6, a son aged 5 and a six-month-old baby. Every morning

she is up at 5.30 to make packed lunches for the older children, hoover the house, prepare food to be cooked for the evening meal and get the baby ready to go to the childminder's.

She drops the children off and drives through the rush hour to get to work. She is in charge of a department at work, and it is her responsibility to make sure that the other people in her department are working efficiently. Every week she has a meeting with them to discuss any problems which have arisen, and she often stays until well after six to check that work has been completed satisfactorily. She is very ambitious and intends to rise high in her profession, so she often volunteers for extra responsibility.

On her way home she picks up all three children from the childminder's, takes them home and cooks an evening meal. She puts the children to bed, washes up and makes sure that the kitchen is clean. She feels she is not doing her job properly unless the house is immaculate. She then usually has papers from the office to look through for the next day or reports to write. She is the chairperson of the local PTA, and complains that she often seems to be doing all the work as well as chairing meetings. She finally stops work at around 11, and goes to bed, though she often has difficulty in getting to sleep.

Her husband also has a high-powered job. She has asked him to give her more help, but he also brings work home, and is often away at weekends for his job. At weekends she has work to prepare for the week, but leaves this till after the children are in bed. She regularly takes them swimming on Saturdays. On Sundays, her in-laws always come for lunch, and she prides herself on cooking them a wonderful meal.

She says she always feels very stressed, but can't see what she could do to make things any easier. How could Amanda reduce the stressors in her life? Based on the sections in this chapter on coping with stress, what other advice would you give her? When you have finished, see the notes below.

● **Social support** increases our ability to cope with stress.
● **Reducing stressors** is also a useful strategy.

Notes on activities:

3 **Pupil dilation** would allow you to become more aware of external stimuli, and thus better able to respond to them. **Deeper breathing** takes more oxygen into the lungs; your muscles require oxygen if they are to work effectively. A **faster heartbeat** speeds up blood circulation, and so carries oxygen to the muscles more quickly. Speeding up **sugar metabolism** creates an instant supply of energy; the danger could well be past by the time proteins and fats were metabolised. Stored red blood cells from the **spleen** mean that the blood can carry more oxygen.

4 There are clear ethical problems here, in terms of the suffering of the rats. The ecological value of the study has also been questioned, in that the environment provided for the rats was not a natural one, so we need to be cautious in the conclusions we draw from the findings. As with all animal studies, we need to be cautious about extrapolating the behaviour of rats to people. This study nonetheless suggests that overcrowding can have far-reaching physical and psychological consequences, and it inspired a lot of research into the effects of overcrowding on people.

8 You have probably listed such things as presenting classes with structured information relevant to the curriculum in the subject being taught; maintaining classroom discipline; setting and marking homework; attending meetings with management; involving parents and management when there are problems; attending training days, and so on.

9 **a** 3; **b** 1; **c** 6; **d** 5; **e** 2; **f** 4; **g** 8; **h** 9; **i** 7.

10 You might have suggested that the waitresses and the chefs should communicate with each other more, to clarify how they feel. The waitresses and the chef could discuss what is a reasonable length of time for customers to wait, and make customers aware of what they have agreed. They could make sure that management are aware of the situation and can intervene when there are problems. Staff training to help them deal with stress might also be a good idea.

11 For questions 1, 3, 4, 6, 10 and 12, 'agree' scores 2, and 'disagree' scores 0. For questions 2, 5, 7, 8, 9 and 11, 'disagree' scores 2 and 'agree' scores 0. For all questions, 'cannot say' scores 1. If you are close to the maximum score of 24, you show signs of being a Type A personality, while if your score is close to 0, you are a Type B personality.

12 One major problem is that this study is retrospective, i.e. it asks people to talk about events which happened before the illness developed, and so relies on their memory being accurate. Another weakness is that there was no control group of people who had *not* developed cancer.

16 suppression = repression (**c**), substitution of thoughts and feelings = reaction formation (**e**), playfulness = regression (**b**), concentration = denial (**d**), logical analysis = rationalisation (**a**).

17 Amanda has taken a lot on, and it is not surprising that she feels stressed. There are several aspects of her life where stressors could be reduced: she could let the children have school meals instead of packed lunches, lower her standards about housework, prioritise what needs to be done at work and delegate more to the people in her department, perhaps mark time in her career for a few years and not take on extra responsibilities, drop her PTA commitment, suggest that her family should visit the in-laws sometimes on a Sunday or eat out, and so on. You have probably come up with several other ideas.

One problem is that she sounds very much like a Type A personality, so she would find making these changes difficult. She might need help in changing the way she thinks about her life and her behaviours. She would also be well advised to take exercise and perhaps put time aside for meditation.

Abnormality

5.1 WHAT IS ABNORMAL PSYCHOLOGY?

Abnormal psychology, or **psychopathology**, is the area of psychology which relates to mental disorders. There is considerable controversy about how 'abnormality' should be defined. Psychologists also differ in what they see to be the causes of mental disorder, or indeed whether we actually need to concern ourselves with causes at all. This is important, because what is seen as the cause (or **aetiology**) of a disorder may determine the treatment (or **therapy**) given.

This is an important area, since mental disorders cause a lot of unhappiness to millions of people, and research in this area aims to alleviate suffering. We will be looking in this chapter at some of the problems associated with this topic.

5.2 DEFINING ABNORMALITY

Problems in this area start with definition:

▷ **Activity 1: defining abnormal behaviour**

Make a list of the characteristics or features of a person whose behaviour you consider to be 'abnormal'. You could picture someone you know and would describe as abnormal, or you may find it easier to think back to a film you have seen that portrayed someone as abnormal.

What criteria would you use to define someone as showing abnormal behaviour?

Keep your notes to compare with the discussion which follows.

Deviation from statistical norms

One way in which abnormality may be defined is as a characteristic or behaviour which is **statistically infrequent**, or which deviates substantially from the average or typical behaviour of the group to which an individual belongs. For example, someone may have an abnormally well-developed memory for word lists: their memory for this kind of information is much better than it is for the majority of others in the population. However, there are problems in defining abnormal behaviour as being behaviour which is significantly different from that of most other people.

One problem here is that using the statistical criterion of abnormality does not include any assessment of whether the behaviour is desirable or not. We would probably be satisfied to define people like Hitler as abnormal, but it doesn't seem sensible or useful to define the statistically rare talents of someone as intelligent as the scientist Steven Hawking or as creative as Picasso in this way.

Another difficulty is that some conditions which clearly constitute a problem are relatively frequent. Depression, for example, is quite common in Western cultures, and is regarded as a mental disorder, but it would not be described as abnormal using this criterion.

A further difficulty arises when deciding where the cut-off point between normal and abnormal should lie. How good a memory would a person need to have, for example, before being described as having an abnormally good memory? At the extremes, there would be little difficulty in deciding that someone had or didn't have an abnormally good memory, but the grey area between these two extremes is problematic.

In one area, however, the statistical criterion is used. **Mental retardation** is defined in the classification system ICD-10, which we will be looking at later, as having a measured IQ which is two or more standard deviations below the mean. In general, though, while this criterion may go some way towards a definition of abnormality, it is clearly not enough to provide a definition on its own.

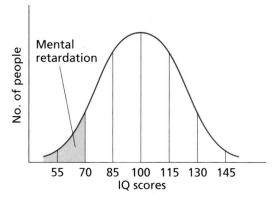

The distribution of IQ scores in the population. Each division represents 1 standard deviation from the mean

Violation of social norms

An alternative definition of abnormal behaviour sees it as behaviour which violates **social norms**. Scheff (1966) introduced the idea of **residual rules**, unwritten rules in a society of which people are somehow aware and to which they generally conform. For example, you do not stand staring vacantly into space in the middle of a busy pavement, or spit on the piano. People who break these rules, and go against social norms, could be defined as behaving abnormally.

Residual rules

One problem with this definition, however, is that we can only judge normality according to the situation. For example, singing loudly and tunelessly is not a problem if someone is in the shower, but would be seen as abnormal in a library or on a bus. Killing people during wars may be regarded as heroic, but can be seen as murder at other times.

Defining behaviour as abnormal according to social norms is also difficult, since social norms change from one period of history to another as social trends change. You can perhaps think of behaviours, like dyeing one's hair pink, or sunbathing topless, which would have been considered abnormal 40 years ago, but which are now accepted as issues of personal choice. Homosexuality is one behaviour which until 1973 was listed as a mental disorder in DSM-II, a classificatory system widely used by psychiatrists, and to which we will be returning later in the chapter. Homosexuality is now legal between consenting adults over 18, and most people in the UK now accept homosexuality as falling within social norms.

Some norms, it could be said, also need to be broken. In the 1950s, it was quite common to find rooms to let with notices saying 'No coloured. No Irish', a practice which, thankfully, has become both socially unacceptable and illegal.

However, this definition of abnormality has been applied: repressive political regimes, such as that in the former USSR, have frequently classified those who disagreed with them as having a mental disorder, and confined them to psychiatric hospitals for publicly condemning the actions of the government.

Maladaptive behaviour

If behaviour is adaptive, it contributes to a person's sense of individual worth and allows them to function adequately as a member of a larger social group. If a person's behaviour fails to meet these criteria, and disrupts their ability to work or to have relationships with other people, it can be said to be maladaptive, and the behaviour can be defined as abnormal.

Within this framework, one criterion for defining abnormality is **personal distress**. As we have noted, disorders such as depression are common, and therefore can't be defined statistically as abnormal. They do, however, make the person thoroughly miserable, and as such are abnormal. Symptoms such as loss of appetite, insomnia and general aches and pains can be indicative of a mental disorder, even if friends or relatives of the person concerned have noticed no real differences in that person's behaviour.

There are, however, problems with this criterion. Distress is a perfectly natural reaction in some circumstances – for example, when someone close to you has died. In contrast, there are some disorders where no personal distress is felt. For example, someone with an antisocial personality behaves violently and with no concern for the feelings of others, but does not themselves feel distressed.

This leads to another criterion related to maladaptive behaviour, that of **causing distress to others**; this criterion would certainly apply to antisocial personality disorder. A person cannot be said to be functioning adequately if their behaviour frightens or upsets other people. However, many disorders would not meet this criterion.

Another aspect of failure to function adequately is that the person with a mental disorder shows **unexpected behaviour**, a term used by Davison and Neale (1994). Although behaviour is affected by the nature of the situation in which we find ourselves, to some extent our behaviour is predictable, and this is one of the things which allow us to interact appropriately with other people. If a person is extremely unpredictable, interacting with them is likely to be very difficult, and their behaviour would therefore be maladaptive. Again, though, it is a matter of where the line is to be drawn between expected variations in behaviour and unexpected behaviour.

Finally, behaviour which is **bizarre** is another example of a failure to function adequately. Some people with schizophrenia, for example, hear voices in their head with which they may carry on a conversation. This leads to the bizarre behaviour of someone walking along apparently talking or arguing with themselves. People with obsessive-compulsive disorder may need to carry out a behaviour such as washing their hands as often as 500 times a day, developing painful sores in the process, and leaving little time for anything else. At the same time, though, a lot of mental disorders are not associated with bizarre behaviour.

All the criteria for defining abnormality which we have looked at so far apply to some aspects of some mental disorders, but none on its own provides an adequate definition. In most cases, psychologists have found that it is best to consider a person's behaviour against all of the criteria we have looked at.

In line with this way of thinking, Rosenhan and Seligman (1989) listed six criteria, shown in Figure 1, for judging behaviour as abnormal:

Figure 1: six criteria for judging behaviour as abnormal (Rosenhan and Seligman, 1989)

1. personal distress
2. maladaptiveness
3. irrationality
4. unpredictability
5. unconventionality and statistical rarity
6. observer discomfort

They put forward the idea that any combination of these criteria could indicate mental illness. This seems to be a useful way forward. The problem remains, though, that the criteria require a subjective judgement to be made; different people could assess a person differently on each point.

Psychologists have also, on the whole, seen that there can be no precise distinction between normal and abnormal behaviour, so abnormality now tends to be seen as a **continuum** with 'normal' at one end, 'abnormal' at the other and various degrees of normality in between. This is a more realistic model, as it takes account of the fact that we have all probably experienced irrational thoughts and feelings or felt distress at one time or another, but do not all need to be defined as abnormal or suffering from a mental disorder.

- Abnormal behaviour has been defined as behaviour which is **statistically infrequent**, **violates social norms**, and is **maladaptive**.
- There are many difficulties associated with defining behaviour as abnormal, notably the fact that assessment may be **subjective**.
- There is no single straightforward criterion for defining abnormality. Taken together, however, different definitions may help to define abnormality.
- Abnormality is now seen to be a **continuum** from normal to abnormal, with varying degrees of mental health in between.

Defining normality

Many of the problems associated with defining abnormality have led to a different approach, that of attempting to define normality. This approach started with Freud, who said that the goal of therapy was a well-balanced individual 'able to love and to work'. Defining abnormality in terms of maladaptive behaviour rests on the assumption that certain aspects of our behaviour are necessary for mental health. Jahoda (1958) suggested a range of characteristics, shown in Figure 2, which describe a mentally well-adjusted person:

Figure 2: characteristics of a well-adjusted person (Jahoda, 1958)

1. self-acceptance
2. potential for growth and development
3. autonomy
4. accurate perception of reality
5. environmental competence
6. having positive interpersonal relations

More recently, Atkinson *et al.* (1983) listed six personality traits which they suggest a normal person exhibits to a greater degree than an individual who is classified as abnormal. In other words, they are stressing the idea that mental health and mental illness exist as a continuum:

Activity 2: what is mental health?

Compare the ideas of Atkinson *et al.* in Box A with the characteristics Jahoda suggests. In what ways are they similar? How do they differ?
When you have finished, see page 120.

Box A: Atkinson *et al.* (1983)

Efficient perception of reality
Normal people have a realistic idea of their own capabilities and can fairly accurately understand what is going on around them. Those people with mental disorders may consistently overvalue or underestimate their own abilities, and misunderstand what other people say and do.

Self-knowledge
Normal people have some awareness of their own motives and feelings – they are more self-aware than those people with a mental disorder.

An ability to exercise voluntary control over behaviour
Although all normal people sometimes act impulsively, they can control their urges if

they decide to do so. Even if they do exhibit bizarre behaviour which does not conform to what society expects, they have voluntarily decided to act in that way.

Self-esteem and acceptance

Well-adjusted people don't always bow to peer pressure. They have an idea of their own self-worth and feel comfortable that they are accepted by others. Mentally ill people frequently feel worthless and unaccepted by other people.

An ability to form affectionate relationships

Normal people can form satisfying, intimate relationships with others. People with mental disorders can be extremely self-centred and concerned with their own feelings, leading to a lack of success in relationships.

Productivity

Normal people have an enthusiasm for life and are productive – whether that be at work or in leisure time. People with mental disorders often suffer from a lack of energy and tiredness.

This approach has intuitive appeal, and could provide some indication of whether a person's characteristics and behaviour would be classed as abnormal. It is not without its problems, however. Like some of the definitions we considered earlier, subjective judgements are necessary, and there may well be differences between the assessment on these criteria – for example, as made by a mental health professional or by the person who is being considered.

In essence, these lists outline ideal mental health. The question arises as to how many of us could be said to enjoy good mental health using these criteria. There is no very clear dividing line between normal and abnormal, and many people who would not be defined as abnormal may still not fully meet all the criteria Atkinson *et al.* and Jahoda have proposed.

◆ An alternative approach to defining abnormality and mental disorder is in terms of **mental health**.

◆ The criteria proposed present an **ideal** which many people may not meet. Assessment is **subjective**.

5.3 Cultural and subcultural differences in the definition of abnormality

Cultures vary in their beliefs, attitudes, values and customs, and may therefore differ in their concept of abnormality. This makes it difficult to define psychological abnormality in terms which can be universally applied. While there are no problems with identifying physical illnesses, such as measles, in a Welsh person and a Chinese person, with mental disorders it is not quite so straightforward.

Some disorders such as schizophrenia are present in most cultures, and are universally considered to be a disorder. Children with attention deficit hyperactivity disorder (ADHD), on the other hand, a condition seen as a disorder in our culture, would be considered naughty or badly behaved but not abnormal in some cultures. Similarly, in some cultures it is considered normal to see and hear a person who has died during the bereavement period. Within Western culture, this would be considered abnormal.

There are also disorders which are recognised and even common in some cultures but are unknown in others. For example, it would be very unusual in Britain to come across someone suffering from **koro**, an anxiety disorder found among the Chinese, where the sufferer is afraid that his penis will withdraw into his abdomen. Sufferers may even tie a string to the penis to stop this from happening. **Amok** – where males have periods of aggression and try to kill or injure others – is not recognised as a specific mental disorder in the West, but is recognised as such in Malaysia. Another example is **dhat**, a disorder found among Indian men, who complain of loss of semen through the urine. They suffer from multiple aches and pains, and believe that the loss of semen is causing them weakness. Disorders such as these, which are strongly related to particular cultures, are known as **culture-bound syndromes.** Helman (1990) has suggested that anorexia nervosa, which we will be discussing towards the end of this chapter, is a Western culture-bound syndrome. Pre-menstrual syndrome and agoraphobia may be other examples.

As an aid to the diagnosis of mental disorders, mental health professionals use systems which classify disorders into diagnostic categories. The two most well-known current systems of classification are **ICD (International Classification of Diseases)** and **DSM (Diagnostic and Statistical Manual of Mental Disorders)**. ICD-10, the most recent version of this system, is currently used in Britain and in most other parts of the world, whereas DSM-IV, the most recent version of this alternative system, is used in North America. Until recently, it was assumed that Western diagnostic categories of mental disorders used in these systems could be applied universally, and that disorders in non-Western cultures were just variations of Western disorders. However, the most recent version of DSM now takes cultural variation into account and includes a list of culture-bound syndromes in an appendix; ICD-10 has a similar section.

There may also be subcultural factors in defining abnormality. At a subcultural level, there are significant differences in the prevalence of diagnosis of certain mental illnesses, and therefore what is defined as abnormal, between ethnic groups in Britain. Cochrane (1977), for example, found that Afro-Caribbeans are calculated to be between 2 and 7 times more likely than whites to be diagnosed as schizophrenic. They are also far more likely to be compulsorily admitted to secure hospitals.

It is possible that the disproportionate number of Afro-Caribbeans diagnosed as schizophrenic may be related to **stereotypes**, e.g. the stereotype that violent behaviour is more likely to be associated with black people. Behaviours of the majority white population may be seen as **social norms**, with deviations being considered abnormal and indeed pathological. It has been suggested that there is a **Eurocentric bias** in defining people as abnormal.

This seems to suggest that culture should be taken into account when diagnosing someone as having a mental disorder. On the other hand, it has also been suggested that taking account of cultural variation may not necessarily be helpful:

Box B: Lopez and Hernandez (1986)

Procedure: A large number of mental health professionals in California were surveyed about the relationship of ethnicity to their diagnostic work.

Results: There was sometimes a tendency to explain the problems experienced by patients in terms of subcultural norms. One clinician, for example, believed that blacks were more likely than whites to suffer from hallucinations, so did not consider a diagnosis of schizophrenia for a black patient.

Conclusion: Being aware of cultural differences can lead to problems being minimised, an appropriate diagnosis not being made, and therefore less chance of appropriate intervention.

Another example of subcultural variation is gender. There are gender differences in the incidence of diagnosis of particular disorders which are related to sex-role **stereotypes** in our society. This can be illustrated by differences in diagnosis for the disorders shown in Figure 3:

Figure 3: four personality disorders from DSM-IV

disorder	characteristics
histrionic personality disorder	extravagant displays of emotion, attention-seeking, manipulative and demanding
dependent personality disorder	lack of self-confidence, passivity, oversensitiveness to criticism
narcissistic personality disorder	grandiose view of their own abilities, lack of empathy in relationships, craving the admiration of others
obsessive-compulsive personality disorder	perfectionist, work-oriented, lack of warmth, requirement that everything be done their way

▶ Activity 3: diagnosis and sex-role stereotypes

For each of the disorders in Figure 3, decide whether the characteristics best fit the sex-role stereotypes of males or females.

When you have finished, see page 120.

For all the disorders shown in Figure 3, there is a higher incidence of diagnosis for the gender who fit the stereotypes than for the other gender. This has also been tested experimentally:

Box C: Broverman *et al.* (1981)

Procedure: Mental health professionals were asked to rate the characteristics of the 'healthy man', the 'healthy woman' and the 'healthy adult'.

Results: The ratings for 'healthy adult' and 'healthy man' were similar. The characteristics included 'assertive', 'decisive' and 'independent'. The 'healthy woman' was regarded as 'submissive', 'dependent' and 'emotional'.

Conclusion: Diagnosis of a person as suffering from a mental disorder may be related to the different gender stereotypes of what ideal mental health (and therefore abnormality) is for a man and for a woman.

- There are cultural variations in what is considered to be abnormal. Behaviour considered normal in one culture may be seen as abnormal in another.
- Disorders specific to a culture are called **culture-bound syndromes**. They are included in the most recent versions of the classificatory systems DSM and ICD.
- There may also be **subcultural variations,** e.g. related to **ethnicity** or **gender**, in defining abnormality.

5.4 MODELS OF ABNORMALITY

There are several models of abnormal behaviour which vary in terms of what are seen to be the causes of abnormal behaviour. This in turn has implications for what is seen as the appropriate therapy for someone with a mental disorder.

Historically, abnormal behaviour has often been explained in terms of possession by evil spirits. **Demonology** is the idea that some sort of evil being is responsible for a person's behaviour. Treatments therefore centred on ridding the body of such evil spirits, and included starvation (to ensure the body was unsuitable for the devils to reside in), trepanation (drilling holes in the skull to let the spirit out) and various forms of exorcism.

It is now widely thought that people who in the Middle Ages were called witches were often merely people with a mental disorder. Religious fervour was strong at the time, and the poorly-educated masses believed abnormal behaviour to be a sign of moral wickedness. Women accused of witchcraft were tortured if they did not confess; and it was said that people who had lost their sense of reason could have the demon exorcised by burning. You may also have read of witches being ducked under water; those who did not drown were thought to be in league with the devil. Those unfortunates who did drown were thought not to be witches, although it was then too late for their innocence to be of much use to them!

Poor "witch"!

Another historical approach, dating back to the second century, took a more medical approach. Galen suggested that normal brain functioning depended on the balance of four fluids, or **humours** – blood, black bile, yellow bile and phlegm. Since mental disorders were considered to be the result of an imbalance of these humours, various treatments intended to restore that balance were employed. These included blood letting to rid the body of an excess of blood, the effect of which was (hardly surprisingly) to calm the most violent of patients!

The development of **asylums** began in the sixteenth century. Originally the asylums admitted mentally disordered people, beggars, and some people with leprosy. The first hospital specifically designed to contain people with mental problems is said to be the Priory of St Mary of Bethlehem in London, founded for the containment of the mentally disordered in 1547. This is the origin of the modern term 'bedlam'. However, the inmates of such asylums were chained to cell walls by iron collars, treated like criminals, and fed an appalling diet.

Treatments included the idea that so-called lunatics could be cured merely by frightening them; this is related to the idea of demonic possession, since evil spirits would be frightened and therefore leave the body. It is perhaps worth mentioning that 'lunatic' means 'controlled by the moon', and is therefore another example of an early aetiology. The fact that the patients were seen as sub-human is well illustrated by the fact that the middle-classes were encouraged to pay to view the antics of the lunatics, and asylums became a huge tourist attraction.

Conditions in the asylums did not improve until in 1793 a Frenchman called Pinel took over La Bicêtre, a large asylum in Paris, and was shocked at the way in which the patients were treated. He advocated a humanitarian approach, removing the chains from the inmates, feeding them healthily and treating them with compassion.

These examples of how historically abnormality has been explained and treated are, thankfully, in the past. However, it is perhaps worth noting that some other cultures had a more positive approach to people with a mental disorder. For example, among many nomadic Asian peoples abnormal behaviour was seen as a sign of special sensitivity to, and the ability to communicate with, the spirit world. The mentally-disordered person would hold a particularly privileged position as a shaman (or priest) within the society. In *The Politics of Experience* (1970), R. D. Laing put forward a similar suggestion about schizophrenics, but this remains an extremely unusual point of view in Western medicine.

We will turn now to more modern models in abnormal psychology.

The biological (medical) model

The medical approach is the most traditional and widely accepted model of mental disorder. As its name suggests, this kind of disorder is seen as a medical problem, so the term 'mental illness' is widely used in this context. There are clear parallels between the medical model of physical illness and the medical model of mental illness.

The **medical model of illness** proposes that **symptoms** are caused by an **organic lesion**, i.e. a change in the structure of body tissue caused by disease or injury. **Diagnosis** involves the identification of the lesion from the symptoms. **Prognosis** gives a likely outcome to the illness. **Treatment** involves treating the lesion by **physical means**. Patients are not considered to be in control of their symptoms.

The **medical model of mental illness** considers abnormal behaviour to be a **symptom** caused either by a **hypothetical lesion**, or by a **physical lesion** which has not yet been identified. Since **diagnosis** is not possible in the absence of a lesion, **classification** (making use of classification systems such as DSM-IV and ICD-10, mentioned above) provides a guide for **prognosis** and **treatment**.

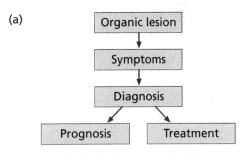

(a)

Organic lesion → Symptoms → Diagnosis → Prognosis / Treatment

Medical model of physical illness

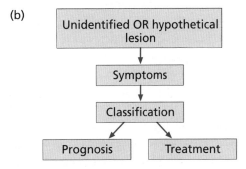

(b)

Unidentified OR hypothetical lesion → Symptoms → Classification → Prognosis / Treatment

Medical model of mental illness

The medical model uses terms associated with physical illness when it talks about mental disorders. Patients are treated by specialist *physicians* (doctors) called psychiatrists, or by general practitioners. The *–pathology* part of the term psychopathology (the study of mental disorders) is taken from medicine. The abnormal behaviour of the patient is seen as a *symptom* of a physical problem. The doctor will aim to observe the patient carefully and then *diagnose* the illness, using one of the classificatory systems, together with further examination and tests to assist diagnosis. They will then decide on a suitable treatment. Some treatments can be given against the will of the patient, by detaining them forcibly and providing treatment under the relevant section of the 1983 Mental Health Act (a process sometimes known as '**sectioning**').

Abnormal behaviour may be seen as caused by **genetic factors**. Some physical disorders, such as cystic fibrosis and haemophilia, can be passed on from parents to children, and the medical model of mental illness suggests that mental disorders can be inherited in the same way. There is strong evidence for a genetic basis to some mental disorders, in particular schizophrenia and bipolar disorder (manic depression). The evidence is far less strong, however, for other disorders such as depression. Genetic factors do not fully explain the development of mental disorders. It seems to be more likely that genetic factors predispose someone to develop a mental disorder; whether it in fact develops seems to depend on environmental factors.

Mental illness can also be seen as having a biochemical cause. Some abnormal behaviours have been linked to the endocrine system, which produces the body's **hormones** and regulates their activity. For example, certain disorders of the thyroid gland have been linked with depression.

Imbalances in particular **neurotransmitters**, chemical messengers which carry information between neurons, have also been linked to mental illness. Schizophrenia, for example, is associated with an excess of the neurotransmitter dopamine. However, there is insufficient evidence to claim that this kind of chemical imbalance causes a particular disorder. Both the disorder and the chemical imbalance could be caused by a further factor; for example, they could both be genetic.

Neurological damage is seen as another possible cause of mental illness. As an example, we will look at **Fregoli's delusion**. People who suffer from this delusion believe strangers to be people whom they know, even though they do not look like them. The sufferer may try to make sense of their experiences by believing that people they know are going about in disguise. A case study of a patient with this disorder is described in Box D:

Box D: Ellis and Szulecka (1996)

Miss C believed that she was being stalked by an ex-lover and his girlfriend, who followed her everywhere. She believed they disguised themselves by wearing wigs or dark glasses, or by changing their clothes and driving different cars. She reported their activities to the police.

She would go up to strangers and demand that they took off their disguises, and believed that the gas man who had come to read her gas meter was one of them, who had adopted a disguise to get into her house.

The false recognition of strangers as people she knew was eliminated by drugs, but the delusion remained. Miss C believed that the police had made the stalkers go away.

A CAT scan of Miss C's brain showed that, as the result of a stroke, there was quite severe damage to the cerebral cortex. (CAT stands for Computerised Axial Tomography, and this type of scan displays a three-dimensional representation of the brain's structures and can therefore be used for such tasks as locating tumours.)

Since mental disorder is seen to have an **organic** (i.e. physical) basis, it is treated with physical or **somatic** therapies. These include drugs, ECT (electroconvulsive therapy, described in chapter 2), and psychosurgery. Psychosurgery involves making lesions in the brain, and cannot be carried out without the patient's consent.

There are several positive aspects of the medical model. Firstly, for many disorders the treatments offered can be very effective. The idea that there is an organic or physical cause for some types of mental illness is supported by the fact that some somatic therapies do relieve the symptoms of many mental illnesses. ECT, for example, is often very successful in treating severe depression, and the symptoms of schizophrenia can be controlled by anti-psychotic drugs such as chlorpromazine.

Additionally, considering abnormal behaviour to be a symptom of 'illness' means that the person cannot be blamed for their disorder; they are not 'bad' but 'ill'. The hope, therefore, is that people will be sympathetic towards those with a mental illness. However, there are stereotypes about people with a mental disorder which mean that this doesn't necessarily happen in practice. For example, research by Jones and Cochrane (1981) showed that British people's stereotype of mental disorder fitted the symptoms of schizophrenia. It is possible that this formed part of your answer to Activity 1. Sufferers from this disorder can be violent and their behaviour is often bizarre. For this reason, many people may be afraid of such individuals, and tend to avoid them rather than showing sympathy.

Some theorists, sometimes known as **anti-psychiatrists**, take a very different view of mental disorders from that advocated by mental health professionals. In his book *The Myth of Mental Illness* (1972), Szasz suggested that most mental disorders are not organic (i.e. having a physical basis) but **functional** (i.e. with no known physical cause). These disorders are attributed by Szasz to what he termed 'problems in living'.

Szasz argued that the word 'depression' simply describes an unhappy person, and that if we consider the term to be a medical diagnosis, this allows us to put into place various practices that we consider will 'cure' the patient, whether or not that person wishes to be treated. To Szasz, mental illnesses are termed 'illnesses' because they go against our idea of normality, and not because they are true, physical illnesses. This makes psychiatry a form of **social control**, made acceptable by the existence of psychiatrists, but really a way of taking away a person's rights and responsibilities.

In his book *The Divided Self* (1965), another anti-psychiatrist, R.D. Laing, suggests that 'sanity or psychosis is tested by the degree of conjunction or disjunction between two persons where one is sane by common consent'. He is here stressing the idea that judging someone to be psychotic is very subjective, and that there are important implications regarding who decides which people are mentally ill. Many researchers find it of great concern that the lack of power of some people's social position seems to attract the label 'mentally ill' more readily than others. As we saw earlier, this applies particularly to members of ethnic minorities and women.

This argument raises an ethical issue. If psychiatrists are justified in believing that a person's abnormal behaviour is caused by an organic problem that is preventing them from functioning adequately, then they are right to treat those people, even if treatment is resisted. The psychiatrist must act for the patient's own good, and take responsibility for their well-being, while attempting to free the patient of the misery of mental illness.

Alternatively, if the anti-psychiatrists are correct, then hospitalisation can be seen as imprisonment which violates people's human rights. People who may never have broken the law have their freedom taken away from them, and if this is true, society is persecuting unconventional people for behaviour that society itself cannot cope with. On the other hand, Szasz's ideas could mean that those with mental disorders are not helped during what is often a very distressing time in their lives.

- **Historically**, mentally ill people have been thought to be possessed by **evil spirits**, suffering from an imbalance of the **humours**, or morally **wicked**.
- The **medical model** sees mental illness as having a physical basis. In particular, **genetic factors**, an imbalance in **neurotransmitters** or other **neurological problems** are seen as important. There is some evidence that these factors play a major part in some disorders.
- Since the causes are presumed to be physical, **physical treatments** such as drugs are offered. They are helpful in treating the symptoms of some disorders.

● **Anti-psychiatrists** take issue with the medical model of mental illness. Szasz believes that there is no such thing as mental illness, and that the concept is used to **control** people. Laing objects to the processes and procedures used as **dehumanising** to the patient.

The behavioural model

As with other areas of psychology, behaviourists relate abnormal behaviour to learning. Behaviourists believe that all behaviours, apart from the few simple reflexes we are born with, are learned. They therefore see mental disorders as learned, inappropriate behaviours which they call **maladaptive behaviours**.

You will remember from chapter 1 that the two main theories relating to this model are classical and operant conditioning. According to **classical conditioning**, behaviours are learned by forming an association between an environmental event (a stimulus) and a physiological reaction (a response). This idea has been particularly influential in explaining the development of phobias. In the same way that Pavlov's dogs learned to respond by salivation to the sound of a bell, a person may learn to produce a fear response when they see a snake or find themselves in an enclosed space.

In **operant conditioning**, an association is formed between a behaviour and its consequences. If a behaviour has favourable consequences (**positive reinforcement**), it is likely to be repeated. For example, these principles have been used to explain conduct disorders in children where inappropriate behaviour may have been reinforced by attention.

The behavioural model of mental disorders, however, is not concerned with causes. It claims that we do not need to know what has brought about a maladaptive behaviour. The problem is the behaviour, so the focus of therapy is on helping people to unlearn these behaviours, and to learn new, more adaptive ones.

For example, in the case of someone who is phobic, one way in which the principles of classical conditioning can be applied in therapy is through the use of **systematic desensitisation**. The phobic person is gradually exposed to the situation or object of their phobia and learns to relax. Exposure is gradually increased until the phobia has disappeared. This works on the principle that it is not possible to have competing responses (fear and relaxation) to the same stimulus. Another possibility is **flooding**, where the person is exposed to the phobic object or situation in an extreme form, on the principle that extreme fear cannot be maintained.

Behavioural therapy has the advantage of being relatively quick and straightforward, and is very successful with some disorders, such as phobias. The behavioural approach, however, has been criticised as being unduly reductionist, since it focuses only on behaviour, and does not take higher mental processes such as thoughts, feelings and memories into account. Many therapists also believe that we need to uncover the root causes of the behaviour in order to find out what underlying emotional problems a person is experiencing. If this is not done, and these problems are not dealt with, there may be **symptom substitution**, where the problem behaviour which has been unlearned is replaced by another, equally maladaptive behaviour.

The cognitive model

You will remember from chapter 1 that cognitive psychologists focus on internal mental processes. In the area of psychopathology, cognitive theorists have suggested that the root of disorders lies in the way people think about events and experiences. In Personal Construct Theory, for example, George Kelly (1955) suggested that every individual made sense of the world using **bipolar constructs**, such as happy-sad or honest-dishonest. These constructs are useful because they provide each of us with a **personal reality**, built on constructs which relate to our individual experience of the world, which can help us to understand the events and people we encounter. This creates a sense of predictability and therefore control over our lives.

According to Kelly, psychological disorders are due to faulty thinking processes, such as the failure of a person's construct system. For example, he explained anxiety in terms of the realisation that our construct system is inadequate for making sense of the events we experience and the people we meet. A person with a mental disorder may be using inappropriate constructs to make sense of the world, or constructs which are too limited or too vague to be helpful. People with psychological disorders continue to use inappropriate constructs rather than altering them, despite the fact that their predictions about events and other people are repeatedly shown to be wrong. This leads to mentally ill people anticipating events with very little accuracy. The implications of this for therapy are that the therapist needs to help the person with problems to change the way they understand the world by adapting their construct systems.

Other cognitive theorists are Aaron Beck and Albert Ellis. They explain mental disorders in similarly cognitive terms to Kelly, but focus on irrational beliefs and negative thoughts rather than explaining inappropriate thinking in terms of bipolar constructs. Beck (1987), for example, related depression to negative thoughts in three areas, which he called the triad of negative assumptions – the self, circumstances and the future:

Figure 4: Beck's triad of negative assumptions

- **Negative view of self**
  (e.g. I am a worthless person)
- **Negative view of circumstances**
  (e.g. everything is bleak and I cannot cope with what people expect of me)
- **Negative view of the future**
  (e.g. things can only get worse, and there is nothing I can do to change them)

Problems occur when these kinds of faulty thinking prevent the person from behaving adaptively.

The therapies cognitive theorists think are appropriate are cognitive (Kelly) or cognitive-behavioural (Beck and Ellis). For Kelly, the person with a mental disorder needs to be helped to develop a more adaptive construct system. For Beck and Ellis, faulty thinking needs to be challenged, and more positive ways of thinking need to be translated into behaviour during the therapeutic process in order to be effective.

Inappropriate ways of making sense of the world and faulty cognitions have been found to be associated with a range of mental disorders. For some disorders, in particular depression but also phobias and anxiety disorders, cognitive therapy can be very effective.

At the same time, however, it has been suggested – by Beck (1991) himself among others – that irrational and maladaptive thinking may be the *result* of a mental disorder rather than its cause. A further criticism of this approach is that it focuses very much on the individual who is experiencing problems; it may therefore not give enough weight to the contribution made by environmental factors (such as poor housing or the characteristics of other family members) to the development of a disorder.

The psychodynamic model

The psychodynamic model centres round the ideas of Freud. According to this model, mental disorder is due to **psychic conflict**, and has its roots in **childhood experience**. The causes of mental disorders lie in the **unconscious**. You may find it useful at this point to look back to the outline of Freud's theory in chapter 1 to remind yourself of its basic principles.

According to Freud, the three parts of the mind are the id, the ego and the superego. In the mentally healthy person, the ego is in control. Mental disorder will result from conflict between the different parts of the mind with which we are unable to cope.

Freud believed that early experiences are crucial to our development. Unresolved and unconscious conflicts relating to our experience of psychosexual development will lead to a mental disorder.

One of Freud's main ideas is that the unconscious mind is all-important. According to Freud, our lives are controlled by internal, unconscious forces of which we are mainly unaware. Ego defence mechanisms are used to prevent the anxiety resulting from psychic conflict from reaching consciousness. However, using defence mechanisms distorts our perception of reality. The conflict which has become unconscious has not been dealt with, so still continues to affect how we experience the world and our behaviour.

Since the causes of mental disorder lie in the unconscious, the aim of therapy is to bring our unconscious conflicts into consciousness so that they can be resolved. Psychodynamic therapy is called **psychoanalysis**. It is a talking therapy, and the main method used is **free association**, where the patient talks freely about anything which comes into their head. With the help of a psychoanalyst, unconscious material is brought into consciousness and interpreted by the analyst, who helps the patient to 'work through' the underlying problems.

There are problems with this model of mental disorder, since it relies very much on interpretation, and many people find the underlying ideas about psychosexual development unconvincing. It has also been accused of being overly reductionist, since it sees people as basically driven by animal instincts over which they have no control. Many people claim to have been helped by psychoanalysis, but it is difficult to evaluate its effectiveness objectively.

▶ Activity 4: which approach?

Match each of the following statements with one or more of these approaches:

medical   **behavioural**
cognitive   **psychodynamic**

a We do not need to know what has caused a person to have a particular problem in order to treat them.
b Therapy consists mainly of talking.
c People need to be helped to make sense of how they experience the world.
d The root causes of problems are to be found in childhood experiences.
e Drugs are a useful way of helping people with problems.
f Mental illnesses have an organic cause.
g This approach can be criticised as being reductionist.

When you have finished, see page 120.

● The **behavioural** model explains mental disorders in terms of faulty **learning**. Treatment therefore involves learning more appropriate behaviour.

● In the **cognitive** model, mental disorders are linked to faulty ways of **making sense** of our world, implying that treatment should focus on developing more appropriate cognitions.
● The **psychodynamic** model sees the roots of abnormal behaviour in **psychic conflict**. Treatment involves dealing with unconscious conflict through psychoanalysis.

5.5   CRITICAL ISSUE: EATING DISORDERS

The classification system **DSM-IV** characterises eating disorders as physically and/or psychologically harmful eating patterns. The two disorders we shall be looking at in this section are **anorexia nervosa** and **bulimia nervosa**. There is some discussion about whether anorexia and bulimia should be thought of as separate disorders or variants of the same disorder. As we will see, some of the evidence relating to the causes of these disorders relates to one or the other, and some to both.

Anorexia nervosa

Anorexia has a high profile in the media, so it is likely that you already know something about it:

▶ Activity 5: anorexia – true or false?

Read through these statements and decide whether you think they are true or false:
a Anorexia is most likely to affect teenage girls.
b People with anorexia do not feel hungry.
c Most people with anorexia recover.
d Anorectics see themselves as fatter than they actually are.
e Anorexia usually starts as an attempt to lose weight.
f There is a similar incidence of anorexia across cultures.

Check your answers by reading through the rest of this section.

Anorexia nervosa means 'nervous loss of appetite', though sufferers do experience hunger. The problem is that they do not respond to it by eating appropriately. Anorectics refuse to maintain the minimum expected body weight and are at least 15% below what is regarded as normal. Typical characteristics are shown in Figure 5:

Figure 5: typical characteristics of anorectics

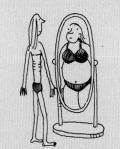

a a fear of gaining weight or becoming fat.

b a distorted body image: although they are thin, they believe that they are fat.

c denial that they have a problem.

d perfectionism.

Although they are thin they believe they are fat

e obsession with food and its preparation, with a tendency to hide food to conceal the fact that they are not eating it.

f avoidance of high-calorie food.

g excessive exercising.

h amenorrhoea in females: one diagnostic criterion is three missed periods.

Of course some of these characteristics are also true of non-anorectics, but Figure 5 gives some idea of the general overall pattern typically found in anorectics. DSM-IV divides anorectics into two types, **bingeing** and **non-bingeing**. Between 30-50% of anorectics also binge and vomit.

Ninety per cent of anorectics are females, with the onset of the disorder usually between the ages of 13 and 18. Some cases are as young as 8, and sufferers may be older than 18. Anorexia also seems to be on the increase among males, of whom around half are homosexual. DSM-IV claims that the incidence is 0.5-1% among young females. The top two social classes (professional and managerial) are over-represented, as are certain professions; according to Garfinkel and Garner (1982), dancers and models account for 7% of cases.

Twenty per cent of anorectics have one episode but make a full recovery. Sixty per cent have a pattern of weight gain and relapse over several years. The remaining 20% are severely affected and usually need to be hospitalised. The mortality rate in this group is more than 10%; anorectics die from starvation, suicide or electrolyte imbalance. Hsu (1990) reports that anorexia is fatal in 5% to 15% of cases.

Figure 5 described the psychological and behavioural characteristics typically associated with anorexia. Someone with this disorder may also show changes in their physical appearance apart from extreme thinness. Typically the skin of anorectics is dry, rough and dirty-looking. They may grow hair on cheeks, neck, forearms or thighs, known as **lanugo hair**, and may lose scalp hair. They have an abnormal intolerance of cold, so have bluish fingers and toes, a condition known as **cyanosis**.

There are several physical and psychological effects of the disorder. Sufferers have a low metabolic rate. They sleep less than normal, and have a low or non-existent sex drive. They suffer from constipation, and sometimes swollen ankles (**peripheral oedema**). They are likely to develop a mood disorder, e.g. depression, or an anxiety disorder. They also show a high rate of alcoholism. They often suffer from anaemia and dehydration, and are liable to die from heart failure.

Bulimia nervosa

'Bulimia' comes from the Greek, meaning 'ox hunger'. It is typified by binge eating followed by behaviour to prevent weight gain, i.e. vomiting, misuse of laxatives and diuretics, excessive exercise or fasting. Non-bulimics may also binge and purge occasionally; it is the frequency of this behaviour which defines the bulimic – it takes place on average 2-3 times a week, and sometimes as often as 30 times.

Bulimics usually have normal weight but a distorted body image, so they see themselves as fatter than they are. They indulge in secretive overeating – up to 10,000 calories at a time – of fattening foods, eaten rapidly with little chewing. Eating stops when the food runs out or when the bulimic experiences severe abdominal pain. They may use coloured marker foods to ensure that all food is eliminated by vomiting. Depression and guilt are common. Bulimics recognise their behaviour is abnormal; the sufferer is aware of loss of control. They often have swollen features with puffy parotid glands, caused by vomiting. Parry-Jones and Parry-Jones (1993) found that four bulimics of the 25 they studied were self-mutilators, i.e. they cut themselves, which they suggest may be a way of reducing anxiety. Parkin and Eagles (1993) described three bulimics who showed similar behaviour, using blood-letting to reduce tension and anxiety.

Nearly all sufferers – 95% – are female. The average age of onset is slightly later than for anorexia; many bulimics have previously suffered from anorexia. It is difficult to establish how prevalent bulimia is, because bulimics usually have normal body weight and they are also secretive about their eating habits. It may be more common than anorexia; it has been suggested that it affects up to 5% of females in their late teens or early twenties.

Bulimia is associated with cardiac problems, sometimes epileptic seizures, kidney damage, hair loss and metabolic disturbances. There is often also throat damage and dental erosion from the corrosive effects of stomach acids as a result of repeated vomiting.

● The main characteristic of people suffering from **anorexia** is a refusal to maintain normal body weight, together with a belief that they are fat, and a refusal to acknowledge that they have a problem. The disorder is associated with a range of psychological and behavioural characteristics, and can result in severe medical problems and even death. Sufferers are typically females in their teens.

● **Bulimia** usually has a slightly later onset. It involves bouts of bingeing and purging. Incidence is difficult to establish because sufferers have normal body weight. As with anorexia, there are serious medical implications.

As with other disorders, the suggested aetiology of eating disorders is a much disputed area. Some theorists focus on possible **biological** factors while others stress the importance of **social** and **psychological factors**.

It is also possible that biological and social/psychological factors interact. The **diathesis-stress model** suggests that some people may be predisposed to develop a particular disorder (**diathesis** refers to this vulnerability), either for genetic reasons or as the result of early experience. Whether they in fact develop the disorder will depend on the amount of **stress** in their lives.

It is important to know as much as possible about the causes of a mental disorder, so that an appropriate therapy can be offered to the patient. For example, if the disorder has a biochemical cause, then it would seem most sensible to use a drug therapy; if the disorder is related to faulty cognitive processes, then cognitive therapy, which aims to change the way someone views the world, would seem to be a good place to start treatment. As we will see, however, a range of explanations has

Anorexia	Higher prevalence in middle and upper socio-economic group	Bulimia
Underweight bingeing (for some)	Mainly female	Normal weight
Denial of problem	Distorted body image	Frequent bingeing
Depression (for some)	Fear of gaining weight	Awareness of problem
Peak onset: early 20s	Secretive about eating behaviour	Guilt and depression
Life threatening	Likelihood of heart problems	Peak onset: mid-teens
Damage to kidneys and gastrointestinal system	Metabolic disturbances	Rarely life threatening

Comparison of anorexia and bulimia

been offered for eating disorders, and in no case does any one theory provide a definitive explanation.

Biological explanations of eating disorders

One possibility is that eating disorders may have a **genetic** basis. One way of exploring this has been through the use of **family studies**. Family studies look at the incidence of a particular disorder within families. If the cause is genetic, it would be expected that if one member of a family has the disorder, other members are also more likely than unrelated people to have it, particularly if they are close relatives. This approach usually relies on interviewing family members about the family, both current and past generations.

Activity 6: family studies

Can you think of any problems with the technique described above? Why might we need to be wary of drawing conclusions, using this method, about the contribution of genes to a disorder?

When you have finished, see page 120.

DSM-IV states that there is an increased risk of an eating disorder in first-degree relatives of sufferers, i.e. parents, brothers and sisters or children. However, because of the problems associated with family studies, this does not necessarily mean that the cause of eating disorders is genetic.

Twin studies are another way in which a possible genetic influence can be investigated. Twins can be **fraternal** (**dizygotic** or **DZ**: they develop from different fertilised eggs within the mother) or **identical** (**monozygotic** or **MZ**: developing from only one fertilised egg). Fraternal twins share on average 50% of their genes, the same proportion as any brother or sister. Identical twins, as the name suggests, have 100% of their genes in common.

The reasoning behind twin studies is that if one identical twin suffers from a disorder, and the disorder is genetically caused, then the other twin must also suffer from the same disorder, since they have all their genes in common. In other words there should be 100% **concordance** between identical twins. For fraternal twins, however, there should be a much lower concordance rate, approximately 50%, similar to that between brothers and sisters who are not twins. If the environment is important, a low concordance between MZ twins reared apart would be expected.

Twin studies have been more informative than family studies in investigating a possible genetic basis for eating disorders:

Box E: concordance for eating disorders in twin studies
Holland *et al.* (1984) – anorexia: MZ twins: 55%   DZ twins: 7%
Kendler *et al.* (1991) – bulimia: MZ twins: 23%   DZ twins: 8.7%

These studies support the idea that there may be a genetic link in eating disorders, but at the same time concordance is a long way off 100%, particularly for bulimia, so other factors are clearly involved.

It is possible that eating disorders are caused by a **neurotransmitter** imbalance in a structure in the brain called the **hypothalamus**, which is known to be one of the structures controlling eating behaviour:

Figure 6: the hypothalamus and eating behaviour
lateral hypothalamus (LH) → stimulates eating (neurotransmitters: noradrenaline and dopamine)
ventromedial hypothalamus (YMH) → inhibits eating (neurotransmitter: serotonin)

Activity 7: neurotransmitters and eating disorders

How could each of the following help to account for either anorexia or bulimia?

a low levels of noradrenaline

b low levels of serotonin

When you have finished, see page 120.

Further evidence of neurotransmitter involvement comes from the use of antidepressant drugs which influence neurotransmitter levels, and have sometimes helped to reduce binge-purge behaviour in bulimics. However, the results of research in this area have been inconsistent.

A further idea links eating disorders with **hormones**. One piece of evidence comes from Lydiard *et al.* (1993), who found low levels of the hormone **CCK-8** in bulimics. Park *et al.* (1995) suggested the possibility of a viral or immune system disorder, since four anorectics he studied had had glandular fever. This could affect the production of **corticotrophin releasing hormone (CRH)**, which would in turn affect the functioning of the **hypothalamus**, which as shown in Figure 6 controls eating behaviour.

One problem with looking to hormones for the cause of eating disorders, however, is that hormone function can be influenced by emotional factors, so it is difficult to establish the direction of any causal connection between hormonal function and eating disorders.

A recent suggestion, put forward by Kennedy (1997), is that anorexia may be due to abnormality in the **temporal lobes** of the cortex. Scanning techniques have shown reduced blood flow to these areas in anorectics. This could explain their distorted body image, since these lobes are involved in the interpretation of what we see.

- **Twin studies** suggest a **genetic** link in eating disorders, particularly **anorexia**.
- **Neurotransmitters** may also be involved, with low levels of **noradrenaline** being associated with **anorexia**, and low levels of **serotonin** with **bulimia**.
- **Hormones** and **temporal lobe abnormality** could also be implicated.

Social and psychological explanations of eating disorders

A range of social and psychological explanations for eating disorders has been proposed: behavioural explanations, cultural factors, cognitive explanations, psychodynamic explanations, and the nature of family relationships.

Behavioural explanations

Attempts have been made to account for eating disorders as learned behaviour, using the principles of conditioning theory. If we use the **classical conditioning** model, the UCS of admiration produces the UCR of feeling good about yourself. When slimming is paired with admiration, slimming itself becomes a CS producing the CR of feeling good about yourself. Using the **operant conditioning** model, admiration for slimness reinforces dieting behaviour. It may also be reinforced by attention; for example, from parents. In this way, slimming may become a habit.

Anorexia has also been explained as a **weight phobia**, brought about by social norms. Advertising puts across the message that 'slim is beautiful', and dieting in Western cultures is often seen as 'normal'. Garner *et al.* (1980) found that Playboy centrefolds and contestants in the Miss America Pageant had become thinner over the previous twenty years, while over the same period the average weight for women had increased. Similarly, Wade and Tavris (1993) reported that Miss Sweden of 1951 was 5'7" tall and weighed 151 pounds, while Miss Sweden of 1983 was 5'9" tall and weighed only 109 pounds.

While these ideas are perhaps not entirely successful in explaining such features of anorexia as distorted perception of body size, and the willingness to pursue the goal of thinness even if it leads to death, they do have some intuitive appeal, and link in well with explanations which focus on culture.

Cultural factors

It has been found that anorexia and bulimia are more common in industrialised societies, where there is an abundance of food, while at the same time slimness is seen as attractive. Immigrants from non-industrialised societies, once they are assimilated, are as likely to develop these disorders as the indigenous population. All this suggests that eating disorders may be linked to cultural factors.

Support for this comes from Sui-Wah (1989), who pointed out that eating disorders are rare in China, and suggested that this may be linked to the respect the Chinese have for food. There is a cultural norm in China of meals being seen as social occasions, so there is pressure to conform to family eating patterns.

The idea of cultural influences is taken further in a feminist perspective on eating disorders. This points out that the images of ideal women presented by our society are constructed by men, since they have the power within society. Images of males concentrate on action, while those of females focus on appearance. Therefore it is only through their appearance that women can exert power, by conforming to the 'ideal' body shape. Orbach (1978) has suggested that bingeing is an expression of anger at social pressure to be thin, while purging is a way of regaining control.

The idea of control is also raised by Lewis and Blair (1991). They argued that women in our society receive conflicting messages about their role: they need to achieve academically and in a career, while at the same time raising a family and putting partner and children first. Anorexia may be a way of regaining control over at least one aspect of their lives.

Cognitive explanations

The underlying principle of cognitive explanations for eating disorders is that attitudes and beliefs influence eating behaviour – for example, the belief that 'thin = successful, happy and attractive'. In bulimics, a broken diet may lead to uninhibited eating (the **disinhibition hypothesis**). A cognitive explanation for this could be the reasoning: 'I broke my diet. What's the use? I failed so I may as well go all the way.' There is some research evidence supporting a cognitive explanation of bulimia:

Box F: Cutts and Barrios (1986)

Procedure: A group of bulimics and a control group were asked to imagine gaining weight. Their heart rate and muscle tension were monitored as indicators of emotional arousal.
Results: The bulimics, but not the controls, showed an increased heart rate and muscle tension.
Conclusion: There are cognitive differences between bulimics and non-bulimics in relation to weight gain.

Cognitive ideas also link well with the distorted body image of anorectics, and we will look at this aspect of the disorder in a little more detail here. Three techniques are used to assess body image:

Figure 7: investigating body image

moving caliper technique
The person is asked to imagine their body silhouetted on a screen, and to mark the width of the face, shoulders, waist and hips using sliding calipers. This is then compared with the actual body measurements.

image–marking technique
The person is asked to face a large sheet of paper and imagine it is a mirror. They are then asked to mark the width of the body at various points.

distorting image technique
An image of the person is projected on a screen through a lens. The image can be adjusted horizontally to make it more or less fat. The person is asked to adjust the image until it seems right to them. This technique is the most realistic and reliable, but requires more elaborate equipment.

There is some evidence of a link between overestimation of body width and anorexia:

Box G: Slade and Russell (1973)

Procedure: Anorectics and controls were asked to estimate their body width. They were also asked to estimate their height, and the width of other objects.
Results: Anorectics overestimated the width of their bodies by 25–55%, while controls estimated body width accurately. There was no difference between anorectics and controls in the accuracy of their estimations of their height and the width of other objects.
Conclusion: There is a strong link between anorexia and distorted body image.

Other research in this area, however, has produced conflicting results. Crisp and Kalucy (1974) found that controls also overestimated body width, but this may be because the group they tested was younger, and estimation of body size becomes more accurate with age. Thompson (1986), however, showed that 95% of women in fact overestimate their weight; it is possible, though, that anorectics overestimate by a greater margin. Even if distorted body image is related to anorexia, it could be that the distortion is a result of the disorder, rather than its cause. A further problem, as Yager *et al.* (1986) have pointed out, is that there are blind anorectics; though of course they will still have a body image based on senses other than sight.

Psychodynamic explanations

Several ideas have been put forward from a psychodynamic perspective. For Freud, eating can be a substitute for sexual expression, so eating disorders could be a symbolic way of repressing sexual impulses. You will remember that one of the characteristics of anorexia is amenorrhoea, which returns the body to a prepubescent state, so the disorder could be a way of avoiding the issue of sexuality. This idea has been given a rather broader focus in the suggestion that anorexia may be a way of avoiding the demands of adulthood by regressing to childhood.

Many patients with eating disorders report in therapy being sexually abused as children, so an eating disorder may be a response to early traumatic experiences. Sexual abuse may lead people to reject their own bodies in adolescence, so anorexia and bulimia may express an unconscious desire to destroy their own bodies.

> ## Activity 8: evaluating psychodynamic explanations
>
> Look back through the psychodynamic explanations outlined above. Can you identify any problems with what they suggest?
> When you have finished, see page 120.

Research findings have questioned psychodynamic explanations. The idea that amenorrhoea could be the aim of anorexia has been challenged by Halmi *et al.* (1977). They found that in almost 40% of anorectics, menstruation ceased *before* significant weight loss occurred, suggesting that an underlying endocrine problem is the cause of amenorrhoea.

Similarly, of the 18 patients with eating disorders studied by Piran *et al.* (1985), eight had shown symptoms of depression at least a year before the eating disorder had developed, suggesting that any link between childhood trauma and developing an eating disorder is likely only to be indirect.

Family relationships

Eating disorders have also been related to problems in family relationships, especially the struggle of young people to establish their own identity. Bemis (1978), for example, argued that anorectics are often well-behaved and co-operative girls, who may feel that they are overly controlled by others. Overcontrolling parents may lead young people to feel that they lack a separate identity, which in turn leads to low self-esteem. Anorexia may be one way of taking control.

The fact that anorexia is more common in middle-class families, where there is likely to be considerable pressure on young people to succeed, lends some support to this idea. Similarly, Pike and Rodin (1991) found a link between eating disorders and mothers who thought their daughters were unattractive and should lose weight.

Coming from a psychodynamic background, Bruch (1973) made a link between anorexia and early relationships between infant and mother. She suggested that distorted body image and faulty hunger awareness both come about as a result of the mother failing to respond to the infant's signals. This leaves the infant with the feeling of being an ineffective individual.

Family systems theories suggest that we need to look at the dynamics within the family in order to understand why one member has an eating disorder. Bruch (1973) believed that anorexia may be mutually rewarding for mother and child: the mother retains the child and the child remains dependent. According to Minuchin *et al.* (1978), anorexia may be a way of diverting the attention of parents who are having marital problems away from each other and on to the child, as a way of preventing family break-up.

All these ideas imply that family therapy is the most useful way to treat eating problems, and it is widely used, with some success.

Activity 9: explanations of eating disorders

Read through the following suggestions which have been put forward to explain eating disorders, and sort them under these headings:

biological, cultural, psychodynamic, family, relationships, cognitive, learning

a Women are under pressure from the media to be thin.

b Women are encouraged to be thin by praise and attention from others.

c Tensions within the family may trigger eating disorders.

d Low levels of noradrenaline are related to anorexia.

e Anorexia may be the expression of a weight phobia.

f Eating disorders express the relative powerlessness of females in our society.

g Anorexia may be a way of retreating from sexuality and adult responsibilities.

h Distorted thoughts and beliefs about food and eating lead to eating disorders.

When you have finished, see page 120.

Explanations of eating disorders: an overview

We have looked at a range of suggestions as to why people might develop eating disorders. There are several levels of explanation. Biological explanations focus on genetic and neurochemical factors in the individual. Learning theory, psychodynamic and cognitive explanations also have their focus very much on the individual, while psychologists interested in family relationships look more at the individual within a social context. The focus can be even broader, taking in aspects of the cultural context.

As we have seen, all these approaches have something to offer, while none seems to provide a complete explanation of eating disorders. However, these different kinds of explanations are not necessarily mutually exclusive. Biological factors may interact with cognitions, influenced by social norms and expectations, and further influenced by particular patterns of family interactions, to lead to the development of anorexia and/or bulimia.

● **Learning theorists** explain eating disorders in terms of classical and operant **conditioning**. They suggest that such disorders may be a **weight phobia**.

● **Cultural factors** may be implicated in eating disorders; they are more common in Western cultures, where slimness is presented as the 'ideal'. They have been related to the relative powerlessness of women in society, and may be used as a way of exerting control over their lives.

● According to **cognitive** theorists, eating disorders are the result of **inappropriate beliefs** and attitudes.

● **Psychodynamic** explanations make a link with **regression** to childhood, and avoidance of adult sexuality and responsibilities. These ideas are, however, difficult to test.

● It has been suggested that the cause of eating disorders may lie in **family relationships**. They may be a way in which young people seek to establish their own identity, separate from an over-controlling parent; the result of inappropriate maternal feedback to an infant; or an attempted solution to distorted family relationships.

● These different explanations are not necessarily mutually exclusive. The **interaction** of different factors may lead to eating disorders.

Notes on activities are on page 120.

Notes on activities

2 There are some parallels between these two systems. The term 'affectionate relationships' used by Atkinson *et al.* seems to be expressing a similar idea to Jahoda's 'positive interpersonal relationships'. Also, 'voluntary control' is similar to 'autonomy', and 'efficient perception of reality' is similar to 'accurate perception of reality'.

Jahoda's term 'self-acceptance' brings in aspects of 'self-knowledge' and 'self-esteem' from the Atkinson *et al.* list, though 'self-esteem' is rather more positive than 'self-acceptance'. 'Productivity' from the Atkinson *et al.* list has something in common with 'potential for growth and development', though the latter focuses more on the individual and the former relates also to interaction with others. 'Productivity' therefore shares some aspects of Jahoda's term 'environmental competence', though it goes further in its emphasis on interaction with the external environment.

3 The first two correspond to female stereotypes, and the last two to male stereotypes.

4 a behavioural; **b** psychodynamic; **c** cognitive; **d** psychodynamic; **e** medical; **f** medical; **g** behavioural and psychodynamic.

6 The technique asks ordinary people, untrained in diagnosing mental disorders, to draw conclusions about the mental health of members of their family. Information about past generations relies on the accuracy of the memory of the interviewee. These kinds of problem have been overcome to some extent by looking at the medical records of family members, but of course this can only be done when people have presented for treatment. Even if it is clear that family members do have similar disorders, we cannot assume that the disorder is inherited; close family members are likely to share the same physical and psychological environment, and this could account for the similarity.

7 Low levels of **noradrenaline** acting on the lateral hypothalamus could be insufficient to stimulate eating and so could be a partial explanation for **anorexia**. Similarly, low levels of **serotonin** may not be enough to inhibit eating and so could partially explain bingeing in **bulimics**.

8 As with all psychodynamic ideas, these suggestions are not easy to test in a rigorous way. The link with amenorrhoea can only relate to females; while most people with eating disorders are female, males are also affected. Similarly, while the onset is most frequently in the early teens, the idea of avoiding sexuality or adult responsibilities cannot explain why the onset is often later, particularly for bulimics. It could also be that any connection between childhood trauma and eating disorders is rather indirect; for example, sexual abuse could lead to depression, which might then be expressed in an eating disorder.

9 a learning; cultural **b** learning **c** family relationships **d** biological **e** learning **f** cultural **g** psychodynamic **h** cognitive

Social influence

One area in which social psychologists have been particularly interested is the effect that other people can have on our behaviour. This general area can conveniently be described by the term **social influence.** This is relevant to very many areas in social psychology, and we will be focusing in this chapter on only two forms of influence: conformity and obedience.

6.1 CONFORMITY

Conformity refers to behaviour change as a result of group pressure. This pressure doesn't necessarily need to be expressed, and may even just be in the mind of the person who experiences it; for example, Mary may feel that she should study languages at university because this is what her two older sisters have done. Sometimes, though, there is explicit pressure; for example, if the rest of the family suggest that this is what Mary should do.

Ambiguous and unambiguous situations

Research into conformity goes back a long way. Allport (1924) asked participants to judge the pleasantness of smells, and found that if people made this judgement in groups, individual judgements tended to be in general agreement with the average judgement for the group as a whole. Similarly, when Jenness (1932) asked participants to judge the number of beans in a bottle, and then revise their estimates after discussion in a group, the second estimate tended to move towards the average group judgement. Another study, shown in Box A, demonstrated conformity using a visual illusion called the **autokinetic effect**: when there is a point of light in an otherwise darkened room, it seems to move about:

Box A: Sherif (1935)

Procedure: Participants were asked individually to estimate how far and in what direction the point of light moved. Average scores were worked out for each participant over a series of trials. They were then divided into groups, each group containing participants with very different averages calculated from the individual trials. Participants were then asked to make individual judgements while in their groups.

Results: After a few trials, individual judgements tended to move towards agreement within the group. The effect was still evident when the tests were repeated later, with participants tested individually.

Conclusion: When making judgements in a group, there is a tendency for individual judgements to drift towards group consensus, i.e. to conform to the average for the group.

Box B: Asch (1951)

Procedure: All participants were given the simple task of matching a standard line with one of three comparison lines (see Figure 1). They were tested in groups of seven, of whom six were confederates of Asch. They were asked for their decisions in order, going round a table, with the genuine participant sitting last but one. On some trials, the confederates were asked to give the (same) wrong answer.

Genuine participant

Results: Participants conformed to the group's incorrect judgements in about 32% of trials on average. This can be compared to a control group, with no confederate participants, where judgements were virtually 100% correct.

Conclusion: In a group situation, there is a tendency to conform to the judgements of others, even where this judgement is clearly incorrect.

It is worth noting that Sherif's study did not *ask* participants to arrive at a group estimate. It is a nice example of conformity where there is no direct and explicit pressure to change behaviour; influence comes about through the individual's perception of the situation.

This study has not been without its critics, however. Asch, who went on to carry out his own series of studies on conformity (see Box B), pointed out that Sherif's study had put participants into a situation of uncertainty, i.e. where a correct answer was not apparent: since the light does not actually move at all, but only seems to move, there is no right or wrong answer.

He argued that for a real understanding of conformity, we need to look at what happens in an *un*ambiguous situation. In other words, there should be one clearly correct solution to the task, and we should look at whether participants move from a position held with certainty to conform to obviously wrong answers given by others.

Figure 1: the Asch task

a Standard line   b Comparison lines

A   B   C

Asch found that about a quarter of his participants *never* conformed to the group's wrong judgement, leaving three-quarters who *did* conform at least once. Some participants conformed on only a few trials where incorrect judgements were made, and only about 1 in 20 conformed each time. We will be returning to the question of individual differences in susceptibility to social influence later in the chapter.

Participants who conformed to the majority gave a variety of reasons for conforming.

▷ Activity 1: explaining Asch's findings

Imagine you had taken part in this study, and conformed at least occasionally to the incorrect judgements of the group. How might you explain what you did?

When you have finished, see page 149.

Asch followed up his original study with some variations, to look in more detail at some of the possible variables which could affect conformity.

▷ Activity 2: other conformity research by Asch

Here are some of the questions Asch investigated in later studies. What do you think his findings were? Try to give reasons for your answers:

a How would more/fewer confederates affect conformity?

b What would be the effect of having one of the six confederates giving the *right* answer?

c What would happen if someone agreed with the genuine participant (as in question 2) to start with, but then gave the majority answer in later trials?

d What would happen if the task were more difficult, i.e. the lines closer in length?

e How would a majority of naive participants react to only *one* confederate in the group giving a wrong answer?

f Would the effect be the same if the genuine participant could give his answer in private?

When you have finished, see page 149.

Another question is whether other people need to be physically present for conformity to occur, or if the belief that others are carrying out the same task is all that is necessary. To investigate this question, Crutchfield set up an experimental situation where participants worked in booths on their own, so were not directly exposed to other participants. They were asked to indicate agreement or disagreement by means of switches which would turn on lights. They were aware of the judgments of other people from a display of lights, and believed that their own responses were similarly available to other participants (see Box C).

Box C: Crutchfield (1954)

Procedure: More than 600 participants were tested, including American college students and military personnel. They were tested for conformity on a range of tasks, including clearly incorrect factual statements and personal opinions, e.g:

a agreement with statements such as: 60-70% of Americans are over 65 years old; Americans sleep 4-5 hours a night, on average.

b an Asch-type task.

c agreement that a star had a larger surface area than a circle (in fact it was a third smaller).

d agreement with the statement 'I doubt that I would make an effective leader'.

e agreement with the statement 'Free speech being a privilege rather than a right, it is proper for a society to suspend free speech when it feels itself threatened'. Participants might have been expected not to agree with this opinion, given that free speech is enshrined as a right in the American constitution.

Results: The degree of conformity varied with the nature of the task. There was 46% conformity to (c), for example, and only 30% conformity to (b). 37% agreed with (d), none of whom did so when asked on their own. Substantial numbers of participants agreed with the 'facts' given in (a), and the opinion given in (e).

Conclusion: There was conformity both to incorrect facts and to opinions. The extent to which conformity was shown depended on the nature of the task.

The information they were given about other judgements was, of course, actually manipulated by the experimenter.

Crutchfield's results were in broad agreement with those of Asch, and extended Asch's work by demonstrating conformity not only in factual judgements, but also opinions. Like Asch, Crutchfield found that some participants never conformed to an incorrect judgement made by the majority, some always conformed and most conformed some of the time.

● Early studies into conformity used situations in which the answer was uncertain. The classic study by Asch, using a task where there was a clearly correct answer, found a high rate of conformity. Variations on this study isolated particular factors such as group size which affect conformity.
● Some conforming participants in Asch's study showed **public conformity**, but no **private change**. Others changed their judgement as a result of social influence.
● Crutchfield's study extended conformity research to opinions.

Cultural differences in conformity

You will have noticed that many of the studies referred to were carried out some time ago, and mostly used American students as research participants, i.e. they provided a snapshot of a particular culture at a particular time. But can these findings be generalised to other populations, and more recent times?

Larsen (1974) replicated Asch's original experiment with American college students, to investigate whether cultural changes in the preceding twenty years would affect conformity rates. Participants still conformed, but at a lower rate than the 32% of the Asch study. Perhaps at that time the US had become a less conformist culture? A further replication in 1979, however, found a rise in conformity.

There may be some variation as culture is modified with the passing of time, but what about **cross-cultural** differences? Using Asch's technique, there have been findings similar to those of Asch in Brazil, Hong Kong and the Lebanon. A higher conformity rate, however, was found among the Bantu in Zimbabwe (Whittaker and Meade, 1967). Every culture needs a degree of conformity, to simplify social life by giving it order and predictability. How this need is translated into practice, though, would be expected to vary across cultures, since what are regarded as important **social norms** – i.e. what is considered to be appropriate behaviour within a particular social group – will vary from culture to culture.

● The conformity rate has been found to alter across time within a **culture**, though overall trends are far from clear. There is also variation between cultures. These differences are related to **social norms**.

Why do people conform?

Let us start by looking again at the Asch study. Those of Asch's participants who conformed to judgements which were clearly incorrect fell into two groups. A distinction was made between those who changed their behaviour, but not their opinion (**public conformity**), and those who changed both their behaviour and their opinion (**private change**).

Kelman (1958) picked up on this distinction, referring to **compliance** (i.e. public conformity) and **internalisation** (i.e. private change). These two different kinds of conformity have been related to two different kinds of influence: what Deutsch and Gerard (1955) have called **normative influence**

Figure 2: public conformity and private change

Asch's terms	Kelman's terms	what happens	influence
public conformity	compliance	behaviour changes opinion doesn't	normative
private change	internalisation	behaviour changes opinion changes	informational

and **informational influence** (see Figure 2). Normative influence refers to the social influence of others which may lead a person to conform to social norms. Informational influence may bring about change as the result of information gained from other people. Asch's study highlights the effect of normative influence, but it may also be that some participants asked themselves: 'Can it be possible that what I think is the right answer is not actually correct here?' This is suggested by the increased conformity found with variation (d) in Activity 2.

Let us look first at **normative influence**. As you will remember from the last section, **social norms** relate to behaviour which is considered appropriate within a particular social group. There are norms, for example, about queuing at supermarket checkouts and apologising when you accidentally step on someone's toes.

Activity 3: identifying and understanding norms

What are the social norms when you are:
a at a psychology lecture?
b in a restaurant?
What kinds of behaviour would go against these norms?
Why are there unwritten social conventions and how do we know what they are?
What are the consequences when we do not observe these conventions?
When you have finished, see page 150.

The observation of social norms helps to explain the conformity people show in some of the studies we have looked at. People very readily identify themselves as part of a group; Tajfel *et al.* (1971) found that people quickly identified themselves as members of a group artificially created by the experimenter even when group membership was decided by something as arbitrary as the toss of a coin. Asch's participants said they felt it was important to maintain group harmony, and that disagreement would damage this. The importance of acceptance and approval emerge clearly in the phrases which they used when Asch asked them after the study why they had conformed to the majority answer; many said they didn't want to 'create a bad impression', 'be different' or 'look stupid'.

This kind of concern has also been verified by physiological measures. Bogdonoff *et al.* (1961) looked at autonomic arousal in participants in a study similar to Asch's. (Autonomic arousal is related to anxiety and stress and is covered in more detail in chapter 4. Blood pressure and heart rate are examples of some of the ways in which it can be measured.) A high level of arousal was found when the participant was faced with an incorrect majority judgement. This dropped if the participant conformed, but remained high if they disagreed with the judgement.

Informational social influence is another factor, which stems from the desire to be right:

Activity 4: decision making and social influence

Imagine you are taking up a new sport, e.g. skiing or tennis, and are planning to buy some equipment. You have heard of a few brand names, but don't know much about the different makes available. How would you go about choosing what to buy?
When you have finished, see page 150.

▷ Activity 5: summarising conformity theory

To link these studies and ideas, complete the blanks in these sentences, picking a word or phrase from those given underneath.

One form of conformity is ...., where there is public acceptance of a group decision, but private disagreement. It depends heavily on .... influence, and is motivated by .... It is more likely in .... situations, such as the study by ....

The other form of conformity is ...., where there is both public and private acceptance. It depends more heavily on .... influence, and is motivated by .... It is more likely in .... situations, such as the study by ....

internalisation   normative   compliance
the need for approval/acceptance   Asch
informational   the need to be right
unambiguous   Sherif   ambiguous

When you have finished, see page 150.

But is the distinction between the two processes as clear-cut as Activity 5 suggests? It has been suggested that both normative influence and informational influence may be factors at the same time:

Box D: Insko *et al.* (1983)

Procedure: Participants worked in groups of six. They were shown a colour slide, and had to decide which of two other slides had the more similar colour. A control condition tested participants alone, to establish the most frequent answers. Four confederates answered before the genuine participant, disagreeing with these answers. There were two independent variables:

    a public vs. private answers
    b determined vs. undetermined

'Determined' referred to trials where the experimenter claimed to have apparatus which could check the accuracy of the judgements made. In the 'undetermined' trials, it was claimed that there was no possibility of making this check, and that the degree of similarity between the colours was simply a matter of opinion.

Results: Conformity was more frequent in the 'public' than the 'private' condition. It was also greater in the 'determined' than the 'undetermined' condition. There was greater conformity, both 'public' and 'private', in the 'determined' condition.

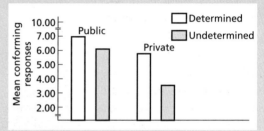

Mean conformity data from Insko *et al* (1983)

Conclusion: The 'public' vs. 'private' comparison showed normative influence. The 'determined' vs. 'undetermined' comparison showed informational influence. The final finding suggests that informational influence can add to normative influence, so the two can work together to increase conformity.

Conformity and social roles

Another important reason why people conform is to do with **social roles**. A role is a set of behaviours which are thought to be appropriate to a person in a particular kind of situation. The role of 'student', for example, implies dressing casually and having a wild social life, as well as studying and writing essays. We all play roles in social situations and our in-role behaviour is shaped by our beliefs about the demands of the situation and the expectations of other people.

A major study in this area, carried out by Zimbardo *et al.* (1973), was interested in how people adapted their behaviour to fit the roles which they had been asked to take on:

Box E: Zimbardo *et al.* (1973)

Procedure: Student volunteers were asked to role-play prisoners and guards in a simulated prison situation. They were chosen to participate on the basis of tests for emotional stability and physical health, as well as having clean legal records. They were then randomly assigned to be prisoners or guards. For the prison, the basement of Stanford University was converted to be as authentic as possible. 'Prisoners' were arrested, charged, finger-printed, strip-searched and deloused. They were then issued a uniform. 'Guards' were also issued uniforms, together with whistles, handcuffs and dark glasses, to make eye-contact with 'prisoners' impossible.
Results: Both prisoners and guards acted in character to an extreme degree. Guards became increasingly more aggressive, and seemed to

Zimbardo's volunteers

enjoy the control they had over the prisoners. They went far beyond the minimum requirements for fulfilling their role, e.g. making prisoners clean out toilets with their bare hands. Prisoners became passive, and showed extreme stress reactions, such as uncontrolled crying and depression. Some prisoners, wanting to withdraw from the study, asked to 'be paroled'. One developed a serious rash when his 'parole' was rejected. It had been intended to run the study for two weeks; it had to be stopped after six days because of the extreme reactions of the prisoners.
Conclusion: People easily respond to roles assigned to them, particularly where the environment supports these roles. The behaviour people demonstrate 'in role' may be very different from their normal behaviour.

Activity 6: Zimbardo's prison simulation experiment

Read through the prison simulation experiment in Box E, and answer these questions:

1 Why do you think potential participants were screened before being accepted?
2 Why were they not allowed to choose which role to take?
3 Both prisoners and guards assumed their roles very rapidly, and showed extreme behaviour. How could you explain this?
4 Participants were paid for taking part in this study. How might this have affected their behaviour?
5 What are the implications of Zimbardo's findings for the prison system?

Compare your ideas with the discussion which follows.

The first two questions relate to Zimbardo's attempts to make his study as unbiased as possible, and so avoid methodological criticisms. Screening the participants ensured that the participants were 'ordinary' people. They had had no direct experience of the law which might have distorted their role-play. They were not unstable, and so were not likely to behave in pathological ways, but could be taken to be representative of people in general. They were also not likely to be badly affected in what was expected to be something of a stressful experience (though not as stressful as it in fact turned out to be).

The behaviour shown cannot be accounted for in terms of existing personality differences, or differences in relevant experiences, then, but can be taken to show how ordinary people are affected by roles allocated to them, and the environment in which they find themselves. If participants had been allowed to choose their roles, it is possible that this might have biased the results; for example, with aggressive people choosing to be guards. (In fact, all the participants had stated a preference for being a prisoner.)

The relative ease and thoroughness with which roles were adopted perhaps has something to do with the media. The prisoners-guards scenario is, after all, a standard one on TV, and the behaviour of both prisoners and guards in Zimbardo's study reflects rather stereotypical pictures of how in general prisoners and guards might be expected to behave. Other role models involving power and subordination are also very widespread in people's lives, e.g. parent-child; teacher-pupil; boss-employee. We can call on our experience of this kind of relationship when it is required in a particular situation.

The fact that participants were paid quite well for taking part may have encouraged them to throw themselves wholeheartedly into their roles. It may also have made it harder for them to withdraw from the study. It is possible, then, that payment may have biased the study in some way.

Zimbardo's study was heavily criticised on ethical grounds, particularly since the participants were clearly distressed by their experience. However, Zimbardo claimed that the study had provided a lot of information which could not have been established any other way. The feedback from the students themselves is interesting; for example, many of the guards mentioned the pleasure they had experienced from their control over others. It is not just 'monsters' or disturbed individuals who have these feelings, but ordinary well-balanced people, if the environment is right.

Perhaps even more importantly, though, Zimbardo's study was instrumental in bringing about changes to the prison system in America, in particular providing support for the notion that an institution itself can have a substantial effect on behaviour.

A final factor in conformity is the power of **reference groups** – people we like or admire, who we conform to because we want to be like them. Relating to role models in this way is known as **identification**.

- In explaining conformity, a distinction can be drawn between **compliance** (public conformity, but no private change) and **internalisation** (public and private change).

- Compliance can be linked to **normative influence**, where people are motivated to observe social norms in order to have the acceptance and approval of others. This kind of conformity is more likely in **unambiguous** situations.
- Internalisation is linked to **informational influence**, where people are motivated by the desire to be correct. It is most likely in **ambiguous** situations.
- The distinction is not necessarily very sharp: both kinds of influence may simultaneously underlie conforming behaviour.
- **Social norms**, the often unwritten rules which allow social groups to function, help to explain social influence.
- Zimbardo's prison simulation study showed how roles and the environment can affect behaviour in situations involving power and subordination.
- **Reference groups** – people we adopt as role models – may also be associated with conformity. This is known as **identification**.

Minority influence

A limitation of most conformity research is that its design only allows a one-way influence; individual participants can either conform to the majority or not. Other research has looked at the possibility of influence in the other direction. To what extent can a minority affect the judgement of a majority? There are many examples in history where a single person has changed majority opinion. For example, Galileo's belief that the earth moved round the sun contradicted opinion at the time, but is now accepted.

An early research study in the area of minority influence is described in Box F:

That's a fine cheese tonight

Fact or majority opinion?

Box F: Moscovici *et al.* (1969a)

Procedure: Participants were tested in groups of six. Two were confederates of the experimenter. Each participant was asked to judge the colour of 36 slides, all of which were blue. The confederates consistently judged them to be green. Participants were also asked to name the colour of the after-image. (This is the colour which is perceived when you have been staring at a colour, and then look at a white surface; the complementary colour is seen.)

Results: A third of all genuine participants judged a slide to be green at least once. They also tended to label the after-image red/purple. Controls who had not taken part in the judgement task used yellow/orange labels.

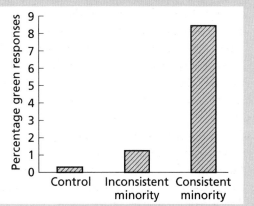

Conclusion: A minority can influence a majority if they are consistent in their judgements. The label given to after-image colours suggests that change was genuine and lasting.

Moscovici proposed that different factors are at work in majority influence and minority influence. He distinguished between compliance (when a majority influences a minority) and conversion (when a minority influences a majority).

In **compliance**, change is to do with the power of greater numbers and factors connected with social norms; people respond to normative influence. There is public agreement with the majority, but private agreement may not last long when a person is no longer in the presence of people holding the majority opinion.

In **conversion**, however, Moscovici believed that an undecided person may pay attention to the viewpoint of a minority because they are interested in the reasons for this different viewpoint. Minorities may therefore respond to informational influence, and there is likely to be lasting change in the opinion held, i.e. **internalisation** in Kelman's terms.

This suggests that minority influence should be linked to **behavioural style**; Moscovici has suggested that a minority is more likely to bring about conformity by a majority if the minority point of view is put across confidently and consistently.

Research has demonstrated the role of confidence in minority influence. Lee and Ofshe (1981), for example, confirmed the effectiveness of a confident non-verbal behavioural style, while Nemeth and Wachtler (1973) found that minorities who appear certain about their position achieve more conformity than those who seem less confident. However, while confidence is important, this should not be allowed to tip over into dogmatism if minority influence is to be effective. Mugny (1984) found that opinion statements putting forward minority viewpoints were far less effective in bringing about change when they were written in slogan-like terms than when they were expressed in more moderate language. It seems that flexibility on the part of the minority, defined as a willingness to make concessions to others to reduce conflict, while at the same time remaining consistent, is more effective than dogmatism.

The study by Moscovici *et al.* in Box F demonstrates the importance of consistency. In a variation of the basic study, Moscovici *et al.* (1969) found that an inconsistent minority had little effect on the judgements of the majority.

Other factors may also be important:

Box G: Moscovici and Nemeth (1974)

Procedure: Groups of five people (four participants and one confederate of the experimenter) were asked to take jury-type decisions. The confederate took a minority view. In one condition, he chose to sit in either position A, B or C at the table (see Figure 3), while in the other he was assigned to one of these seats.

Results: There was little minority influence when the confederate was assigned to a seat. When he chose where to sit, he was highly influential when he sat in position C, but not when he chose seats A or B.

Conclusion: Minority influence is more likely when a person holding a minority opinion is seen to act autonomously and when he is the focus of attention.

Figure 3: seating in the Moscovici and Nemeth (1974) study

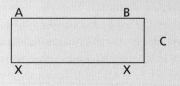

The status and power of the individual is also relevant. If someone putting forward a minority viewpoint is perceived by others as having high status or as being able to exert power over others, these characteristics can help to bring about change in a majority viewpoint. However, Wiggins *et al.* (1967) found that these characteristics are of little use if the person hinders the group from reaching its goal.

Other factors also work against minority influence. If the minority is seen as having something to gain from the opinion they are putting forward, their perceived self-interest is likely to make them less effective in bringing about change in the majority. The same is true if two or more people are in the minority and cannot agree among themselves.

Group size may also be a relevant factor in whether a minority can influence a majority:

Activity 7: conformity and group size

Imagine yourself as one of a group of 12 people, who need to come to a unanimous decision. You are in a minority of one. Then imagine the same situation with a smaller group, say 6. In which group would you be more likely to conform to the majority? Why?

When you have finished, see page 150.

This question is relevant to jury size. The Supreme Court in the USA has shown some interest in reducing the size of juries. This would cut costs, and could well lead to greater efficiency in terms of the time taken to reach a verdict. At the same time, a jury decision will affect people's lives, so every effort must be made to find the size of group which will make the best quality decisions.

In the film 'Twelve Angry Men', made in 1957, a murder case jury, about to vote 'guilty', was persuaded to change its verdict by one doubting member. The behaviour shown by the one man wanting to bring in a 'not guilty' verdict was very much in line with Moscovici's suggestions for conversion: he was consistent, he argued his case and discussed the objections of the other jury members, rather than just dogmatically repeating his view. This is of course fiction, but nonetheless provides a nice example of how a minority can influence majority opinion.

Henry Fonda acts persuasively in 'Twelve Angry Men'

In a jury of 12, one member who does not agree with the others is under considerable social pressure to conform, whereas fewer people will mean less pressure. The Supreme Court was influenced by Asch's work. They came to the conclusion that a jury of six would be efficient in terms of cost and time, and would also have the advantage of being less likely to be under pressure to conform (though it is worth noting that Asch's studies did not find that a group of six was under less pressure to conform than a group of twelve!). This could well ensure a more just verdict.

- A distinction can be made between **compliance**, where a majority can affect the judgement of a minority, and **conversion**, where a minority can affect the judgement of the majority.
- **Conversion** is best achieved if a minority view is put consistently and not dogmatically.
- This research could be relevant to considerations of effective **jury size**.

Evaluation of conformity research

Much of the research into conformity has been criticised on methodological grounds. As you read through the previous section, you may have had doubts about the **ecological validity** of studies such as those of Asch and Sherif. Can we really find out much about a social phenomenon like conformity within the confines of a laboratory situation? While this approach does have the advantage of controlled conditions, in which exact measurements can be made and compared (e.g. the estimates of the distance the light appeared to move in Sherif's study in Box A), it also has a number of disadvantages.

If we take the Asch study as an example, we are often put into situations where we can conform or not, but we are seldom faced with a task as artificial as line-matching. There would seem to be room to test the basic ideas suggested by this kind of research in a more naturalistic way. Crutchfield's technique could arguably be seen as being even less realistic than the Asch studies.

There is also the question of **demand characteristics**. Even when participants are not aware of the true nature of an experiment, they are aware of taking part in a psychological experiment of some sort. This knowledge may lead them to think about what the study may be investigating and so to behave in ways which do not necessarily correspond to the way they would act naturally.

Another problem is the sharp distinction made between 'fact' and 'opinion' in accounting for different findings. There are of course judgements which fall neatly into one or other category. The Asch study (Box B), for example, is concerned with a fact: one line of the three comparison lines was the same length as the standard line. Some of the judgements in the Crutchfield study (Box C), on the other hand, looked at what were clearly matters of opinion.

However, there seems also to be a grey area between fact and opinion, which could be explored in more depth. There is quite a lot of knowledge which we might define as 'fact', but which is in truth culturally determined. Opinions which are widely held within a particular culture are often considered to be 'fact', but are majority opinions and facts the same thing? Before Galileo, for instance, it was an accepted 'fact' that the sun moved round the earth. Similarly, the distinction between normative and informational influence is not clear-cut, as the Insko study (Box D) suggests.

You may also have had ethical concerns. As we saw earlier, Bogdonoff *et al.* (1961) showed that participants experienced the situations they were put in as stressful.

You may have come away from these studies with the impression that conformity is somehow wrong or ridiculous; this emerges quite clearly in Asch's work, and is a judgement he himself explicitly made. It is not the job of psychological research to provide answers about social desirability, and it is in any case open to question whether conformity is necessarily undesirable.

As pointed out earlier, conformity serves a very positive and necessary function in helping social interaction to run smoothly. Normative influence helps us to make the compromises necessary in social life to fit into social situations. If a friend were to take you to an event at the local Conservative Club, for example, you might wear a suit and keep your radical green views to yourself. Informational influence helps us to learn appropriate behaviour in times of uncertainty; for example, learning how to taste wine involves a lot of acceptance of others' definitions of what makes a wine 'good', when to the beginner it may not taste very pleasant at all. However, most conformity research has tended to focus on demonstrating conformity, rather than broadening its scope to consider in detail the functions it might serve in different situations.

At the same time, these studies do give us a good basis for understanding conformity. This research has implications for group situations: we can't expect disagreement and therefore discussion to arise naturally in groups, and at the same time, we can't assume that agreement shows consent.

- Conformity research has attracted a certain amount of criticism. Its **ecological validity** is often poor, and there are also **ethical concerns**.
- It may also rest on questionable **assumptions**, e.g. drawing a sharp distinction between fact and opinion, and normative and informational influence. It tends to be **descriptive** rather than providing functional explanations.
- Research has given us some understanding of conformity, which may be applicable in practical situations.

6.2 OBEDIENCE

Milgram's research

After the second world war, German war criminals who had been involved in the Holocaust – the wholesale killing of Jews, together with other 'undesirables' such as gypsies, homosexuals and the mentally ill – were put on trial for war crimes. These trials continued for a number of years and roused considerable public interest.

Those on trial did not appear to be monsters. On the contrary: Hannah Arendt, writing about the trial of Adolf Eichmann, was struck by just how ordinary he seemed, using the phrase 'the banality of evil'. Yet at the same time, he had been very directly involved in the concentration camp programme. His defence against the charges brought against him, like that of many other war criminals, was that he was 'only obeying orders'.

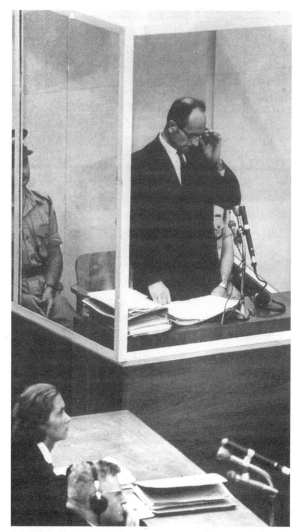

Adolf Eichmann in the dock

Milgram was intrigued by the apparent contradiction between the ordinariness of the men involved and the terrible deeds they had carried out. He was interested in how the idea of obeying orders fitted into the picture, and in the extent to which ordinary people would obey orders to harm an innocent fellow human being. He brought these factors together in a series of studies. The basic study is described in Box H opposite.

Milgram later ran a number of variations of the basic study, to find out more about the particular factors which might influence obedience. Some of these, together with the results, are listed in Box I.

Box H: Milgram (1963)

Procedure: Male volunteers, aged 20-50, were recruited through a newspaper advertisement to take part in a 'scientific study of memory and learning'. Each worked in pairs with Mr Wallace, apparently another participant, who was in fact a confederate of Milgram and an accountant in his late fifties. His part in the study had been planned in advance and was scripted.

The study was run at Yale University Psychology Department by a young man in a white lab coat. He told the participant and Mr Wallace that the study was investigating the effects of punishment on learning. The two men drew lots to decide who was to be the teacher and who the learner in the experiment, though this was rigged so that Mr Wallace was always the learner. In view of the teacher, Mr Wallace was strapped into a chair and attached to electrodes, linked to a shock generator. At this point, Mr Wallace said he had a heart condition, but was assured that though the shocks were painful, there would be no permanent damage. The teacher's job was to administer a shock every time the learner made a mistake in learning a list of paired associates.

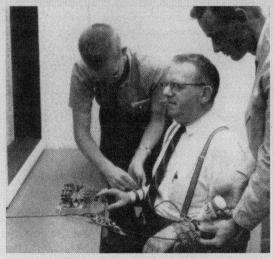

Milgram's (1963) apparatus and Mr Wallace being connected up to it

The teacher was then taken to another room containing the shock generator. This had a 30-point scale showing an increasing level of shocks from '15 volts–mild shock' up to '450 volts–XXX'. The size of shock was to be increased every time an error was made. The teacher was given a 45 volt shock in case he had any doubts that the shock apparatus was real. No further shocks were given, though the teacher was unaware of this.

Results: All the participants gave increasing shocks in the early part of the experiment. No one stopped below '300 volts–intense shock'. Some participants were unwilling to continue, but did so when told by the experimenter: 'Please continue' or 'The experiment requires that you continue'. These instructions (which Milgram called 'prods') were followed despite Mr Wallace banging on the wall, refusing to continue to take part in the experiment, and asking for the shocks to stop. Many teachers continued to give increased shocks even when, at 315 volts, Mr Wallace let out a violent scream, and when at 330 volts there was complete silence from the next room – the teacher had been told that no response counted as a wrong response. In all, two-thirds of the men (65%) continued to increase the shocks up to the maximum level of 450 volts.

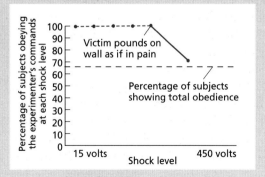

Conclusion: Ordinary people are likely to follow orders given by an authority figure, even to the extent of killing an innocent human being.

Box I: variations on Milgram's experiment

disobedient models: When the 'teacher' was in the presence of two other participants (actually confederates of the experimenter) who refused to administer shocks, the level of obedience fell from 65% to 10%.

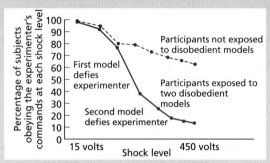

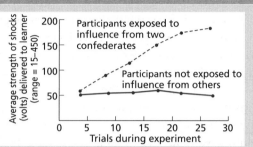

Just under 50% of participants continued to increase the shocks to the maximum 450 volts.

proximity of the learner: When the learner was in the same room as the teacher, the obedience level dropped to 40%. It dropped still further to 30% when the teacher had to force the learner's hand on to the shock plate.

proximity of the experimenter: When the experimenter left the room and gave instructions over the phone, the obedience level dropped to around 20%.

two teachers: A teacher was paired with another (confederate) teacher who administered the shocks. The genuine participant had only to read out the words. The obedience level was 92.5%.

encouragement: The participant was not instructed to increase the shock each time an error was made. The average shock given remained around 50 volts across the series of trials. When two confederates urged the participant to increase the shock level, the average strength of the shock given after 20 trials was more than 150 volts.

location: The study was carried out in a run-down office, rather than at Yale University.

▶ Activity 8: explaining Milgram

Use the information in Box H and Box I to identify:

a the factors which influenced obedience in this series of experiments

b the relative strength of each

Can you explain exactly how each factor might have influenced behaviour?

Compare your ideas with the discussion which follows.

The degree of personal **responsibility** which participants experienced is obviously of major importance here. In the original study, it was easy for participants to hand over responsibility to the experimenter, since he was giving them instructions and reminding them of their role when they protested (i.e. 'prods'). Participants were also assured by the experimenter that he was responsible for the welfare of the learners. There was therefore plenty of reason for the participants not to accept personal responsibility.

In the 'two teachers' variation, the high level of obedience can perhaps be explained in terms of the situation allowing the participant to shift responsibility from themselves to the person actually administering the shocks. In the 'disobedient models' variation, the refusal of the models to follow instructions is likely to have demonstrated to the participant that it was possible to take responsibility and act accordingly. This may be one reason why there was such a dramatic drop in obedience in this situation. Taking personal responsibility would also have been an important factor in holding down the hand of the 'victim', though the effect here was much smaller. We will be coming back to the question of responsibility later in this chapter, when we discuss reasons why some participants did *not* obey the experimenter.

The marked drop in obedience when the experimenter was in the next room (from 65% to 20%) also underlines the importance of the physical **presence of the experimenter**. Together with the effect of a disobedient model, this is one of the most important factors.

A related factor is the **authority of the experimenter**. Given the mention of a 'scientific study' in the advertisement, the experimenter's white coat and the prestigious setting of Yale University, the experimenter would be seen as a legitimate authority figure. When in one variation the experimenter was 'called away' and a stand-in (introduced as a research participant) suggested the stepwise increase in shocks as his own idea, obedience was greatly reduced, again suggesting the importance of authority.

The **location** does not seem to have played a major part here, though, since obedience only dropped by 15% when the location was changed.

Another factor is the **gradual** change in the behaviour required from the participant. A 15-volt shock is extremely mild, and willingness to deliver it paves the way for the next shock, also pretty mild, and so on.

Social influence clearly played a major role, since the encouragement of others was enough to produce a major increase in disobedience. The fact that 35% of participants ceased to be obedient before the end of the experiment suggests that some of the remaining 65% who did obey may well have had qualms about their behaviour; in fact, many participants showed clear signs of conflict and distress, stuttering, twitching and verbally abusing the experimenter. In a few cases, participants had seizures. In this case, a disobedient model would be enough to tip the balance towards disobedience. It is possible that the behaviour of disobedient models reminded participants of a possible alternative response: some participants made remarks at the end of the basic study, where they were not exposed to disobedient models, such as 'I didn't realise I could'. At the same time, participants tended to increase shocks when encouraged by others to do so; social influence can work both ways.

The effect of the presence of the learner in the same room as the teacher, and in particular of the teacher having to hold the learner's hand on the shock plate, is perhaps surprising. Obedience dropped in both these conditions, but was still at quite a startling level. Being brought face to face with the consequences of your actions does not seem to have as much influence as you might suppose.

▷ Activity 9: the ethics of Milgram's study

Milgram's work has been widely criticised on ethical grounds. What are the ethical objections to this study? You may find it helpful to look at Figure 5 towards the end of this chapter, which shows the British Psychological Society guidelines for carrying out research with human participants. How justified are these objections? How, if at all, could they be overcome?

Compare your ideas with the discussion which follows.

Ethical factors in Milgram's research

There are two main considerations here: **deception** and the **stress** or loss of self-esteem which may have been experienced by participants as a result of taking part.

The participants were deceived about the nature of the experiment, so they were unable to give their informed consent to participate in it. They were also not informed that they could withdraw from the experiment at any time. On the contrary, they were explicitly instructed to continue, and clearly felt under some pressure to do so. One way of avoiding this kind of criticism would be to give participants full information about the experiment, and to ask them to role-play their usual behaviour, but in this case role-play would be unlikely to be a true representation of normal behaviour. Alternatively, naturally occurring behaviour could be observed, but such an approach does not lend itself easily to this particular topic.

One way of mitigating this kind of ethical problem, where participants cannot be given full information about the nature of the study, is the use of **debriefing**. This involves giving participants as much information as possible about the study after it has taken place. They are told about the aims of the investigation, and any deception that was necessary. They are also encouraged to ask questions, and the use to be made of the findings is discussed. They are reassured that the way they behaved was perfectly natural in the circumstances, and not in any way unusual or shameful. Given the nature of Milgram's study, though, this last aspect of debriefing might be both inappropriate and ineffective.

A further study looked at the value of debriefing:

Box J: Ring *et al.* (1970)

Procedure: Milgram's experiment was replicated, using female students as participants. One group was thanked after the experiment, but not debriefed. A second group was thanked and debriefed, and reassured that their behaviour was quite normal. A third group was debriefed, but not reassured about their behaviour.
They were told they should have defied the experimenter.

Results: Both group 1 (who thought they had really hurt the learner) and group 3 (who were not reassured about their behaviour) were very upset about the experiment, compared to group 2. However, only group 1 regretted having taken part in the experiment.

Conclusion: Careful debriefing, which includes both information and reassurance, can go a long way towards overcoming ethical problems.

NB: *All* participants received a complete debriefing at the end of the study.

Perhaps even more serious is the stress caused by participation in Milgram's experiment – at least one participant suffered convulsions – and the loss of self-esteem which many participants experienced as a result of taking part in this study. Baumrind (1964) argued that adequate measures had not been taken to protect participants from psychological harm.

In replying to this kind of criticism, Milgram argued that the study was not intended to cause stress for the participants, and that Baumrind was confusing

the outcome (i.e. stress experienced by participants) with what was expected to happen. He pointed out that before carrying out the study, he had asked many people, including psychiatrists, what they expected the outcome to be. There was general agreement that perhaps only one person in a hundred would obey throughout the experiment, and that most would stop at 150 volts. Milgram also carried out a follow-up study (Milgram, 1964) when he surveyed those who had taken part. He reported that 84% were glad to have taken part in the experiment, 75% said they had learned something useful and only 1.3% were sorry or very sorry to have taken part. Milgram argued that the ethics of a study are best judged by those who have taken part, rather than in absolute terms.

However, many if not all of the participants must have experienced some loss of self-esteem, knowing that they had been prepared to hurt another human being, and had been unable to resist obeying an authority figure. This must have been all the more hurtful, since the experimenter had no real authority; although the participants were paid for taking part in Milgram's study, they were paid before the study started, so there was no real incentive to continue.

In answer to those who point to the loss of self-esteem suffered by those who took part in the experiment, it has been argued that it is not the duty of psychologists to hide from people truths about their own nature, however much they may not wish to know those truths.

This leads on to the question of the extent to which stress was *caused* to the participants by taking part in this study. It could be argued that it was the way the participants *responded* to the situation which led them to experience stress. As Milgram points out, the whole point of the study is that participants had a choice, and that most chose obedience.

A further justification of this study is that the ends had justified the means: his study had gathered valuable information about human behaviour which could not really have been established in any other way. Perhaps more than any other experiment, Milgram's study highlights the capacity of ordinary people for homicidal – even genocidal – behaviour. This carries clear implications for international courts, but it also changes our perceptions of ourselves. By knowing about this study, we are ourselves less likely to obey in similar situations.

With these kinds of considerations in mind, Elms (1972) considers Milgram's experiment to be one of the most significant ever carried out in modern psychology, and one of the most moral, both in its attempts to understand important phenomena and its concern for the welfare of its participants.

● Milgram was interested in the defence offered by war criminals that they were 'only obeying orders'. He carried out a series of studies to investigate obedience.

● In his original study, 65% of his participants were prepared to give what they thought were lethal electric shocks to someone they believed to be a fellow-participant in a learning experiment.

● Variations of the study looked at various factors in more detail. There was, for example, a drop in obedience when the participant was exposed to disobedient models. The authority of the experimenter, cues to reduce the sense of personal responsibility and the gradual increase in the strength of shocks given all seem to be important factors.

● Milgram's study has been criticised on **ethical** grounds: participants were deceived and subjected to stress and loss of self-esteem. However, Milgram found that very few participants regretted taking part in the study. The stress experienced can be seen in terms of the participants' choice of behaviour. Valuable information has been gained with important implications.

Gender, culture and victim characteristics

◗ Activity 10: gender, culture and obedience

Would you expect gender and/or culture to be a factor in obedience in this kind of study? Give reasons for your answer.
When you have finished, see page 150.

The participants in Milgram's original study were all men, but the effect of gender has been explored in similar studies. The Ring *et al.* study (Box J) found no difference between levels of obedience in men and women, and a later study by Milgram (1965), using a relatively small sample of 40 females, had similar findings. Another study focusing on gender produced even more startling results:

Box K: Sheridan and King (1972)

Procedure: Male and female participants were asked to give a puppy genuine electric shocks of increasing strength. Participants could see the puppy yelping, howling and struggling to free itself in response to the shocks.
Results: High levels of obedience were found in both men and women. Every female participant gave the puppy the maximum shock.
Conclusion: Women are just as likely as men to obey orders involving the infliction of pain.

You probably feel that this is a very distasteful study, but it does address the issue of gender very directly. It is perhaps also worth noting here that many women were among the concentration camp personnel involved in the Nazi programme of killing Jews and members of other 'undesirable' groups.

To investigate possible cultural differences, several researchers have replicated Milgram's study at different times and in different countries. For example, Mantell (1971), using a German sample, found an obedience level of 85%, while Kilham and Mann (1974), using an Australian sample, found somewhat lower rates of obedience than the 65% recorded by Milgram.

It is difficult to draw any very definite conclusions from these findings, though, since the behaviour of some participants in these later studies may well have been affected by knowledge of Milgram's original work. Another problem in making comparisons is that the studies were not exact replications of Milgram's work. In any case, even relatively small differences in the make-up of the sample – age, educational level, and so on – make direct comparisons unreliable. At the same time, the possibility that there are cultural differences in obedience cannot be excluded.

Let us look finally in this section at a study investigating the characteristics of the *victim*:

Box L: Farina *et al.* (1966)

Procedure: Milgram's basic procedure was followed. The teacher was introduced to the learner before the experiment began, on the pretext that getting to know someone helps communication. The learner then talked about himself and his past in either a negative way (unhappy childhood, history of illness, parents divorced and so on) or positively.

Results: More intense shocks were given to the learners who had talked about themselves negatively. Teachers also showed through questionnaire answers that they were less interested in getting to know the 'negative' learners than the 'positive' ones.

Conclusion: The results support what has been called the 'just world hypothesis': people who suffer do so because in some way they deserve to suffer. The 'negative' learner identifies himself as a loser in a world where people get what they deserve. He is therefore a legitimate target.

You may have found the results of this study a little surprising. There is quite a widespread belief that people are sympathetic to the underdog, but in practice this doesn't seem to be the case. It is perhaps worth noting that the Nazis went to a great deal of trouble to put across the idea of Jews as underdogs, and this may perhaps have had a part to play in the readiness of the camp guards to kill them.

● Most studies have found no **gender** difference in obedience levels.

● There are **cultural differences** in obedience levels, but precise comparison is difficult.

● Characteristics of the **victim** may also be relevant. The widespread belief that we show sympathy for the underdog seems to be false.

Milgram and after

We have already looked at criticisms made of Milgram's studies on ethical grounds. There has also been considerable criticism of their methodology. One suggestion (Orne and Holland, 1968) was that participants did not actually believe that they were giving genuine electric shocks to the learners. Far from the participants being deceived, they suggest, it was Milgram himself who was deceived into thinking that his participants accepted the experimental situation at face value!

▷ Activity 11: Milgram's methodology

Imagine you were a participant in Milgram's study. What aspects of the experimental situation might have struck you as rather odd and would perhaps have made you suspect you were being deceived? When you have finished, see page 150.

One way to clear up the question of whether Milgram's participants behaved as they did because they did not believe that the 'victim' was genuine was to set up a study in which participants also serve as their own victims:

Box M: Kudirka (1965)

Procedure: Participants were instructed to eat 36 quinine-soaked biscuits.

Results: Grimaces, moans and occasional gagging showed that this was clearly unpleasant. Nonetheless, virtually all the participants ate the biscuits.

Conclusion: Suggestions that participants are obedient because they don't accept the experimental situation as real are not supported. There are still high levels of obedience when the reality of the situation is quite unambiguous.

A second question mark hangs over the **ecological validity** of the study: can the findings of an artificial laboratory study be related to real-world situations?

It has been argued that there were some crucial differences between Milgram's studies and obedience in Nazi Germany. Firstly, the experiments were presented to participants in a positive way, i.e. as aiming to increase knowledge about human learning, while many Germans recognised the aims of the Nazis as immoral. Secondly, there were no penalties for disobeying Milgram's orders, whereas it would have been very dangerous to have disobeyed orders in Nazi Germany. Finally, Milgram's participants were told explicitly that the shocks they would give would cause no permanent damage, while people like Eichmann knew they were sending other people to their deaths.

These differences may not be so very clear-cut, however. The Nazi programme was presented to the German people in a very positive way, in terms of racial purification and the creation of a Nazi homeland. Most of Milgram's participants, on the other hand, recognised what they were doing to be wrong – as we have seen, many became very upset in the course of the experiment and protested at what they were being asked to do – but they nonetheless continued to give the shocks. Similarly, although participants were told that the shocks would do no permanent damage, it is hard to see what other interpretation could be put on the pleas from the victim for the experiment to stop, followed by a scream and then silence. Indeed, when they were reunited with Mr Wallace after the experiment, many 'teachers' stated that they thought they had killed him.

In one very important way, Milgram's study mirrored the experience of the Nazis who were 'only obeying orders'. In both cases, people were put into a situation unlike any they had ever experienced and instructed to carry out an extremely distasteful task. In real life, people being given orders to harm or kill others is not an everyday situation. For example, during the Kosovo conflict newspapers carried reports of groups of Kosovan men being machine-gunned to death and then set on fire, and of refugees being herded on to a bridge to be bombed, so that they would appear to be victims of NATO aggression. Presumably the people who obeyed these orders were not in a normal, everyday situation. It could be that it is the strangeness of the situation which makes obedience more likely. It could therefore be argued that as Milgram's participants were in an unusual situation, his studies had *higher* ecological validity.

This leads to the question of whether people show the same level of obedience in a more everyday situation. This can only really be tested by carrying out a naturalistic study, in such a way that the participants are not aware of being studied:

Box N: Hofling *et al.* (1966)

Procedure: A man claiming to be a doctor rang a hospital on 22 separate occasions. Each time, he asked a nurse to give medicine to a patient. This would require the nurse to break three hospital rules:

a they were not allowed to accept instructions over the phone.

b the dose was double the maximum limit stated on the box.

c the medicine itself was unauthorised, i.e. not on the ward stocklist.

On each occasion, the nurse's behaviour was monitored.

Results: In reply to questionnaires, most nurses said they would not obey such an order. In reality, 21 of the 22 nurses followed the orders they were given.

Conclusion: There is some support for obedience to authority in less extreme situations than that tested by Milgram: a very high proportion of people follow unjustified orders if told to do so by an authority figure.

When they were debriefed, some of the nurses said that this kind of situation often arose. They followed instructions because otherwise the doctors would be annoyed. This doesn't really explain away what they did, however, but rather says something about the relationships between authority figures and their subordinates which may lead to orders being obeyed.

Stimulated by Milgram's original experiments, a more recent set of 19 studies, the Utrecht Studies of Obedience, was carried out by Meeus and Raaijmakers in the 1980s. In these studies, participants were asked to inflict what Meeus and Raaijmakers termed 'administrative violence' on people who they thought were their fellow-participants. This involved making negative remarks about their performance on tests, and denigrating remarks about their personality. Two sample studies are described in Box O:

Box O: Meeus and Raaijmakers (1986)

Procedure: In a bogus personnel selection procedure, 39 participants aged 13–55 were instructed to make job applicants nervous, and to disturb them while taking a test as part of the application procedure. In consequence, applicants failed the test and remained unemployed. Forty-one participants aged 18–55 took part in variations of this basic study, when the experimenter was out of the room and when another participant was present who refused to obey the orders given by the experimenter.

Results: In the basic experiment, more than 90% of participants – a much higher percentage than in Milgram's experiment – complied with the orders they had been given, even though they considered them unfair and did not enjoy carrying out the task. In the variations of the study, obedience was much lower than in the equivalent variations of the basic Milgram study.

Conclusion: Participants show willingness to obey orders to inflict mental harm on others when instructed to do so. As in Milgram's studies, however, obedience is reduced in the absence of an authority figure, or in the presence of a disobedient peer.

On the basis of observing participants' behaviour, analysis of questionnaire responses and debriefing, Meeus and Raaijmakers concluded that participants had found the task stressful but had attempted to hide the stress they were experiencing and act as though nothing were wrong, behaving as an official. They therefore explained their findings in terms of attitudes to social institutions, and distant relationships with fellow citizens.

● Milgram's studies have been criticised on methodological as well as ethical grounds.
● The studies may have given rise to **demand characteristics**, and their **ecological validity** has been questioned. Later studies have gone some way towards refuting these criticisms. It may be unwise to assume, however, that the findings of laboratory studies can be directly extrapolated to behaviour in Nazi concentration camps.

6.3 INDIVIDUAL DIFFERENCES IN RESPONSE TO SOCIAL INFLUENCE

Up till now we have been considering social influence in general terms. Another approach has been to look at individual differences between people in terms of the extent to which they are affected by such influence.

In all the conformity studies discussed earlier in the chapter, you will remember that there were individual differences in conformity, with some people being much more likely to conform than others. This kind of pattern has been found in other research, looking at conformity both on judgements of facts, as in the Asch studies (Box B), and on opinions, included in the Crutchfield study (Box C).

Several researchers have looked at individual differences in conformity and obedience, including Crutchfield (1955) and Elms and Milgram (1966), and links with various characteristics have been found. For example, higher levels of obedience have been found among prejudiced and intolerant people, those achieving lower educational levels, and scientists and engineers (compared to doctors and teachers). Sub-cultural differences have also been found, with the military and Catholics (compared to Jews and Protestants) being more likely to conform. But the correlations are often weak, so any one factor of this kind is unlikely to play a large part in determining susceptibility to social influence.

One important theory, however, which links conformity and obedience to personality is Adorno's work on the **authoritarian personality**. Adorno *et al.* (1950) were interested in prejudice, and whether it was related to a particular kind of personality. Adorno himself was a Jewish American at a time when anti-Semitism was rife in the USA. He produced scales to measure personality, the most famous of which is called the **F-scale** (F standing for 'fascist'). Some sample items are shown in Figure 4:

Figure 4: sample statements from the F-scale

The most important thing to teach children is obedience to their parents.

Homosexuals are hardly better than criminals, and ought to be severely punished.

Any good leader should be strict with people under him in order to gain respect.

When a person has a problem or worry, it is best for him not to think about it, but to keep busy with more cheerful things.

People can be divided into two distinct classes, the strong and the weak.

Some day it will probably be shown that astrology can explain a lot of things.

The F-scale measures characteristics such as conventionality, submission to those in authority, aggression to those over whom you are in authority, toughness, destructiveness and superstition. The scale was successful in identifying people who were likely to be prejudiced, since prejudiced people would be likely to have these characteristics and so to agree with all these statements. Adorno referred to a high scorer on these scales as an **authoritarian personality**.

One characteristic typical of the authoritarian personality was a tendency to conform. A relationship has been shown between high scores on the F-scale and obedience in studies like that of Milgram (Box H). There is some evidence that a tendency to conform is related to upbringing.

Frenkel-Brunswik (1942) found that as a child, someone with an authoritarian personality was likely to have been strictly disciplined, and punished for disobedience.

From Adorno's work, it emerges that the authoritarian personality has a greater need than most for approval and acceptance. You will remember that **normative influence** is related to these needs, and is one factor in conformity; conformity is a way of satisfying these needs. Support for this comes from Stang (1973), who found that people with high self-esteem (and therefore less in need of the approval and acceptance of others) were less likely to conform than those with low self-esteem.

● There is some support for the idea that personality plays a part in conformity.
● One of the characteristics of the **authoritarian personality** identified by Adorno is conformity.
● This kind of personality has a high need for the approval and acceptance of others. It is related to a harsh, disciplinarian upbringing.

6.4 INDEPENDENT BEHAVIOUR

Why people conform to the behaviour of others or obey orders are interesting questions, but equally interesting is why others do not. After all, 13 of the 50 participants in Asch's experiments (Box B) did not conform with the majority, and 35% of the participants in Milgram's experiment resisted the order to continue giving shocks, at least to the extent of refusing to give the most extreme shocks.

Asch interviewed his participants after his experiment, and found that those who had not conformed fell into one of three groups. For one group, the essential factor was that they were **confident** that their judgement was correct. This can be related to the findings of Perrin and Spencer (1981), who replicated Asch's study. Very few of their participants conformed. In order to avoid using participants who knew about the Asch series of studies, they used medical and engineering students. Both these groups deal with physical phenomena, where accurate observation and measurement are crucial. Given the nature of the task, their knowledge and skills could have made them more sure of the judgement they were asked to make. This study also confirms the findings of Wiesenthal *et al.* (1976), that people who see themselves as competent at a particular task are much less likely to conform to a majority.

A second group maintained their independence by **withdrawal**, mentally withdrawing from the group, avoiding eye contact with the others, and so on. A third group experienced tension in the situation, but chose to *focus* on the requirements of the task.

Another factor in independent behaviour is past experience. Convincing evidence for this idea comes from one of Milgram's studies, and in particular from two participants who would not follow the experimenter's instructions.

One of them, Gretchen Brandt, refused to obey when the voltage was raised to 210V. It emerged that she had grown up in Nazi Germany. When she was asked to explain why she had not obeyed the order to give shocks, she replied: 'Perhaps we have seen too much pain'. The other, Jan Rensaleer, had lived in Holland during the second world war. He also had direct experience of the potentially terrible consequences of unquestioning obedience. To return to a previous point made in the discussion of Milgram's studies, unlike some of the other participants, both accepted responsibility for their own behaviour, rather than giving control to the experimenter.

Here we are looking at people affected by unusual and extreme experiences. What about people without this kind of experience? A study set up to investigate independent behaviour is described in Box P:

Box P: Gamson *et al.* (1982)

Procedure: Participants were told the study was to investigate community standards, and was being carried out by a human relations company. In groups of nine, they were asked to fill in questionnaires on a wide range of topics. This was to establish the extent of anti-authority attitudes for each participant.

They were also asked to sign an agreement to be videotaped, which stated that the tape would remain the property of the company. They were then asked to discuss the case of a petrol station manager, who was living with someone he wasn't married to. They were told that the company had fired him on moral grounds, and he was suing for breach of contract. The co-ordinator asked three of the participants to argue as if they were offended at the manager's conduct. Their discussion was videotaped. This was repeated for three more members of the group. They were then asked to repeat these views individually in front of the camera, and sign an agreement that the videos could be used as evidence in a court case.

Results: Out of 33 groups, only one followed the procedure all the way through. There was a high correlation between anti-authority attitudes and disobedience, but there was also disobedience in groups where anti-authority attitudes were low. In some groups, some of the participants signed the affidavit, but in many groups, disobedience became the group norm.

Conclusion: There is considerable readiness to disobey when people feel they are being manipulated. Although disobedience is linked to anti-authority attitudes, this is not enough to explain disobedience.

▶ Activity 12: comparing Milgram and Gamson *et al.*

Look back to Milgram's study (Box H). Compare this with the Gamson *et al.* study in Box P. What factors could have influenced people to be more ready to disobey in the Gamson *et al.* study? When you have finished, see page 151.

- **Personality**, **competence** and **experience** may all influence non-conformity and disobedience.
- Disobedience is more likely when people are aware that they are being manipulated.

6.5 Critical issue: The development of ethical guidelines for research

Because of the subject matter of psychology, research is carried out on people (or in some cases animals), and this raises special concerns in terms of the way those who take part in psychological research are treated. Ethical issues arise for psychologists more than for other scientists mainly because they study living organisms – human beings and animals. They are sentient beings; they can feel pain and fear. The humans involved are also thinking beings, and may experience an experimental situation as threatening, embarrassing, stressful or belittling. It is generally considered unacceptable for a person to induce feelings of self-doubt or inadequacy in another person, so researchers need to think carefully whether what they are planning to do could affect participants in this way.

It is unacceptable to induce feelings of self-doubt and inadequacy

Until fairly recently, people taking part in psychological research were known as 'subjects', and you may find this term used in older textbooks. However, the term 'participants' is now widely used, and recommended by the British Psychological Society. This change in terminology emphasises the fact that people freely give their time and effort when they offer to take part in a psychological study, and so deserve respect and concern for their well-being.

'Unethical' refers to procedures which are not only morally wrong but which are also professionally unacceptable. As we saw earlier, Milgram's work has been widely criticised on ethical grounds, and is perhaps the study most psychologists think of first when the topic of ethics in research involving human participants is raised. As we have seen, there are still differences of opinion about the ethical justifications of his research, with some psychologists seeing it as highly unethical and some seeing it as work of the highest moral quality. It is perhaps worth noting that the American Psychological Society investigated the ethics of Milgram's research shortly after it appeared, and concluded that it was morally acceptable, while in 1965 the American Association for the Advancement of Science awarded him a prize for his outstanding contribution to psychological research.

One undoubted result of Milgram's study, and the debate on ethics which arose from it, was an increased focus on ethical issues in psychological research. To help researchers consider these issues, professional bodies such as the British Psychological Society (BPS) in Great Britain and the American Psychological Association (APA) in the USA produce regularly updated guidelines. Both these sets of guidelines stress that the aims of psychological research should be a better understanding of people and the promotion of human welfare, which require an atmosphere of free enquiry. At the same time, research needs to be carried out responsibly, and with concern for the welfare of people who take part in it.

We will be looking in this section at the Ethical Principles for Conducting Research with Human Participants (1993), produced by the BPS. The BPS has a register of chartered psychologists who work professionally in research or applied fields. People can be struck off the register if they fail to maintain professional standards, and it is hoped that this system will create an accredited body of professional psychologists in whom the general public can have confidence.

Figure 5: summary of BPS Ethical Principles for Conducting Research with Human Participants (1993)

1. **introduction:** in good psychological research, there should be mutual confidence and respect between participants and researchers. Guidelines are necessary to help to establish whether research is acceptable.

2. **general:** researchers have a duty to consider the ethical implications of their research before it is carried out. They should eliminate possible threats to the physical and psychological well-being of participants. When researchers do not have sufficient knowledge of possible implications of their research for people varying in age, gender or social background, they should consult people with relevant characteristics.

3. **consent:** whenever possible, participants should be given full information about an investigation so that they can make an informed decision about whether or not to take part. Especial care should be taken with research involving children or others who may be unable to give full informed consent. Participants should not be pressurised into taking part in research when the researcher is in a position of influence or authority over them, or by financial reward.

4. **deception:** deception should be avoided wherever possible, and particularly if participants are likely to feel troubled when debriefed.

5. **debriefing:** when participants are aware of having taken part in a study, at the end of their participation the researcher should offer full information. They should discuss any aspects of the research which may have had negative consequences for the participant.

6. **withdrawal from the investigation:** participants should be told at the outset that they have the right to withdraw from the study and have their data destroyed, even when the study has been completed, and whether or not they have been paid to take part.

7. **confidentiality:** information gathered about participants during research should be kept confidential, and if published should not be identifiable.

8. **protection of participants:** participants should be protected from any physical or psychological harm greater than that experienced in everyday life. Where personal information is collected, participants should be protected from stress and assured that personal questions need not be answered.

9. **observational research:** unless consent is given for behaviour to be observed, observation only of behaviour which could normally be observed by strangers is acceptable. Researchers should be sensitive to cultural values, and to intruding on the privacy of people being observed, even if they are in a public place.

10. **giving advice:** if the researcher becomes aware of physical or psychological problems of which the participant is apparently unaware, these problems should be raised with the participant. An appropriate source of professional advice should be recommended.

11. **colleagues:** a researcher who is aware of a colleague carrying out research not following these principles should encourage the colleague to consider the ethical issues arising from their research.

We will look in a little more detail at some of the issues considered by these guidelines.

Consent

In order to give consent to take part in a study, participants need to be given full information beforehand on which to base their decision. There is some evidence that sufficient information is not always routinely provided. Epstein and Lasagna (1969), for instance, found that only a third of people volunteering to take part in a study had any real understanding of what was involved. However, this study was carried out some time ago, and with ethics emerging in recent years as a very real issue in psychological research, it may be that researchers are now more aware of the importance of giving full information.

In some circumstances, it can be difficult to obtain consent based on a full understanding of the implications of taking part in a study. The study of children poses problems here, since they may not be able to understand the situation. It is generally agreed that if children are too young to understand the research aims, or below the legal age of consent, their parents must be asked for consent in their place. Informed consent can also be a problem for some adults; for example, people with a mental disorder or people with learning difficulties.

There may be further problems when there is an existing relationship between potential participants and the researcher, particularly when the researcher is in a position of authority over participants. For example, many studies are carried out by university lecturers in psychology, using their students as participants. In this case, steps must be taken to ensure that consent is freely given, with no inducements offered for taking part, such as participation being counted towards course grades, nor any suggestion that there might be negative consequences in deciding not to take part.

Within the university system of the United States, psychology undergraduates have to take part as participants in research, and participation counts towards their final grades. The choice is not whether to take part or not, but only which research to participate in. They are paid for participation. However, students are aware that this is a course requirement, and it could be argued that participation may provide the students both with insights into psychological procedures and a sensitivity towards their participants when they carry out research themselves.

Deception

Menges (1973) found that 80% of a sample of 1000 experiments involved giving participants incomplete information about the study. They were given full information about the dependent variable in only 25% of the studies, and complete information about the independent variable in only 3%. (The terms 'dependent variable' and 'independent variable' are explained in chapter 7.) In other words, deception appeared to be widespread in psychological research. Again, however, it is worth noting the date when this research was carried out; it is possible that deception is now no longer as widespread as Menges suggested.

Deception is linked to informed consent: if participants have been deceived about the nature of the study, it is not possible for them to make an informed decision as to whether or not they are willing to take part. Deception is also likely to have wider repercussions, in that participants who have been deceived are likely to be angry, and disillusioned about the way psychology studies are carried out, and so psychology may be brought into disrepute. For these reasons, the use of deception should be considered very carefully, and only used when it is essential to the study.

It has been argued that some forms of deception are worse than others. For example, if you turned up to take part in a psychology study which you thought was investigating memory, and were then told that the study was actually researching the type of person who replied to advertisements requesting volunteers, it is unlikely that you would be unduly distressed. On the other hand, deception such as that suffered by Milgram's participants, where there may be damage to people's self-image and self-esteem, is clearly potentially more serious.

One way of approaching the question of whether deception is acceptable is to consult people, similar to those to be tested, before carrying out the study. They should be given full information about the aims and procedures of the proposed study, together with the nature of the deception involved and why it is considered necessary. If they say they would have agreed to take part given this information, then there is some support for the use of deception.

Kelman (1967) has suggested that one way to overcome the problem of deception is to ask people to role-play. In some experiments, this may be a valuable strategy. At the same time, there are clearly limitations to the kind of research where this might be useful, and there will in any case inevitably be some doubt about the extent to which role-play accurately represents participants' normal behaviour.

Debriefing

Debriefing can be linked to the idea of protecting participants from harm (guideline 8). Participants are given full information about the study in which they have taken part (if this has not taken place beforehand) and are reassured about their own performance. In many cases, this is not problematic.

However, many people who have had no previous experience of taking part in psychology experiments – and these are ideal participants, since they are less likely than, for example, psychology students to be influenced by previous knowledge of psychology – are concerned that in some way judgements will be made either about their ability or their mental health. Careful and thorough debriefing does therefore need to be given serious consideration.

It is perhaps worth noting that debriefing can provide additional benefits for both researcher and

participant. During debriefing, participants can often provide additional information about their performance which may be useful to the researcher in understanding the phenomenon being investigated. For the participant, the understanding gained during debriefing can be an educational experience shared with the researcher.

Right to withdraw

This guideline has links with the need for informed consent. Informed consent may be given at the outset of the study, but participants have the right to withdraw their consent and decide at any point that they no longer wish to take part. This right should be made clear to them, and that it applies even if (as in the case of Milgram's participants) they have accepted payment for participation. They should also know that they have the right to withdraw any data they have provided, and to have it destroyed, even when the study is completed.

Now are you quite sure you want to take part?

In some circumstances, the right to withdraw needs to be given particular consideration. For example, in the earlier example of psychology lecturers using their students as participants, it is particularly important that the right to withdraw at any time without negative consequences is emphasised.

Confidentiality

The importance of confidentiality is highlighted in the BPS guidelines, unless participants have agreed in advance to waive this right. Confidentiality is a legal right under the Data Protection Act, but a further argument for its importance comes from Coolican

(1990), who points out that potential participants in psychology studies would soon become very hard to find if they were not assured of confidentiality!

It is standard practice in most psychology studies to assign participants a number. If their results are to be singled out for discussion in a research report, they can then be referred to by this number, and so not be identified. In some areas of research, the case study method is used, where one person or a small group of people with some unusual psychological characteristic are studied in some detail. In this case, participants are usually identified only by their initials, for example the case of HM reported by Milner (chapter 2, Box F).

However, there may be exceptions to the practice of maintaining confidentiality, when psychologists feel they have a wider ethical duty. If we take as a hypothetical example research involving participant observation of gang behaviour, during which a researcher became aware that a crime was being planned, the researcher might consider that his ethical responsibility should be to society as a whole, and that he should therefore report the planned crime. Similarly, on a more personal level, if a researcher became aware that a participant was planning to commit suicide, he might not feel bound to respect the participant's confidentiality, if he considered this not to be in the person's best interests.

Protection from harm

There is seldom any risk of physical harm to participants in psychology experiments. Some experiments have used electric shocks or loud noise, or have deprived participants of food or sleep, or have induced nausea. However, if this is the case, participants are warned beforehand so that they can decide whether or not they wish to take part.

When it comes to psychological harm, Aronson (1988) proposed that researchers should ensure that participants leave the experimental situation in a frame of mind that is at least as sound as when they entered it. In most studies, this is not problematic if participants are given as much information as possible beforehand and fully debriefed at the conclusion of the study, and reassured that their performance is in no way out of the ordinary.

A well accepted principle of psychological research is that if a researcher is unsure about a study and its effects on participants, they should seek advice from a colleague. This should preferably be someone who has carried out similar research before, and who is not likely to be affected by the outcome of the research, and will therefore be unbiased in the advice they give. Milgram, whose studies were outlined in the previous section, kept to this principle, and consulted 14 psychology students and 40 psychiatrists before he carried out his first experiment. These people suggested that participants were very unlikely to obey the orders they were given. As we now know, however, their predictions were very inaccurate. However, following this basic principle can help to ensure that any possibility of harm to participants is minimised.

In some studies – again, notably those of Milgram – protection from harm is a contentious issue. It is clear that participants did not leave Milgram's studies in the same frame of mind as when they entered it, since the vast majority of them had gained an awareness of their willingness to inflict harm on an innocent human being when ordered to do so. But does the psychologist have a responsibility to protect people against self-knowledge, however unwelcome?

A cost-benefit analysis might be useful here, weighing up the costs of the immediate distress of the participants in Milgram's study against the benefits both to them personally (suggested by the proportion who felt that they had learned something useful) and more generally, in increasing our understanding of human psychological functioning in this area.

Observational studies

In many observational studies, people are unaware that their behaviour is being observed. This usually means that they have not consented to take part in the study and are not debriefed afterwards. In some cases a situation may be set up by the researcher, such as someone pretending they need help because their car has broken down, so deception may also be involved. This kind of study involves what is called **involuntary participation**, and may involve **invasion of privacy**.

It could be argued that if normally occurring behaviour in a public place is observed, consent is implicitly given. If the study you are carrying out involves observing whether men or women are more likely to hold a door open for someone passing through the door after them, the ethical considerations are fairly minimal. But if you are observing rather more sensitive behaviour – perhaps the way mothers interact with their children, or public courtship behaviour – you need to be aware of possible ethical objections. A study illustrating this problem was carried out by Humphreys (1970) who investigated the behaviour of consenting homosexuals, himself acting as a 'lookout' at a public convenience. Those being studied were completely unaware that they were being studied and that their car registration numbers were recorded in order to obtain more background information later on.

Giving advice

There is one problem that is encountered by psychologists far more frequently than by other scientists. People sometimes take the opportunity of talking to a psychology researcher about educational or mental health problems, mistaking the researcher for a clinical psychologist or a counsellor. In this case, the researcher is advised to recommend an appropriate source of professional help, and explain the misunderstanding to the person involved.

The BPS guidelines go even further than this, suggesting that advice should be offered if the researcher becomes aware that the participant may have a problem, even when the participant apparently does not realise it and has not asked for advice.

The morality of carrying out research: psychology and the ethical imperative

One further aspect of ethics in psychological research needs to be mentioned. As Brehm (1956) has pointed out: 'We must not overlook the other side of the ethical issue: the ethical imperative to gain more understanding of important areas of human behaviour'. This idea is echoed by Aronson (1988), who pointed out that psychologists have an 'ethical responsibility to society as a whole'. The BPS guidelines suggest that increasing our understanding of people's behaviour improves people's lives, and 'enhances human dignity'. In other words, if we are to understand people's behaviour and improve the quality of their lives, we must carry out research. But it must be carried out with an awareness of the rights of the participants involved.

All the ethical consideration discussed here are relevant to many pieces of research. One overall question, however, applies to every piece of psychology research: 'Do the ends justify the means?'. In other words, will the knowledge gained from the research outweigh any possible costs to the participants?

Aronson (1988) has suggested that psychologists may face an ethical dilemma when there is a conflict between their responsibility towards research participants and to society as a whole. For example, it could be argued that Milgram's research into obedience has highlighted aspects of important social issues with potential benefit to society, and this benefit may be considered to outweigh the cost to participants.

● Psychology research can raise serious ethical issues. Various professional bodies have produced **ethical guidelines**.

- Psychology research should avoid causing physical or psychological **harm** to participants.
- Participants should give **informed consent** to taking part in a study, and should be made aware that they can **withdraw** at any time. Special care must be taken with participants who cannot give informed consent. Researchers need to be aware of possible problems in invading the **privacy** of others.
- **Deception** is sometimes unavoidable, but **debriefing** can help to minimise its effects.
- A **cost-benefit analysis** should be made before embarking on research.
- Psychologists also have an ethical responsibility to carry out research to increase knowledge about human behaviour and so potentially improve the quality of our lives.

We have looked in some detail at the ethical concerns raised by Milgram's experiments, but his is not the only study to have raised such concerns. To end this chapter, we will look briefly at another study which has attracted criticism on ethical grounds, which was carried out by Zimbardo (1973 – Box F).

Since his study was carried out some time after Milgram's studies, Zimbardo went to considerable lengths to make the study as ethical as possible. Participants were given reasonably full information before the study was carried out, so that they knew that the study would involve invasion of privacy, the loss of some civil rights, and harassment. They were not informed, however, that they would be 'arrested' by the police, in part because approval for this aspect of the study was only received just before the study started, and partly to make the study more realistic.

Not only were participants aware that they were free to withdraw at any time – indeed, some asked to do so – but Zimbardo himself stopped the study as soon as it became clear that the effects on the participants were far more severe than had been anticipated.

Participants were debriefed individually and in groups immediately after the experiment, and everyone who had taken part was asked to return questionnaires several weeks later, several months later, and at yearly intervals. On the basis of this information, Zimbardo claimed that the suffering experienced by people who had taken part did not extend beyond the experimental situation.

▶ Activity 13: the ethics of Zimbardo's study

Look back to the account of Zimbardo's study (Box E). In the light of this information and the additional information given above, to what extent do you consider Zimbardo's study to have been unethical? To reach your assessment, you will need to consider the ethical guidelines described above.

Notes on activities

1 A variety of reasons were given. Some participants claimed that they thought a mistake had been made; they did not want to upset the experiment, which might create a bad impression; they did not want to seem different from everyone else; they did not want to look stupid. All these reasons show **public conformity**, i.e. changing the answer they would have given if asked on their own, but no **private change** – their actual judgement of the lines was not affected.

Some participants, however, seemed to believe that the incorrect decision of the majority was actually correct; they showed private change as well as public conformity. They suggested reasons why their own judgements might have been wrong; perhaps they were suffering from eye strain, or the position of their chair did not allow them to see properly.

2 a Asch found that the conformity effect emerges with only three confederates; increasing the size of the group beyond this does not increase the size of the effect. There was a less marked effect when there were only two confederates. What seems to be crucial here is not the size of the group, but the fact that there is complete agreement among group members.

b The reverse is also true: if the judgements made are no longer unanimous, and there is one confederate who gives the correct answer, the rate of conformity drops to about 5%. Allen and Levine (1971) found this to be true even when the non-conforming confederate wore glasses with pebble lenses; his judgements might not be very reliable! Curiously, this also seems to happen if one confederate gives a different *wrong* answer from the other confederates. However, this only seems to apply to physical judgements, like Asch's lines task; if a social or political judgement is involved, another answer diverging from both the majority and the participant results in the participant conforming to the majority decision (Allen and Levine, 1968). This may be because we expect there to be a variety of opinions on social questions, but we expect consensus on physical judgements.

c When the dissenter from the group changes to agreement with the majority, the conformity effect reappears, with the same strength as in the original situation.

d Making the task more difficult tends to increase conformity; presumably participants then have less confidence in the correctness of their judgments.

e If only one person in the group gives a wrong answer, the rest of the group tend to be sarcastic and make fun of him. It seems that the participants in the original study who were afraid of being ridiculed were justified!

f This perhaps helps to explain why, when Asch allowed the genuine participant to write down his answer, while still being aware of the answers of the confederates, conformity dropped to just over 12% – he would no longer be vulnerable to this kind of reaction.

3 In a lecture, you listen to the information you are given and make notes. You are quiet; any talking is done in a whisper. It would be inappropriate to stand up and start singing a rugby song, or to take all your clothes off. Similarly in a restaurant, you order food, eat it with the cutlery provided and pay before you leave. You wouldn't take your own food and ask the waiter to cook it for you, or sit with your elbows in the soup.

Social conventions help to ensure that social interaction with others runs smoothly. Because these conventions are unwritten, many of them are acquired as part of the socialisation process. What is (and is not) appropriate behaviour is picked up by observing the behaviour of others. The consequence of not observing social conventions is loss of the acceptance and approval of others.

4 You would probably ask the advice of people you know who are already involved in the sport, and could well end up buying the same make of equipment as they did. This kind of conformity doesn't have anything to do with needing their approval. The fact they have more *information* than you is what is crucial in your decision to conform, so this is known as **informational influence**. It has a role in particular in situations where there is some degree of uncertainty, i.e. lack of information.

5 In the first paragraph, you should have linked **compliance**, **normative**, the **need for approval/acceptance**, **unambiguous** and **Asch**, leaving the other terms for the second paragraph.

7 You probably decided that you would be more likely to conform in a group of twelve. Convincing eleven people that you are right is much more of an uphill struggle than convincing five!

10 Gender might be expected to make a difference. In our society and many others, a woman's role has traditionally been that of carer, protecting others from harm rather than inflicting it. Social behaviour reflects the varying cultural norms and values of different societies. It therefore seems probable that obedience, like other social behaviours, will vary from culture to culture.

11 Firstly, this was presented as a study on the effects of punishment on learning, but participants were not doing anything which the experimenter could not have done just as well for himself. It must also have seemed very odd when the experimenter showed no reaction when the learner pounded on the wall and demanded that the experiment should be stopped. There were possibly other subtle clues which could have been picked up. It is very difficult, for example, to treat a confederate in exactly the same way as a complete stranger. These factors could well have led to participants trying to guess the *real* purpose of the study, i.e. **demand characteristics**. They may have come to realise that they themselves were actually the ones being studied.

In reply to this, Milgram claimed that a follow-up survey showed that 80% of participants had no such doubts. Additionally, many participants showed clear and unambiguous stress responses, such as trembling, stuttering and sweating.

12 The Gamson *et al.* study was carried out nearly 20 years after Milgram. During this time, there were many social changes, one of which could have been that it had become more acceptable to question authority, a change to which knowledge of Milgram's studies could itself have contributed. Milgram's study received widespread publicity. One of the participants in the Gamson *et al.* study even referred to Milgram's work as a reason for not conforming!

Perhaps also the participants were less intimidated by a company representative than by a researcher from a prestigious university.

In addition, people were working in groups. You will remember from our discussion of Milgram's study that obedience was reduced to 10% when the participant was exposed to disobedient models.

Finally, the participants in this later study can have been in no doubt that they were being cynically manipulated, whereas in the Milgram study they might have believed that what they were doing was of some academic value.

07

Research Methods

7.1 METHODS IN PSYCHOLOGICAL RESEARCH

You will remember from chapter 1 that psychology goes beyond common sense in that it attempts to set about the task of understanding behaviour and experience in an organised and systematic way. It does not rely on casual observation to support its ideas because this approach is very limited and can be misleading. For these reasons, psychologists carry out studies to investigate their ideas in a structured way which will enable them to collect information or data which can provide objective evidence to support or challenge psychological ideas.

Not all psychologists give priority to research, however. As we saw in chapter 1, for humanistic psychologists, with their focus on the experience of the individual, research is of much less importance than for, say, cognitive psychologists, although Rogers did carry out research into clients' experience of client-centred therapy. The work of most psychologists, however, is focused on research, and a wide range of methods has been used to try to understand how people function.

The experimental method, which is the traditional method of scientific enquiry, has been the main method used by psychologists. However, alternative ways of carrying out research also have their place, and may be more suitable for some research areas. We will look first at what the different methods used in psychological research involve.

The experimental method

There are two criteria which define a piece of research as an experiment. Firstly, an **independent variable (IV)** is manipulated by the experimenter, with all other variables being kept constant. Secondly, there is an element of **random selection** and/or **allocation** of participants to conditions. There are other methods which do not fully meet these criteria yet which may loosely be called experiments, but we will start by looking at each of these two criteria in turn.

A variable is anything which can vary, i.e. can have different values. The **IV** is the variable in which the experimenter is interested, in terms of its effect on the **dependent variable (DV)**, i.e. the performance of participants in an experiment.

In terms of manipulation of the independent variable, in an experiment the researcher creates two or more different conditions. The differences between the conditions constitute the **independent variable**, with all other variables being kept constant. The effect of these different conditions on the **dependent variable** is measured and compared.

To give a simple example, a researcher may be interested in how different instructions for carrying out the memory task of learning a word list affect the number of words remembered. One group of participants could be instructed to learn the words by reading through the list over and over again, repeating them in their heads, i.e. rehearsal. A different group of participants could be asked to use story linkage, making up a story in which all the words appear. Both groups would then be asked to write down as many of the words as they could remember. The independent variable here is the instructions given to the participants, since it is the difference between the groups. The dependent variable is the number of words remembered, since that is what is being measured.

Activity 1: identifying the IV and DV

For each of these studies, identify the IV and the DV:

a A researcher is interested in whether older or younger people are more helpful. Drivers are observed at a junction. The number of older people (apparently over 45) and younger people (apparently under 25) who give way to another vehicle (and who do not give way to another vehicle) are counted.

b Do people work more efficiently first thing in the morning or later in the day? The productivity of workers making soft toys in a factory is compared between 9–10am on the morning shift and 7–8pm on the evening shift on a given day.

c Participants are asked to remember word pairs, either by rehearsing the pairs of words to themselves or by forming a mental image linking the two items. They are tested by being given the first word of each pair and then asked to supply the word with which it was paired. When you have finished, see page 178.

The experimenter would also need to control **confounding variables**. These are any variables which could affect the outcome of the study but are not the IV in which the researcher is interested. It is important to control or eliminate confounding variables in an experiment in order to be sure that any differences between conditions in the dependent variable can only be the result of the manipulation of the independent variable.

A confounding variable can take the form of a random error or a constant error. A **random error** is any uncontrolled or inadequately-controlled variable which could affect the results in an unpredictable way. For example, performance on a task could be affected for some participants by a disturbance outside the room in which they are being tested, or by not being able to get to sleep the night before, or by not being motivated to perform the task they are asked to carry out. A **constant error** is something other than the IV which consistently affects the DV – for example, participants in one condition being given unclear instructions.

Confounding variables can also be classified as **subject variables**, i.e. differences in the participants in the two conditions, or **situation variables**, i.e. differences in the testing situation. For an example of a subject variable, let us go back to the memory experiment described above. If all the participants in one condition were male and all the participants in the other were female, gender could be a confounding variable: it is not the variable in which the researcher is interested but could be the reason for any differences in the test scores of the two groups.

Similarly, in the same experiment, time of day could be a situation variable. For example, if one group were tested early in the morning and the other group late at night, any differences found between the scores of the two groups could be explained in terms of the time they were tested (e.g. people may be more alert in the morning) rather than in terms of the instructions they were given.

Condition 1   Condition 2

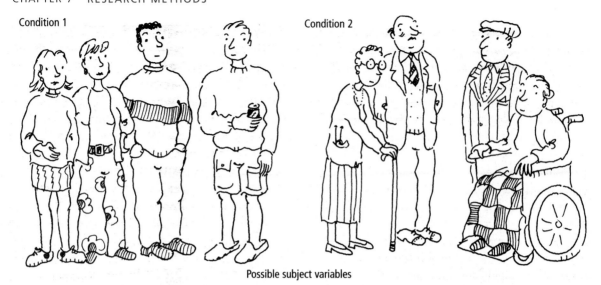

Possible subject variables

▶ Activity 2: identifying confounding variables

Look back to the studies in Activity 1. In each study, identify possible confounding variables. Say whether each is a subject or a situation variable. When you have finished, see page 178.

Laboratory experiments are carried out in many areas of psychology, because they give the researcher more control over the procedure. Laboratory conditions make it easier to control confounding variables and isolate the one variable in which the researcher is interested, i.e. the IV. If this is done successfully, the researcher can claim that there is a cause and effect relationship between the IV and the DV. The control the laboratory experiment offers makes it easy for other researchers to repeat or **replicate** the experiment to check the findings. It also means that researchers can set up the conditions they need, and do not have to wait for a suitable opportunity to present itself naturally. Another advantage of this kind of experiment is that it can easily be structured to provide **quantitative data**, i.e. results in a numerical form. These can be analysed using statistical tests which indicate how likely the results are to have come about by chance. A laboratory experiment also means that sophisticated technical equipment can be used, e.g. presenting a visual stimulus for a precisely measured fraction of a second.

Laboratory experiments also have their drawbacks, however. A major problem is **ecological validity**, i.e. the extent to which a laboratory study shares the characteristics of a real-life situation. For example, in the **Strange Situation**, described in chapter 3, the conditions in which the children experienced separation and reunion with caregivers were somewhat artificial, and so it might be unwise to generalise from the results of this technique to the effects of temporary separation in familiar surroundings. Similarly, Ebbinghaus' use of nonsense syllables to investigate the nature of memory (see chapter 2) allowed the role of meaning in memory to be controlled. However, this kind of material is very different from the kinds of things which we would normally try to learn.

A related problem is what Orne (1962) called **demand characteristics**. In a laboratory situation, participants are usually well aware that they are taking part in an experiment, and so may try to make sense of what they are being asked to do. They may pick up cues from what the researcher says and does, or from the layout of the laboratory. They could then change their behaviour in a way that they see as being helpful to the researcher, or possibly set out deliberately to go against what they perceive to be the experimenter's aims, which Masling (1966) has termed the **'screw you' effect**. If participants are responding to demand characteristics, clearly the ecological validity of the study is compromised.

A study carried out by Berkowitz and La Page (1967) provides a good example of the possible role of demand characteristics. This study investigated Berkowitz' **aggressive cue theory**, and was interested in the effect of contextual cues – in this case, the presence of weapons – on aggression. Participants were made angry by being given a series of seven mild electric shocks by a confederate of the experimenter, supposedly as a way of assessing the effects of stress on problem-solving behaviour. Participants were more aggressive (in terms of giving more small electric shocks to the confederate, as a way of evaluating his performance on a problem-solving task) when there was a shotgun and a revolver in the room than when no weapons were present.

However, it is possible that the participants guessed the nature of the study. The presence of weapons in a psychology laboratory must have seemed very odd, and the cover story – that the weapons were needed for an experiment later on – seems rather unconvincing.

Page and Scheidt (1971) replicated the 'weapons effect' study, and interviewed the participants afterwards. Eighty-one per cent claimed to have suspected that the investigation was about revenge against the confederate, and many of these had guessed that the weapons were there to increase their aggressive response. The results of the Berkowitz and La Page study could therefore be explained by the participants co-operating with what they (correctly) saw to be the aim of the study.

In answer to this criticism, Berkowitz pointed out that it was just as likely that participants could have decided to behave in such a way as to go against the hypothesis being tested. Either way, though, demand characteristics could have reduced the ecological validity of the study and distorted the research findings.

Related problems are **evaluation apprehension**, where participants' performance may be affected by concern that their behaviour will be judged by the experimenter, and **social desirability** effects, where behaviour may be distorted in an attempt to give what the participant believes to be a good impression.

Experimenter effects are a further problem. These occur when the characteristics or behaviour of the experimenter may influence the behaviour of the participants. For example, experimenter characteristics could include gender, race, age or physical attractiveness, while experimenter behaviour which might affect participants' behaviour could include being very friendly or patronising.

A related problem is **experimenter bias**, when the experimenter shows unintentional bias when recording the data from an experiment. One way to overcome this kind of problem is to use a **double blind** technique. In most research, participants are unaware of what the experimenter is expecting the study to show (though of course demand characteristics may make this less true). Keeping participants unaware of the nature of the study is known as the **single blind** technique. In a double blind study, the collection of data is carried out by someone other than the experimenter, so that neither the participant nor the person running the study is aware of what the results are expected to be.

Not all studies carried out in a laboratory, however, are experiments. Observational studies which look at naturally occurring behaviour can also be carried out in laboratory conditions. For example, Smith and Lloyd (1978) made many video recordings of the interaction between mothers and babies, in such a way that the activity and verbalisation of both mother and baby could be viewed simultaneously. They found that a turn-taking pattern emerged, in which both baby and mother took an active part, and concluded that this kind of early interaction formed the basis in very young babies for their later acquisition of language.

Conversely, not all experiments are carried out in a laboratory. Some experiments are **field experiments**. These are studies which take place in natural conditions, but where the criteria for an experiment are met. Field studies are carried out when it is thought to be important that what is being studied happens in the natural environment. A good example here would be the study by Hofling *et al.* into nurse compliance, described in the section on obedience in chapter 6.

The main advantages of field experiments are that they have high ecological validity and reduce the possibility of people responding to demand characteristics. However, control is more of a problem, with an increased likelihood of the study being influenced by confounding variables. This also makes replication more difficult. While high ecological validity may mean that the results of field experiments can be more readily generalised, i.e. the conclusions drawn from the experiment can be assumed to apply to similar situations, it may also be more difficult to apply general conclusions from a field study to other situations which differ from the situation in which the study was carried out. There are also ethical problems, which we shall come to later in this chapter; in particular, participants will not have given consent to having their behaviour observed if they are unaware that they are taking part in a study. Field experiments can also take longer to carry out than laboratory experiments, since the researcher may have to wait for behaviour to occur, and they do not allow complicated technical equipment to be used.

A final kind of experiment is the **natural experiment**. This is a procedure which takes advantage of a naturally occurring event. For example, **adoption studies** have been carried out to establish the extent to which schizophrenia has a genetic cause. To do this, the incidence of schizophrenia in adopted children with birth mothers with the disorder, and those with birth mothers with no history of mental disorder, is compared. This kind of study has similar advantages and disadvantages to the field experiment. Such studies are not strictly speaking experiments, since random allocation is not possible; experimenters cannot randomly allocate children to birth mothers.

There are also **quasi-experiments**, which take a broadly experimental approach but where the criteria for an experiment are not completely met. Studies (a) and (b) in Activity 1 are examples of quasi-experiments. Random allocation of participants to age groups in study (a) would not be possible – participants would come to the study already allocated as over 45 or under 25! Similarly, in study (b) it would be unlikely that the researcher would be able to allocate workers randomly to shifts.

- In the **experimental method**, researchers manipulate an **independent variable** to find its effect on the **dependent variable**, while controlling **confounding variables**.
- **Laboratory experiments** take place in controlled conditions, while **field experiments** take place in the natural environment. **Natural experiments** take advantage of a naturally occurring situation, while **quasi-experiments** do not completely meet the criteria for an experiment.
- All these kinds of experiment have both advantages and drawbacks.

Non-experimental methods

As well as experiments, psychologists have a range of other methods open to them. Because none of these methods involves manipulating the independent variable, they do not offer the control of an experiment, and so it is more difficult to establish cause and effect relationships. They do, however, enable researchers to carry out research in more natural conditions than those of a laboratory, and they can be more suitable than the experimental method for some kinds of investigations.

Correlational analysis

Correlational analysis is a statistical technique which measures the relationship between two variables. An example of research using correlational analysis is Kanner *et al's* study, described in chapter 4, of the relationship between the experience of everyday hassles and the psychological symptoms of stress. A positive correlation occurs when as values for one variable increase, values for the other also tend to do so; in Kanner *et al's* example, people who experienced more hassles tended to suffer more from stress, while those who scored low on the hassles scale tended also to score low for stress. A negative correlation occurs when as values for one variable increase, values for the other tend to decrease. There would probably be a negative correlation, for example, between the amount of alcohol people had drunk and how well they performed on a test of hand-eye co-ordination.

Statistical tests measuring correlation produce a value or **coefficient** between +1 (a perfect positive correlation) and −1 (a perfect negative correlation). A coefficient of 0 shows that an increase in one variable does not predict a consistent increase or decrease in the other variable. A correlation coefficient must always have a value between +1 and −1. In practice, coefficients are rarely as high as +1, and negative correlations are rarely as low as −1, but usually fall somewhere in between these extreme values. A correlation of 0.7, for example, would show a fairly strong positive relationship between two variables, while a correlation of -0.3 would show a fairly weak negative relationship.

▷ Activity 3: correlation

For each of these pairs of variables, say whether you would expect to find a positive correlation, a negative correlation or no correlation. Estimate what value between +1 and −1 you would expect the coefficient to have:

a height and shoe size

b scores on a French test and scores on an English test

c how stressed a person feels and their state of health

d bodyweight and scores on a video game

When you have finished, see page 179.

This technique allows us to measure the strength and direction of relationships between two variables. It can also be used at the start of research to establish whether there is a phenomenon which could be investigated more thoroughly using the experimental method. As we shall see later, it is also used to establish the **reliability** and **validity** of tests.

Its main drawback is that it cannot establish cause and effect. There is likely to be a strong positive relationship between the number of puddles that you see and the number of umbrellas, but there isn't a causal relationship between puddles and umbrellas, since both are caused by a further variable, i.e. rain.

Correlation also cannot show non-linear relationships. As discussed in chapter 4, the relationship between arousal and performance is initially a positive one, but when arousal becomes too great, and can be described as stress, performance drops off and the relationship becomes a negative one. These two trends would cancel each other out to give a correlation coefficient close to 0, masking the real relationship between these two variables. This kind of relationship is called a **curvilinear relationship**.

● **Correlational analysis** shows the direction and strength of the relationship between two variables. A major drawback is that it cannot establish **cause and effect**, nor can it show **curvilinear relationships**.

Observational studies

This method makes no attempt to manipulate variables, but simply records aspects of behaviour in a particular situation as they occur. As we saw earlier, this technique can be used in a laboratory setting, but more often takes place in a more natural setting. It therefore has high ecological validity and avoids demand characteristics. It allows researchers to collect a wide range of interesting data.

In **participant observation**, the researcher joins in with the group of people being studied. Hargreaves (1967), for example, investigated social relationships at a school by becoming a teacher at the school for a year. Similarly, Marsh (1978) investigated the extent to which the behaviour of football fans comes about as the result of them conforming to the rules developed by the groups of fans themselves. To do this, he went to football matches, travelling with groups of fans, and observed their behaviour. In **non-participant observation**, such as observations of children's play, the researcher remains apart from those being studied, who may or may not be aware that their behaviour is being watched.

It is often possible to record on video the behaviour which is being observed. This has the advantage of allowing the behaviour to be viewed as many times as is necessary for a full analysis to be carried out. Where this is not possible, the methods of time sampling and event sampling may be used to make the observation more manageable.

In **time sampling**, observations are made for only short periods of time during the observational period. For example, if a researcher was interested in the kinds of play shown by children in a playground, it would be impractical to observe the children's behaviour and at the same time make detailed notes. Time sampling could be used by watching the children for a two minute period in every quarter of an hour, using the rest of the time before the next observation to make notes on what had been observed. If the observer was interested in the frequency of particular kinds of play, this method would be a manageable way of making comparisons across the period of the observation.

In **event sampling**, observations are made of a specific event each time it occurs. If the researcher observing children's play, for instance, was interested in whether boys show more aggression in their play than girls, each example of behaviour from both boys and girls which could be classified in this way would be noted.

Naturalistic observation is a useful technique when the researcher is interested in something which would be very hard to recreate in a laboratory – for example, the behaviour of drivers or the interaction of children at school. It can also be used in exploratory studies, to establish which phenomena could be explored in more detail in a laboratory setting.

One practical problem of observational techniques is the **observer effect**, where observing a phenomenon may in itself affect what is being observed. A good example is the **Hawthorne Effect**, which takes its name from the Hawthorne works of the Bell Telephone Company where it was first observed. It refers to the fact that in an industrial setting, productivity may improve simply as the result of changes being introduced, even if this was not the intention behind introducing the change. In psychological research, the Hawthorne effect is often referred to when a research participant's behaviour may have been affected by their awareness of being observed.

Observer bias is also possible. As rigorous measurement is not taking place, observers may interpret what they see in line with the expectations and beliefs they bring to the study. One way of trying to overcome this problem is to have two people making observations of the same event(s), and to check that their observations are similar. This is known as **inter-observer reliability**, and we will be returning to it later in the section on reliability.

A further problem of observational techniques is the difficulty of **replication**; it is very unlikely that all aspects of an observational study would remain the same if the study were to be repeated. For this reason, too, there are difficulties with **generalisation**, i.e. applying the conclusions drawn from a study of this kind more widely. For example, it might be unwise to draw general conclusions about the nature of children's play from observation of a particular playgroup, since there are likely to be a number of uncontrollable variables which could have affected the observations. For instance, the skills of the playgroup staff, the kinds of toys and materials available and the number of children attending the group could all have an effect on children's behaviour.

It is also more likely in this kind of study than in an experiment that relevant aspects of the behaviour being observed could be missed. For example, in an observation of children's play in a group situation there could be so much movement that it would be difficult to keep track of everything which took place. As noted already, this kind of difficulty can be minimised by making a filmed record, which can be replayed as often as is necessary for a complete record.

- **Naturalistic observation** focuses on naturally occurring behaviour. In **participant observation**, observers themselves take part.
- **Time sampling** and **event sampling** may be used.
- It is a useful technique when studying behaviour which could not easily be translated to a laboratory setting.
- There may be **observer effects**, and **replication** may be difficult. Carrying out this kind of study can present **practical problems**.

Case studies

Unlike the methods we have talked about so far, a case study is a detailed study of one individual or a small group of individuals. A range of methods can be used, including interviews, detailed observation, records such as a medical history, information from others about the person being studied, and so on. Quite often at least some of the data is **qualitative**, being largely descriptive, rather than **quantitative**, i.e. providing precise measures. A case study is an **idiographic** approach, since it is an in-depth study, focusing in detail on particular characteristics of the individual(s).

This method is widely used in clinical psychology; Freud's research, for example, consisted entirely of case studies of patients. It can be a very useful approach for increasing understanding of all relevant aspects of a person's experience and behaviour. It is also useful for investigating the characteristics of people who are unusual in some way, for example Curtiss' study of Genie, described in Box P of chapter 3.

One of the advantages of this method is that it can increase our knowledge within a certain topic area, such as mental disorders, when a more experimental technique would be unethical. For example, if people with a mental disorder were randomly allocated to conditions, in one of which they were offered a specific treatment which they were likely to find beneficial, and in the other condition were not offered treatment, there would be serious ethical problems in withholding treatment from people who might benefit from it.

The case study method can be useful in the initial stages of researching a topic, to identify particular areas which might usefully be followed up using other methods. The detail it provides means that it can also be used as the basis for challenging an existing theory, if the results of the case study call the theory into question. It also gives detailed information about a real person or people, where techniques such as the experimental method are more interested in general trends, i.e. take a **nomothetic** approach, and so may lose valuable information about individual differences. Finally, since the numbers of participants are so small, it

lends itself to a **longitudinal** approach, where people are studied over time, e.g. the Freud and Dann Bulldog Bank study of concentration camp survivors, described in Box N of chapter 3.

However, there are also some drawbacks to this method. A major problem is **generalisability**; we cannot conclude that what is true of one person or a small group of people is also true of people more generally. **Researcher bias** is also a problem; for example, Freud's case studies have been criticised on the grounds of the high level of interpretation they involved. Finally, if a case study involves in-depth interviews, this relies heavily on the person being interviewed giving accurate answers. For instance, an adult asked about their childhood may not be able to remember relevant information or may inaccurately reconstruct their memories. The problem of **recovered memory** and **false memory syndrome** is discussed in chapter 2.

● **Case studies** are in-depth studies of one or a small number of people. They provide detailed, often **qualitative**, data.
● They are a useful way of studying unusual characteristics, particularly where a more experimental approach would raise ethical difficulties.
● The results are not necessarily **generalisable**. **Researcher bias** may also be a problem.

Interviews and surveys

Interviews and surveys cover a wide range of related techniques – **interviews**, **questionnaires**, **attitude surveys**, and the **clinical method** used in diagnosing psychological problems – but they all involve asking people for information about themselves. Interviews can be **structured**, where every respondent (the person being interviewed) is asked the same questions, or more **unstructured**, where there is room for flexibility in terms of what is asked.

Questionnaires and surveys may use open-ended or closed-ended questions. **Closed-ended questions** provide the respondent with answers from which they must choose, while **open-ended questions** allow them to answer in any way they feel is appropriate:

◗ Activity 4: closed- and open-ended questions

A closed-ended question:

Why did you choose to take A-level psychology? Was it because:

a it sounded more interesting than the other options?

b it was recommended by a friend?

c you like the teacher?

d you thought it might be easier than the other options?

An open-ended question:

Why did you choose to take A-level psychology?

What are the advantages and disadvantages of each of these types of question?

When you have finished, see page 179.

One example of the use of surveys is to measure people's attitudes to various issues. Likert (1932) developed the principle of measuring attitudes by asking people to respond in a structured way to a series of statements relevant to the attitude being measured. A series of statements – perhaps 30 – is prepared, relevant to the particular attitude to be measured, with half the statements being favourable and half unfavourable. This balance is necessary in order to eliminate **response set**; if all the statements were favourable to the attitude being measured, participants might respond without reading each statement carefully, and so reduce the accuracy of the information being gathered. Statements are presented in random order and participants rate each statement on a five-point scale, to which numerical values are attached.

Examples of the sorts of items which might be used to measure attitudes to the royal family, together with the scoring system, are shown in Figure 1. You will see that a high score shows a favourable attitude to the royal family, and a low score an unfavourable attitude. A person's attitude is the sum of their scores from all the items. The numbers would not appear on the questionnaire completed by participants; they are only there to show you how the system works.

In a different area, **Eysenck's Personality Inventory (EPI)** is a personality **questionnaire** using a similar approach. It is an example of a **psychometric test**, i.e. a test which aims to measure particular psychological characteristics. In this case the characteristics being measured are extroversion and neuroticism, the two dimensions which Eysenck believes are sufficient to describe an individual's personality. A typical extravert is sociable, gregarious, impulsive and enjoys taking risks, while a typical neurotic is guilt-ridden and anxious. Sample questions relating to extroversion are shown in Activity 5:

◗ Activity 5: measuring extroversion

Here are some sample questions on extroversion. For each one, answer 'yes' or 'no'.

You can answer '?' if you really cannot decide, but try to avoid this if possible.

Don't spend too long thinking about how to respond – it is usually best to stay with your first reaction.

Figure 1: sample of a Likert scale to measure attitudes

1. The royal family are good ambassadors for this country

strongly agree	agree somewhat	undecided	disagree somewhat	strongly disagree
5	4	3	2	1

2. It would be a good idea to have a president instead of the royal family

strongly agree	agree somewhat	undecided	disagree somewhat	strongly disagree
1	2	3	4	5

1. Are you inclined to be slow and
   deliberate in your actions?   Y ? N
2. Do you often buy things on impulse? Y ? N
3. Do you often change your interests? Y ? N
4. Are you rather cautious in novel
   situations?   Y ? N

Did any problems occur to you as you were answering these questions? Are there any ways you think this method of measuring personality could be criticised?

When you have finished, see page 179.

Given the kinds of problem often found with these kinds of questionnaires, Eysenck included a lie scale in the EPI. This uses questions such as: 'Have you ever been late for an appointment?', working on the principle that we have all at some time been late for something, even if only slightly late for something not very important. This is perhaps a little limited, but it is one way of alerting the tester to the possibility of a **social desirability** effect.

A structured approach has the advantage of focusing on specific questions which are of interest to the researcher, and is likely to produce quantitative data, i.e. in the form of scores, which are more easily analysed using statistical methods. This is particularly the case where the range of possible answers to questions is limited. In their written form, techniques such as attitude surveys and personality questionnaires allow a lot of information to be gathered relatively easily from large numbers of respondents. Given the constraints on what are asked using this kind of structured technique, interviewer bias is less likely than with a more unstructured approach.

An unstructured interview, on the other hand, while being more open to bias, allows the interviewer to follow up responses which are of particular interest, and thus to collect potentially richer data. It has the advantage of being very flexible and giving access to information which might not easily be gained using other methods.

In practice, a **semi-structured interview** technique is often used to tap into the advantages of both the structured and unstructured approaches. An example of a semi-structured

technique is the **clinical interview**, used to assess a person with a mental disorder. Specific questions are asked, but there is also the possibility of following up responses in more detail if this is thought to be useful. This technique may be used not only to diagnose the particular disorder from which the person is suffering, and so form a basis for deciding which kinds of therapeutic intervention might be appropriate, but also to provide material for research purposes. Mental health professionals use this technique to collect information about the psychiatric, medical, personal and family history of the patient; their social circumstances; and their personality. In addition, they use a more structured approach to make a cognitive assessment, e.g. of memory and IQ, test the functioning of the central nervous system and make a physical examination.

One of the drawbacks to unstructured or semi-structured techniques, where the range of possible answers is open, is that they may be limited by how easily respondents can express themselves. This in turn may be affected in face-to-face interviews by the sensitivity and skill of the interviewer. The interviewer must also be aware of ethical considerations. Respondents should not feel coerced into giving replies, nor feel that judgements are being made about them on the basis of the information they give.

Sometimes postal interviews are carried out, usually anonymously, which go some way to addressing these concerns. With this method, though, flexibility is lost and the return rate is usually very low. More importantly, the kinds of people who choose to return completed postal interviews or questionnaires are a **self-selected sample**, and so may not be typical of the group of people in whom the researcher is interested. We shall be returning to sampling later in the chapter.

● **Interviews**, **questionnaires**, **attitude surveys** and **clinical interviews** are techniques which ask people directly for information. They can be **structured** or **unstructured**. A structured approach offers precision and ease of analysis, while an unstructured approach offers richness of data.

7.2 QUANTITATIVE AND QUALITATIVE DATA

Many of the research methods used by psychologists are concerned with collecting **quantitative data**, i.e. numerical data which can be put in categories, or in rank order, or measured in units of measurement. This emphasis on quantitative data is the result of psychologists adopting a similar approach to research to that used in traditional sciences such as physics and chemistry. This approach is **positivist**, which means that it sees only measurable events as worthy of scientific study.

However, we have also looked at methods which do not have this focus, and are more interested in collecting much more loosely-structured **qualitative data**, which do not easily yield this kind of numerical information.

▷ Activity 6: qualitative data in research

Look back through the different methods used in psychology outlined at the start of this chapter. Which of the methods described could provide qualitative data?
When you have finished, see page 179.

An interest in qualitative data came about as the result of the dissatisfaction of some psychologists with positivism. Since psychologists study people, the traditional approach to science is not seen as an appropriate way of carrying out research, since it fails to capture the totality of human experience and the essence of what it is to be human. Exploring the experience of participants is known as a **phenomenological** approach.

It is argued that to focus on isolated pieces of behaviour, as is most often the case in studies interested in collecting quantitative data, is rather superficial, and ignores the social context within which behaviour takes place. Given that psychological research is something which happens in a social context, the objectivity of the researcher, central to traditional methods, is seen as essentially false within psychology. As people studying people, researchers necessarily have attitudes and values which they bring to their research. It is therefore more honest that researchers' attitudes and values should be acknowledged, and form part of the context of research.

Experimental methods limit the possible ways in which a research participant can react to and express appropriate social behaviour. Findings are therefore likely to be context-bound and simply a reflection of the assumptions which the researcher brings to the investigation.

The traditional method of using research to confirm or falsify a particular theory, model or hypothesis is also seen as inappropriate. Rather, theories, models and hypotheses should emerge from the data, as a co-operative effort of researcher and participant. These ideas also link to the **deconstructionist** approach and the **feminist perspective**. According to many who work within this perspective, the traditional positivist approach is seen to be very male-oriented, with its emphasis on control, manipulation and objectivity, and as such is dehumanising.

Qualitative methods necessarily involve interpretation of data, which from a traditional viewpoint could be seen as a criticism. However, psychologists interested in a qualitative approach believe that objectivity is unattainable in psychological research, and given the nature of the subject matter, they consider that even to attempt to be objective is undesirable.

- Some psychologists have challenged the traditional emphasis on **quantitative data** using a scientific model in psychological research.
- They have argued that **qualitative methods** may be more appropriate, given the subject matter of psychology.

7.3 VARIABLES, OPERATIONAL-ISATIONS AND HYPOTHESES

In the section on the experimental method in psychology, we discussed how the aim of a piece of research is to find out whether an IV affects the DV. This is done by manipulating the IV between conditions, and controlling possible **confounding variables**. Correlational research, on the other hand, looks for a relationship between two variables.

The variables in a particular piece of research need to be **operationalised**, i.e. defined in terms of how they are to be used in a particular study. For example, the Loftus and Palmer study in Box T of chapter 2 was interested in whether the wording used in a question about an event (IV) affected memory of that event (DV). The IV here was operationalised as the inclusion of the word 'hit' or 'smashed' in a question about the speed of a car in a video showing a car crash, and the DV was the answer a week later to the question: 'Did you see any broken glass?'

▶ Activity 7: operationalisation

Here are some research ideas. For each one, identify the IV and the DV and suggest ways in which each could be operationalised:

a Do people remember more about a topic they are interested in than about one in which they have little interest?

b Are there gender differences in the amount of aggression shown by children in play?

c Are neurotic people more likely to suffer from phobias?

When you have finished, see page 179.

Much psychological research aims to test a specific **hypothesis**. This is a precise prediction about the expected findings of a study, and includes the IV and DV in their operationalised form, or the two co-variables in the case of correlational analysis. A study uses two hypotheses, the **null hypothesis** and the **alternative hypothesis** which is also known as the **research** or (in an experiment) the **experimental hypothesis**.

The **null hypothesis** predicts that there will be no difference between the conditions, or no relationship between the co-variables, in the case of a correlational study. For example, in the Loftus and Palmer study the null hypothesis would predict that there would be no difference between the conditions they tested in the percentage of people claiming to have seen broken glass. Statistical tests tell us what the probability is that the results of a

study have come about by chance. If this probability is relatively high, then the null hypothesis has to be retained. If it is relatively low, then the null hypothesis can be rejected, and the alternative hypothesis accepted.

In a study, the null hypothesis is what is being tested when data are analysed using statistical tests. The **alternative hypothesis** (i.e. the alternative to the null hypothesis) predicts that there will be a difference between conditions, e.g. in the Loftus and Palmer study that a higher percentage of participants in one group would report having seen broken glass. In a correlational study, the alternative hypothesis will be that there is a relationship, not necessarily causal, between the two variables.

Alternative hypotheses can be **one-tailed (directional)** or **two-tailed (non-directional)**. In an experiment, a two-tailed hypothesis predicts that there will be a difference in the DV between the conditions of the study, e.g. that there will be a difference in the number of words remembered by participants using rehearsal and those using story linkage in a memory task. In the case of a correlational design, it predicts a relationship between the variables, e.g. that there will be a relationship between extroversion scores and preference for bright colours on a colour preference questionnaire. It does not, however, specify what the difference or relationship will be.

If the hypothesis is one-tailed, the direction of the difference or relationship is also predicted. In the above examples, one-tailed hypotheses would be: 'participants using story linkage will remember *more* words than those using rehearsal' and 'there will be a *positive* relationship between extroversion scores and preference for bright colours on a colour preference questionnaire'.

▶ Activity 8: hypotheses

Read through these examples of alternative hypotheses, and identify whether each is one- or two-tailed:

a There will be a difference in scores on an intelligence test between people who eat fish and those who do not eat fish.

b There will be a relationship between extroversion and a preference for loud music.

c People will remember more words in a foreign language if the information is presented in picture form, rather than as words alone.

Now rewrite these hypotheses. For each one, if it is one-tailed, rewrite it as a two-tailed hypothesis. If it is two-tailed, rewrite it as a one-tailed hypothesis. When you have finished, see page 180.

● Variables need to be **operationalised** in terms of how they are to be used in the context of a particular piece of research.

● The **alternative (researcher/experimental) hypothesis** proposes that there will be a difference or a relationship between two or more sets of data. The **null hypothesis** proposes that there will be no such difference or relationship.

● Experimental hypotheses can be **directional** (one-tailed) or **non-directional** (two-tailed).

7.4   POPULATIONS AND SAMPLES

A target population is a group of people who share specific characteristics, and who the researcher is interested in testing. Populations can be small (e.g. female A-level physics students in a particular sixth-form college) or large (e.g. people living in Britain). Populations are usually too large, however, for every individual to be tested, so only a subset of the population – a sample – is tested instead. Ideally this should be a **representative sample**, i.e. one in which all the characteristics of the parent population are represented. If the sample is representative, any conclusions drawn from the results of the study can be generalised to the population as a whole, since the sample will be accurate in terms of representing important aspects of the population.

Activity 9: representative samples

Imagine you are planning to use A-level students at your college as participants in an investigation into the relationship between study habits and exam success, and you intend to select a sample to test. Which characteristics would need to be included in your sample to make it representative of A-level students as a whole?

When you have finished, see page 180.

The larger the sample, the more likely it is to be representative of the population from which it is drawn. If the sample in Activity 9, for example, consisted of only five students, it would be very unlikely that all the different characteristics which might be important to the research would be represented. If the sample is not representative of the population, it is said to be **biased**, i.e. some characteristics of the population are either over- or under-represented, so the sample does not reflect accurately the characteristics of the population.

The problem in deciding on an appropriate size for a sample is essentially a practical one. A very small sample is likely to be biased, but on the other hand a very large sample will take a long time to test, and could be expensive in terms of additional materials which may be necessary. Whatever the sample size, there is likely to be **sampling error**, i.e. inaccuracies in the sample in terms of its representativeness of the parent population. This is reduced (though not necessarily eliminated) by testing a larger sample.

A small population: left-handed trainspotters living in Norwich with their birthdays in May

Sampling methods

There are several ways of selecting a sample. In a **random sample**, every member of the parent population has an equal chance of being included in the sample. To select a random sample, a list of all the members of the population is necessary, e.g. in the study in Activity 9, a list of all the students taking A-levels at your college.

There should be no bias in who is selected as part of the sample. This could be achieved by putting all the names into a hat, stirring them round, and then picking out names to make up the sample until the planned sample size is reached.

Alternatively, if the population is too large for this to be practicable, every member of the population could be given a number. A computer program which generates random numbers could then be used to select the sample, matching up the numbers given by the computer with the numbers given to the members of the population.

The strength of this method is that it avoids possible experimenter bias in selecting a sample. The drawback is that a random sample may well not be representative of the population. For example, a random sample of A-level students could by chance consist entirely of males. However, this kind of bias becomes less likely as the size of the sample increases.

Another possibility is a **systematic sample**, where members of the population are picked on the basis of some system. A sample of voters, for example, could include every tenth person on the electoral roll. This is not strictly speaking a random sample, since only those who are in the relevant position on the roll can be selected, but it is likely to be relatively unbiased, and a faster process than random sampling. It is sometimes called a **quasi-random** sample.

An **opportunity sample** is frequently used. This means that the sample is selected on the basis of who is available at the time of testing and willing to take part. Since it is so straightforward, it is frequently used by students carrying out A-level psychology coursework.

Activity 10: problems with opportunity sampling

Imagine you are planning to carry out the research into study habits and exam success described in Activity 9, and you decide to test an opportunity sample. What kinds of factors might lead to this not being a representative sample?

When you have finished, see page 180.

In practice, the problems associated with opportunity sampling may often not be too serious. For example, in a study measuring physiological responses to stress, people forming this kind of sample would be unlikely to produce results which would differ radically from those of samples selected in other ways.

In a **self-selecting sample**, people volunteer either directly or indirectly to take part in a study. This kind of sampling technique was used in Milgram's study on obedience (see chapter 6) when he advertised in the newspaper for volunteers. The problem here is that those who volunteer directly may not be typical of the target population, so the sample would be biased. This problem has already been mentioned in the discussion of postal interviews.

People may also volunteer indirectly. For example, if you were interested in possible gender differences in superstition you could set up a ladder and note how many males and how many females avoided walking underneath it. The people you were observing would be unaware that they were taking part in a study, but would indirectly be volunteering to take part by walking where the ladder was set up.

In **quota sampling**, the sample is selected so that particular characteristics of the population are represented in the same proportion in which they occur in the target population. Let us take as an example a research study into the study habits of psychology students at a college. Thirty females and 10 males are in their second year of studying psychology, and 40 females and 20 males are in their first year. A quota sample would need to draw a sample of males and females in the ratio of 3:1 from the second year, and 2:1 from the first year.

a self-selecting sample

This is the only sampling method which tries to ensure representativeness, rather than simply making it likely.

▷ **Activity 11: identifying sampling techniques**

In each of these studies, identify the sampling technique used, choosing from:

random   **systematic**
opportunity   **self-selecting**

a A student research group is interested in a possible relationship between age and attitudes to the use of drugs. People are stopped in the street and asked to complete a questionnaire.

b A psychologist is investigating attitudes of English schoolchildren to learning French. At a local high school, he gives a questionnaire to the third boy and the third girl listed in each of the class registers.

c A psychology student carrying out a study on the effects of stress on problem-solving puts up a notice on the college notice board asking people willing to take part in her study to sign up.

d Students in a psychology class have been asked to carry out a memory test on one participant each. Some ask people in the library and the study area, some ask those in the canteen, while others go to find participants in the common room.

In each case, why might the sample not be representative of the parent population? When you have finished, see page 180.

● A study tests a sample of the population in which the researcher is interested. If this is a **representative sample**, results can then be **generalised** to the population as a whole.
● In a **random sample**, every member of the population has an equal chance of being part of the sample. A **systematic sample** selects on the basis of some kind of system. An **opportunity sample** consists of members of the population who are available at the time of testing, and willing to take part. In a **self-selecting sample**, participants offer themselves, either directly or indirectly, as part of the sample. In **quota sampling**, characteristics of the population are represented in the sample in the same proportion in which they occur in the population.
● Sampling methods can introduce **sampling error** which can lead to a **biased sample**.

7.5 EXPERIMENTAL DESIGN

Some of the factors which need to be taken into account when planning experimental research have already been discussed. The IV and the DV need to be operationalised, and possible confounding variables need to be eliminated as far as possible. The size of the sample to be tested and the sampling method need to be considered. Another decision which needs to be made is the design of the study, and we will be looking in this section at three possible designs.

One possibility is an **independent measures** design. You may also find this referred to as an **unrelated design** or a **between-groups** design. In this design, different participants are tested in each condition of the experiment, and participants are randomly allocated to conditions. To go back to the earlier example of a study comparing the effectiveness of rehearsal and story linkage on recall, one set of participants would take a memory test using rehearsal, while a different set of participants would be asked to use story linkage.

The experiment could consist of two or more conditions, where each condition receives a different experimental treatment (as in the memory test example), or one or more experimental conditions and a control condition. In a **control condition**, participants are given no particular treatment; in this example they would be asked to memorise a list of words with no strategy being suggested. The principle here is that the data from this group provides a baseline with which the experimental condition(s) can be compared.

Manipulation of the IV is one criterion for defining a study as an experiment. The second is random allocation of participants to conditions. Randomly allocating participants to conditions means that all participants should have an equal chance of taking part in either condition, or in any condition if there are more than two; in the memory experiment example, a third condition could be introduced where participants were asked to use a third method to help them remember the words, e.g. putting pairs of words into a meaningful sentence. The principle of random allocation is to prevent any kind of bias in selecting which participants will take part in which condition, and so avoid bias in the way in which the experiment is carried out.

To achieve random allocation the person conducting an experiment may 'take names out of a hat' or use random number tables. In natural or quasi-experiments, however, discussed in the section on methods in psychology, this is not possible.

In a **repeated measures design** (sometimes known as a **related design** or **within-groups design**), participants take part in both (or all) the conditions. Their performance in the different conditions is compared. Since participants take part in both (or all) conditions, random allocation does not apply in quite the same way. The order in which they carry out the conditions, however, should be randomised.

Evaluation of independent measures design

The main advantage of the independent measures design is that it eliminates the possible problem of **order effects**. If all participants take part in both or all conditions in the same order, there may be a **practice** effect. They may do better in the second condition in which they take part, not because of the nature of the condition itself, but because they may be helped through practice. Alternatively, **boredom** or **fatigue** as they work through the conditions could account for differences in performance. Taking part in only one condition eliminates this possibility.

Using this design also helps to reduce the effect of **demand characteristics**. If people take part in more than one condition, they are more likely to guess the aim of the experiment and perhaps adjust their performance than if they take part in only one condition. In some cases, fewer materials are needed, since the same materials (e.g. the list of words to be remembered) can be the same in both or all conditions, as each participant will be exposed to them only once.

The major drawback to an independent measures design is the possibility of the results being affected by **individual differences** between the participants in each condition. In the memory test example, any difference between the two conditions could come about as the result of participants in one group having in general better memories than those in the other, rather than the manipulation of the IV, i.e. the strategy they have been asked to use. Random allocation of participants helps to minimise this source of bias. This design also requires more participants (i.e. twice as many in a two-condition experiment) than a repeated measures design, in which each participant provides data in both or all conditions.

Evaluation of repeated measures design

The main advantage of a repeated measures design is that it eliminates the influence of **individual differences**, since each participant's performance in one condition is compared with that same person's performance on the other(s). As noted above, it also requires fewer participants.

The main drawback, however, is the possible influence of **order effects**, i.e. practice, boredom and fatigue. Sometimes it is possible to minimise these effects by **counterbalancing**, i.e. varying the order in which participants carry out conditions. In the memory test example, half the participants could start with the rehearsal condition, and then go on to use story linkage, while for the other participants, this order would be reversed.

Counterbalancing is not always a solution, however. For example, in the memory experiment, participants who started with the story linkage condition could find it so effective that they used it in the rehearsal condition as well in spite of the instructions they were given. Counterbalancing may not even be possible. If the effectiveness of two methods of teaching French were to be compared, it would only be possible for participants to take part in one condition. In these cases, an independent measures design would need to be chosen.

With a repeated measures design, **demand characteristics** are likely to be more of a problem. It is also possible that additional materials would need to be prepared. For instance, in the memory test example, different word lists would need to be constructed for each condition; otherwise participants might remember more words on the second condition simply because they had already seen them once. The word lists would also need to be matched in terms of word length and how common the words are, which could be a time-consuming process. A word list in one condition with words like 'cat', 'tree' and 'chair' matched with a word list in the other condition with words like 'bagatelle', 'chandelier' and 'antigropeloes' would clearly introduce an unwanted bias!

Matched pairs design

A final design possibility is a **matched pairs design**. This aims to pick up on the advantages of both independent measures and repeated measures designs, while avoiding some of the drawbacks of both. In this design, each participant is matched with another participant on characteristics which are considered relevant to the experiment. These characteristics could include age, sex, personality or intelligence. One participant from each pair is then allocated at random to each condition, and each participant takes part in only one condition. This

method assumes that the matching process creates pairs which are so similar that for the purposes of the study they can be treated as if they were the same person.

To return to the memory experiment example, potential participants could be matched on the basis of their memory ability. They would be given an initial memory test requiring them to learn a list of nonsense syllables, for example, and would be put into pairs on the basis of having similar recall scores. One member of each pair would then be randomly allocated to each condition.

▶ ## Activity 12: matched pairs design

Look back through the discussion of the advantages and drawbacks of the independent measures and repeated measures designs. Identify the strengths of each which are incorporated in a matched pairs design.
What are the drawbacks of this design?
When you have finished, see page 180.

Pilot studies

Whichever design is selected, a **pilot study** is normally carried out before starting the process of gathering data. A pilot study is a small-scale study carried out with a few participants to highlight any possible problems in the planned study. For example, the instructions given to participants may not be clear, or the statements used in an attitude questionnaire may be ambiguous. A pilot study also clarifies aspects of the research such as whether the method used to collect data in an observational study is workable, or how long the optimal time would be for a participant to be exposed to materials in a study on memory. If the time allowed is too long, there is likely to be a **ceiling effect**, where most of the participants remember virtually everything, and so the procedure fails to discriminate between the performance of different participants. Similarly, if it is too short, there may be a **floor effect**, where very little is remembered by anyone.

● An experiment has one or more **experimental conditions**, where participants receive particular treatments. For the purposes of comparison, it may also have a **control condition**, where there is no experimental intervention.

- In an **independent measures** design, different participants take part in each condition of a study. In a **repeated measures design**, each participant provides data in both or all the conditions.
- Each design has both strengths and weaknesses in terms of **order effects**, **demand characteristics** and the influence of **individual differences**.
- A **matched pairs** design attempts to combine the strengths of independent measures and repeated measures designs. It is, however, an unwieldy and time-consuming method.
- A **pilot study** is usually carried out before starting full-scale research in order to identify any possible problems with the design of the study.

7.6 RELIABILITY, VALIDITY, AND STANDARDISATION

The term **reliability** in psychological research relates to consistency. For example, Eysenck's EPI is a reliable test, since it provides relatively consistent results if the same person takes it more than once. Researchers need to be sure that the measures they are using are reliable, and so provide a consistent measure. A tape measure which measured out a metre differently every time it was used would be of little use. The same idea is important in psychological measures.

Test-retest reliability assesses external reliability, i.e. the reliability of a test over time. It involves giving participants the same test on two different occasions. If the test is reliable, the results should be very similar. The timing here is important; if participants take the test for the second time too soon after the first test, it is possible that they may remember their previous answers. On the other hand, if there is too long a time gap, participants may have changed in some important way.

Split-half reliability assesses the internal consistency of a test, i.e. the extent to which all parts of the test contribute equally to what is being measured. This is done by comparing the results from half the test with the results from the other half. A test can be split in half in several ways,

e.g. the first half and the second half, odd number and even number questions, or at random.

Inter-rater (or **inter-observer**) **reliability** refers to the extent to which two people rating the same event agree on the ratings they give. If more than one person is to be involved in using a rating scale (for example in a study rating passers-by on helpfulness when asked for change for the phone) it is necessary that they are able to use the scale consistently. A scale would need to be worked out in advance and then tested for reliability before the main study begins.

In all these cases, reliability can be checked by using **correlational analysis**; if a measure is reliable, the two measures should show a very high positive correlation.

Validity refers to the extent to which a test is actually testing what it sets out to test. A test can be reliable but not valid. This is a criticism often made of intelligence tests; they are reliable, in that they give consistent results, but it has been argued that they are not valid tests of intelligence because they only measure a very narrow range of abilities. In order to be useful, a test needs to be both reliable and valid.

There are two overall types of validity. The first is **content-related validity**, i.e. is the content of the test appropriate for what the test aims to measure? The second is **criterion-related validity**, i.e. does the test tally with other measures to which it is considered to be related?

A very straightforward way of assessing whether the content of a test is valid is to see whether it *seems* to be testing what it aims to test. This is called **face validity**. For example, items which tap into individual differences in the ways in which people respond to situations and other people seem on the face of it to be testing personality. People who are expert in the field which a test covers may also decide whether material which is appropriate – both in terms of the nature of the content and the range the content covers – is included. **Construct validity** relates to the extent to which test items are in line with the hypothetical constructs underlying them, e.g. the questions on extroversion in Eysenck's EPI relate to the theoretical constructs of his theory of personality on which the test is based.

One way of testing the validity of a test in terms of its relationship with known criteria is to assess its **concurrent validity**. A new personality test, for example, might well be evaluated in terms of the extent to which it produces similar results to an existing test. Tests of **predictive validity** are another way of establishing the criterion-related validity of a test. The old 11+ test is a good example of a test whose use was based on the assumption that it had predictive validity. All children used to take this test, which determined whether they went on to either a grammar school offering an academic education or a less academically-orientated secondary modern school. The use of this test rested on the assumption that results at 11+ could predict how well someone was likely to do later on in their academic life (see Figure 2).

Concurrent validity and predictive validity can be tested using correlational analysis. If a test has concurrent validity, there should be a strong positive correlation between the results it provides and results using the existing measures with which it is being compared. If it has high predictive validity, there should be a strong positive correlation with later performance on the related criterion.

A final kind of validity is **ecological validity**. This has already been mentioned. You will remember that this refers to the extent to which the results of an investigation can be generalised to other places and other conditions.

Measures of reliability and validity are used in the **standardisation** of tests. When new tests or new versions of existing tests are being developed, items to be included need to be adjusted in order to make the test a reliable and valid measure of the population with whom it is intended to be used. It would not be enough, for example, to translate an American test into Danish and assume that it would then be suitable for use with Danes. The translated version would need to be tested on a large sample of Danes, and appropriate adjustments made.

Standardisation also refers to the procedures used when studies are carried out. For example, the instructions given to participants should be identical, so that there is no possibility that slight variations in wording could affect the results of the study. The timing and presentation of stimulus material, together with the techniques used in scoring, also need to be standardised for the same reason.

- **Reliability** refers to the consistency of a test. Measures of reliability include **test-retest**, **split-half** and **inter-rater** reliability.
- **Validity** refers to the extent that a test measures what it claims to measure. Validity can be **content-related** (**face** validity and **construct** validity), and **criterion-related** (**concurrent** and **predictive** validity).
- Measures of reliability and validity are used to **standardise** tests for use with a particular population.
- Standardisation also refers to carrying out the procedures of a research study consistently.

7.7 LEVELS OF MEASUREMENT

When carrying out research, psychologists collect data. While sometimes the data are qualitative, many of the techniques described produce quantitative data, and it is this kind of data which will be discussed here. The information collected varies in how precise it is, and the term 'levels of measurement' refers to these differences in precision. It is important to assess the level of

Figure 2: types of validity	
CONTENT-RELATED VALIDITY (appropriate content)	**CRITERION-RELATED VALIDITY** (relationship to other measures)
face validity: does the test appear to test what it aims to test?	**concurrent validity: does the test relate to existing similar measures?**
construct validity: does the test relate to underlying theoretical concepts?	**predictive validity: does the test predict later performance on a related criterion?**

measurement of a particular set of data because this will determine how it can be analysed statistically. The different levels can be illustrated by the example shown in Figure 3:

Figure 3: levels of measurement

example: study of possible gender differences in helping behaviour, where the behaviour of potential helpers is observed.

Nominal level data

Ordinary level data

Interval (and ratio) level data

nominal level: Each person is classified as either 'helping' or 'not helping'.
ordinal level: Each person is rated on a helpfulness scale of 1-10, where 1 = 'request for help ignored' to 10 = 'overwhelmingly helpful'.
interval level: the amount of time spent helping is measured. This would also be a measurement at ratio level, since the baseline measurement of time spent helping is zero.

At its simplest, measurement is at **nominal level**. This is sometimes also referred to as category data, because it means that each piece of data is put into a category. Measurement at this level is basically a head count. It gives us very little information. For example, in Figure 3, someone classified as 'helping' could be someone who barely helped at all or someone who was so overwhelmingly helpful that you wished they would stop.

The next level of measurement is **ordinal level**. This goes beyond the simple categorisation of nominal data in that each piece of data is in the form of a score, and so the data can be put in order. However, the measurement is still not very precise. In Figure 3, for example, we cannot assume that someone rated 8 for helpfulness is exactly twice as helpful as someone rated 4; all that can safely be said is that someone rated 8 is more helpful than someone rated 4. Since the measuring scale is so imprecise, the data are reduced to rank-ordered scores, i.e. the researcher will focus on the order of the scores rather than the scores themselves.

Interval level measurement is more precise, since it refers to measures which, in contrast to ordinal level measurement, have equal intervals between the points on the scale being used; there is exactly the same distance between 2 cm and 3 cm, for example, as between 14 cm and 15 cm. The most common examples of interval level measurement are measures of temperature, length and time.

Length and time are also examples of **ratio level** data. This is the same as interval data, but additionally the scale has a genuine zero or starting point; it is not possible, for example, to measure something as being −3 cm. Measures of temperature provide interval level data, but not ratio level. 0°C or 0°F are not a baseline measure since temperatures such as −13° are possible.

It needs to be noted that data do not come ready labelled with a particular level of measurement, but the level to be used must be decided by the researcher. If we go back to the example from Figure 3, the amount of time spent helping is interval (and indeed ratio) level data. We could, however, choose to ignore the actual number of seconds spent helping, and focus instead on the order of the scores, i.e. reduce the data to ordinal level. It would also be possible to assign participants to categories, e.g. 'helped for less than 10 seconds', 'helped for 10-30 seconds' and 'helped for more than 30 seconds', thereby treating the data as nominal.

Activity 13: levels of data

For each of the following examples, decide the level at which data is being analysed:

a A psychologist believes that tiredness affects co-ordination. Two groups of people, woken after different amounts of sleep, are tested on a task which requires them to move a small metal ring along a curved loop of wire without touching the wire. The number of times each participant makes contact with the loop of wire is noted.

b Researchers are interested in possible gender differences in choice of play activity. Eight-year-old participants are given a list of 12 play activities, four of which can be described as make-believe, four as construction and four as physical activity. From the 12, they are asked to choose their favourite activity. The number of choices of girls and boys which fall into each category are compared.

c A psychology teacher is interested in whether there is a relationship between the amount of time students spend on writing an essay and essay grades. Students are asked to note down the time spent on an essay. The normal essay grades of A–E are translated into a numerical scale, i.e. A=10, B=8, etc. The teacher investigates a possible correlation between these two measures.

d A researcher is interested in how instructions on how to learn a list of words affects the number of words recalled. One group of participants uses rehearsal. The other group uses story linkage. The number of words remembered by participants in each group is noted.

When you have finished, see page 180.

● Data can be described in terms of different **levels of measurement**. The level of measurement determines appropriate statistical analysis.

● **Nominal level**, where data are put into categories, is the least precise level. Ordinal level gives more information since it uses scores. It focuses on the order of the scores rather than the scores themselves. More precise still, **interval level** refers to data where there are equal intervals between the points on the measuring scale. Where there is a genuine zero, this is also **ratio level** data.

7.8 Descriptive statistics

The term 'descriptive statistics' refers to ways in which sets of data can be summarised. Two important ways in which this can be done are by using measures of central tendency and measures of dispersion. A range of charts and graphs can also be used to present a clear overview of the data obtained from a study.

Measures of central tendency

These measures are ways of reducing a set of numerical data to one value which represents the whole set. Look back to sample study (d) in Activity 13. If you had carried out this study with 40 participants in each condition, it would be quite hard work to see from the sets of scores which method was more effective in leading to recall. A good way of summarising these data to provide an easy comparison of how many words were remembered in each condition would be to work out the average, or **mean**; all the scores would be added together and the total divided by the number of scores.

The **median** is another measure of central tendency. If a set of scores is put in numerical order, the middle score of the sequence is the median. If there are two middle scores (i.e. an even number of scores in the set), the mean of these two scores is the median.

The final measure of central tendency is the **mode**. This is the most frequently occurring score in a set of scores. Sometimes there may be two equally frequent scores (in which case there are two modes, known as **bimodal** values), or even more, giving **multimodal** values.

◗ Activity 14: mean, median and mode

a These are the scores on a psychology test for a class of students. Work out the mean, the median and the mode:

7 7 8 10 11 11 11 13 13 15 15

b The mean number of children in the average British family is 2.4. Why might this not be the best way of expressing this kind of information? Which measure of central tendency do you think might be better, and why?

c These are people's scores on a general knowledge test. Which measure of central tendency do you think would be the best way of summarising the data? Give your reasons:

5 6 12 17 18 18 25 29 31 31 36 37 64

When you have finished, see page 181.

The three measures of central tendency all have their uses and are appropriate in different circumstances. If you are collecting very precise data, i.e. interval data, like reaction time in seconds, it makes sense to use the mean to summarise the data, as it is the most precise of the three measures.

It would make less sense to use the mean where the data itself is ordinal and so is less precise, as in the use of rating scales. In general, the median is used to summarise this kind of data.

The mode is in practice rarely used except with nominal data. It would, however, make sense to use it to summarise data which fall into a limited number of categories. For example, if people were being rated on a three-point helpfulness scale (1 – didn't help; 2 – quite helpful; 3 – very helpful), identifying the category which was used most would seem to be the most effective way of summarising the data.

To highlight the usefulness and limitations of each of the measures of central tendency, work through Activity 15:

◗ Activity 15: mean, median and mode: advantages and drawbacks

For each measure of central tendency, answer the following questions:
a is this measure always an actual score?
b does it use all the scores?
c does it use the values of all the scores?
d is it distorted by an extreme value?
Decide whether your answer to each question is an advantage or a drawback of this measure, and enter each answer in this table:

measure of central tendency	advantage	disadvantage
mean	1_____ 2_____	1_____ 2_____
median	1_____ 2_____	1_____ 2_____
mode	1_____ 2_____	1_____ 2_____

When you have finished, see page 181.

Measures of dispersion

A measure of dispersion is another way of summarising data. This measure gives an indication of the spread of scores, i.e. the extent to which scores deviate from the measure of central tendency. In these sets of scores:

13 14 15 16 17   and   5 10 15 20 25

the mean for each sample is 15, but the second set of scores shows a much greater spread than the first. A measure of dispersion is therefore a further way of summarising data and gives more useful information than a measure of central tendency alone.

A simple way of expressing this spread of scores is to use the **range**. This is simply the smallest score subtracted from the largest score. In the above example, the range for the first set of scores is therefore 4, and for the second set 20. For technical reasons, if there is an even number of scores, 1 is usually added to this figure. If values are calculated to one decimal place, e.g. 7.6 and 5.8, the range is the difference between the extreme scores plus .1, while .01 is added if values are calculated to two decimal places, e.g. 7.64 and 5.83.

The range is very simple to work out, but where there is an extreme score (as in Activity 14, c), the range can give a distorted picture of the data. To overcome this drawback, the **interquartile range** may be calculated. This is the range calculated using the 25% of the scores immediately below the median, and the 25% of the scores immediately above it, to give an indication of the range of the central 50% of the scores.

The **standard deviation** is a more sophisticated measure of dispersion, since it calculates the average distance from the mean of all the scores. It is a more powerful measure of dispersion than the range, since the values of all the scores contribute towards the calculation. Because it is a more precise measure, it is usually used when the data itself is precise, such as the time taken to react to a visual stimulus. Where the data is less precise, e.g. in the form of ratings on a rating scale, the range is more likely to be used as a measure of dispersion.

Another measure of dispersion is the **variance**, which is simply the standard deviation squared. This statistic is sometimes required in order to carry out statistical tests on the data.

Finally, the **variation ratio** is a simple measure of dispersion, and is used where the mode is used as a measure of central tendency. It is the percentage of non-modal scores in the sample. In this set of scores:

2   3   5   5   5   7   8   8   9   9

the mode is 5, since it is the score which appears most frequently, as three of the ten scores. The number of non-modal scores is therefore 7 out of ten, so the variation ratio is 70%.

- **Descriptive statistics** are ways of summarising data.
- The **mean**, the **median** and the **mode** are three **measures of central tendency**, i.e. a way of representing a set of scores with one statistic.
- The **range** (including the **interquartile range**), the **standard deviation**, the **variance** and the **variation ratio** are **measures of dispersion**, which give information about the spread of scores.

Graphical representation

Psychologists carrying out research often present their data graphically. This way of summarising results has the advantage of presenting the data very clearly, in such a way that the overall findings are immediately accessible to the reader of a research report. Four of the most frequently used types of graphical representation are histograms, frequency polygons, bar charts and scattergraphs. We will look at each of these in turn, and consider when they are an appropriate way of presenting data, the underlying principles of their use and how they are interpreted.

Histograms

A histogram is used when representing interval- or ratio-level data. It divides data into categories, each represented as a bar. The bars are of equal width, and are drawn touching each other. Since histograms can only be used with continuous data, i.e. where there are no gaps between scores for the categories, categories which do not contain scores must also be shown, as in the first category in Activity 16 (see opposite). The categories are shown on the x-axis, with the mid-point of each category being identified, and the frequency with which each category occurs is shown on the y-axis.

Let us take as an example the results of a memory test, where participants have been asked to learn a set of 30 words and then write down as many as they can remember (see Figure 4 opposite).

Activity 16: interpreting a histogram

Look at this histogram and answer the questions below:

Histogram showing the number of words recalled on a memory test

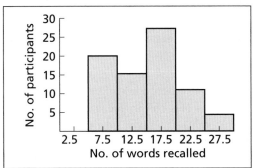

1 How wide is the range of scores within each category?
2 What is the range of scores making up the category on the extreme right?
3 How many participants had scores in the largest category?

When you have finished, see page 181.

Frequency polygons

A frequency polygon is an alternative to a histogram. Instead of using bars, the mid-points at the top of each bar are joined. It is a useful technique to show the results of two or more conditions at once. To take the data from Activity 16 as an example, these scores could be data from a condition in an experiment in which participants were asked to use rehearsal as an aid to recall. Data from another condition, where participants were asked to use story linkage, could be shown on the same frequency polygon, so that comparison of the results of the two conditions could be made (Figure 5).

Bar charts

Bar charts look similar to histograms, in that they consist of bars of equal width, but there are important differences. They are used with ordinal or nominal data, and so can be used with non-continuous frequencies on the x-axis. They are often used to show the means for different conditions in an experiment. They are usually

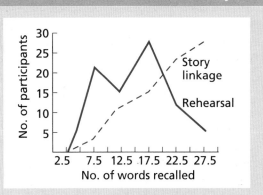

Figure 4: frequency polygon showing the number of words recalled on a memory test

Figure 5: examples of bar charts

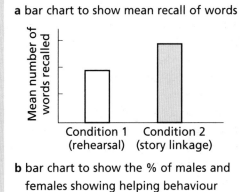

drawn so that one bar does not touch the next, so that they do not seem to suggest that the data are continuous. Two examples of bar charts are shown in Figure 5. The first shows means for the two conditions of a memory experiment, comparing the effectiveness of rehearsal and story linkage on recall of words. The second compares the helpfulness of males and females in terms of opening doors for someone carrying heavy shopping.

▶ Activity 17: interpreting a bar chart

Look at this bar chart and answer the questions below:

Bar chart to show the number of aggressive acts observed in children at play

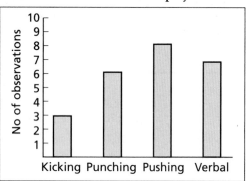

1 Which behaviour was observed most frequently?
2 Which behaviour was observed least frequently?
3 How many acts of verbal aggression were observed?

When you have finished, see page 181.

Scattergraphs

Scattergraphs (or scattergrams) are used to show sets of data where a correlational technique has been used. Each of the two variables being correlated is represented on one axis. The crossing point of the two scores for each individual being tested is marked on the scattergraph.

Figure 6: scattergraphs

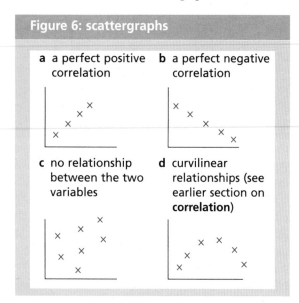

a a perfect positive correlation
b a perfect negative correlation
c no relationship between the two variables
d curvilinear relationships (see earlier section on correlation)

In practice, a perfect positive or a perfect negative relationship is extremely rare, particularly as the number of observations increases, so a scattergraph can be used to assess the direction and strength of any relationship between the two variables being correlated. It can be helpful to draw a line of best fit on a scattergraph to help show whether the relationship between the two variables is generally a positive or a negative one, and to show the strength of that relationship.

To work out where a line of best fit should go, the average value of each variable is worked out, and the resulting point – the **pivot point** – is marked on the scattergraph. A straight line is then drawn through this point in such a way that each point is as close to the line as possible, and with the same number of points above and below the line:

Figure 7: scattergraph with line of best fit

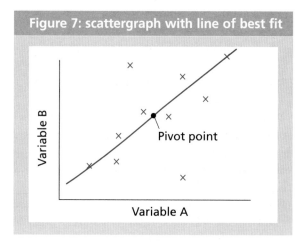

In Figure 7, since the line of best fit is in the same direction as in Figure 6 (a), the relationship between the variables being correlated is a positive one. As most of the points are reasonably close to the line, the correlation is fairly strong. There are two points which are quite a distance from the line of best fit; these are called **outliers**, and mean that the strength of the correlation is reduced.

▶ Activity 18: drawing and interpreting a scattergraph

Here are data from a correlational study to investigate a possible relationship between IQ (scores on an intelligence test) and points scores at A-level (where A=10, B=8, C=6, D=4, E=2):

participant	IQ scores	A-level scores
1	125	20
2	110	14
3	127	24
4	135	18
5	118	22
6	142	20
7	122	16
8	112	10
9	128	18
10	108	10

Use this data to draw a scattergraph, and draw on a line of best fit.

a Does your scattergraph show a positive or a negative relationship?

b Are there any outliers?

c How strong is the relationship between IQ and performance at A-level?

When you have finished, see page 181.

● **Graphical representation** provides a clear way of displaying data.

● **Histograms** take the form of bars, and are used with continuous data, of at least interval level. **Frequency polygons** are an alternative to histograms, and are useful for showing two or more sets of data at once.

● **Bar charts** can be used with non-continuous data at ordinal or nominal level. They can also be used to show the **means** for different conditions in an experiment.

● **Scattergraphs** are used to display correlational data. They give an indication of the direction and strength of the relationship between two variables.

7.9 ETHICS IN PSYCHOLOGICAL RESEARCH

Carrying out psychological research is not just a matter of operationalising the variables in which you are interested, choosing an appropriate design, controlling possible confounding variables and handling the data which has been collected. It is also extremely important that researchers make sure that they take full account of the ethical guidelines laid down by professional bodies such as the British Psychological Society. These point out the kinds of issues which researchers need to bear in mind when planning and carrying out research. The Association for Teachers of Psychology (ATP) has produced similar guidelines specifically aimed at students studying psychology at pre-degree level. The Experimental Psychology Society has laid down similar guidelines for work with animals.

You have already read about the development and role of ethical guidelines in the critical issue section of chapter 6, where the ethical aspects of research are discussed in detail. The following activity, however, should serve to remind you of some of the issues raised there:

▷ **Activity 19: identifying ethical issues**

Read this account of a (fictional) psychology study. List what you consider to be the ethical problems which it raises. Compare your notes with the discussion which follows it on the next page.

Dr Smith is carrying out a research project. She tells her group of 20 students that they will take part in her experiment, but does not say what the research involves. The students turn up at the required time, and are told by a man in a white lab coat that they should sit down and wait for Dr Smith to arrive. They are kept waiting for nearly two hours in the laboratory.

After about an hour, two students get up to leave. They say they have waited long enough, and won't wait any longer. They are told to sit down, and the laboratory door is locked.

When Dr Smith finally arrives, the students are told to fill in the questionnaire they are given as honestly as possible. When they have all finished, the laboratory door is unlocked, and they leave.

They think their ordeal is over, but the following week, Dr Smith starts one of her lectures with an amusing anecdote, in which she divulges one of the answers given to an item in the questionnaire by a student, whom she identifies. Everyone in the lecture theatre roars with laughter. The student whose answer has been quoted runs out of the room in embarrassment, vowing never to take part in another psychology experiment ever again.

Dr Smith did not ask for volunteers for her study. The students were *told* they had to be involved in her research. This violates one of the most basic ethical guidelines, that participation should be voluntary. In addition, the students were told nothing about the nature of the research, so they did not have enough information to decide whether or not they wished to participate in the study. In other words, they could not give informed consent.

The students could also have been intimidated because they were put in a position where refusing to take part in the study would be very difficult. The power relationship between Dr Smith and her students is a very unequal one, as she is in a position to influence their academic progress. The students could also have found the man in the lab coat intimidating. This is sometimes known as the power of the investigator. You may remember that in the studies carried out by Milgram, discussed in chapter 6, this kind of intimidation was a factor in many of the participants being prepared to give powerful electric shocks to another person when they were instructed to do so. Researchers have to be aware that their participants may see them as threatening or in a position of influence, merely because they are carrying out research.

Dr Smith also breached confidentiality when she let other people know of a student's answers in her study. All participants should be guaranteed anonymity when they volunteer to take part in research. In case studies, participants are usually referred to by initials for this reason. Participants should also be able to withdraw from the study at any stage (and withdraw their data), should they wish to do so. They should not be subjected to stress or discomfort. Waiting in a laboratory for two hours is not acceptable research practice!

It is also good practice to debrief participants at the end of a study. This involves explaining to them the aims and purpose of the experiment, if they wish to know, and answering any questions they may have. It can also include reassurance about the way they have responded in the experimental situation; participants in psychology experiments are often concerned that their performance has been inadequate, or that their behaviour has been in some way unacceptable. The aim of debriefing is that participants should leave the research situation, as far as possible, in the same psychological state in which they entered it. There is no indication that Dr Smith debriefed the students who had taken part in the study.

You may not have spotted all the ethical dilemmas in Activity 19, but you were probably able to work out most of them. It is really a question of treating people sensitively and with respect, and appreciating them giving up their time to take part in research.

Ethical issues have been touched on only briefly here, but this topic is raised in connection with a number of studies in this book. Even where ethics are not specifically mentioned, you will need to bear these issues in mind when you read about psychological research.

● There is a range of **ethical issues** which need to be considered when planning and carrying out research.

Notes on activities

1 a IV = age. DV = whether or not they give way at the junction.

b IV = time of day. DV = number of soft toys produced.

c IV = instructions. DV = number of words correctly remembered.

2 There are any number of possibilities. Here are a few suggestions:

a **possible subject variables:** the gender of drivers; how pressed for time they were.

possible situation variables: how far away from the junction each driver was; the speed at which they were travelling.

b **possible subject variables:** different kinds of workers could be employed on each shift, e.g. younger workers on the early shift and older workers on the evening shift.

possible situation variables: only one shift might cover a loo break; different toys, one more complicated than the other, could be produced by the different shifts.

c **possible subject variables:** some participants might find it easier to form mental images than others; those with better memories might by chance be allocated to one group.

possible situation variables: if the groups were tested in different places, there might be more distractions in one place than the other.

3 a a fairly strong positive correlation, say 0.8. The correlation would not be perfect because there are some tall people with relatively small feet and some short people with big feet.

b since both tests are to do with words, some positive correlation would be expected; this would probably not be particularly strong – say 0.4 – since some people who are good at English might well have little interest in French.

c a fairly strong negative correlation, say -0.8, might be expected, since there is good evidence for a relationship between stress and poor health (see chapter 4); again, there would be exceptions, since some people seem to thrive on moderate amounts of stress.

d there doesn't seem any reason why there should be a relationship between these variables; perhaps people who spend a lot of time developing skills on video games might lead a more sedentary lifestyle and so be more likely to be overweight, so there might be a very small positive correlation, say 0.1.

4 Closed-ended questions provide data which is easier to analyse. For example, the percentage of participants choosing each response would be very easy to work out. However, it is possible that none of the answers corresponds with how the person answering the question would ideally like to respond. In the example here, the person could be taking A-level psychology because it was the only option available which would fit in with their timetable for other subjects, and for which there were still places available. Open-ended questions may lead to more detailed information being given, but it is likely to be more difficult to analyse.

5 You may have thought it was pretty obvious what the questions were testing; you probably realised here that 'no' answers to questions 1 and 4, and 'yes' answers to questions 2 and 3, would contribute to a high score for extroversion. This awareness could possibly affect the way you answered the questions, i.e. you could respond to the **demand characteristics** of the procedure. Your answers could also be influenced by **social desirability**; people could answer so as to put themselves in a good light (this is known as 'faking good'). It is of course rather unfair to form a judgement on the basis of a few questions; in reality, these items would be embedded in a much longer questionnaire, and one covering neuroticism as well as extroversion.

The range of possible answers could be seen as constraining; sometimes people find it hard to limit themselves to Y/N answers (even with ?). Another problem here is that the questions are a little vague and don't relate to a defined context, e.g. what kind of novel situation is meant in Q4? This could perhaps affect how you would want to answer the question. Eysenck has shown, however, that people do respond consistently over time to this kind of question, in other words the questionnaires have been shown to have good **test-retest reliability**, a concept which we will be looking at later in this chapter.

More generally, you may have thought that answering this kind of question requires you not only to be prepared to answer the questions honestly (which may be problematic, particularly if something important – like being offered a job – depends on the outcome) but also to have enough insight to be able to do so.

6 Open-ended questionnaires, unstructured interviews, case studies, participant observation and to some extent clinical interviews are all likely to produce qualitative data.

7 a **IV = interest.** People could be asked to use a scale of 1 (very boring) to 10 (extremely interesting) to rate for interest potential topics on which they might be tested. The operational definition of interest would be the interest ratings.

DV = memory. People could be given questionnaires on passages they were asked to memorise. The operational definition of memory would be the questionnaire scores.

b **IV = gender,** i.e. whether children were boys or girls.

DV = aggression. Both boys and girls could be observed at play. A list of aggressive behaviours could be drawn up (e.g. pushing, name-calling etc). The number of times these behaviours were shown during the observation period would be the operational definition of aggression.

c **IV = neuroticism.** This could be operationalised as the N scores on Eysenck's EPI. People scoring above a certain point on the scale would be classed as 'neurotic' and those below a certain point as 'non-neurotic'.

DV = the extent to which participants suffer from phobias. A questionnaire could be used to establish which phobias people suffer from and the extent to which they fear phobic objects and situations. The operational definition would be the scores on the phobia questionnaire.

8 a two-tailed. One-tailed = people who eat fish will score higher on an intelligence test than those who do not eat fish.

b two-tailed. One-tailed = there will be a positive relationship between extroversion and a preference for loud music.

c one-tailed. Two-tailed = there will be a difference in the number of words remembered in a foreign language when the information is presented in picture form and as words alone.

9 Some suggestions here are that the sample should include: both sexes; mature students as well as students studying for A-levels immediately after finishing their GCSEs at school; students in both their first year and second year of study; those taking different combinations of A-levels, e.g. science, languages and so on.

10 This kind of sample is very easily biased. You might, for example, tend to approach people you are friendly with, and they might differ in important respects from the parent population, i.e. the population from which they are drawn. For example, in Activity 9 these could be students following similar A-level courses, leaving out those studying other courses.

11 a This is an **opportunity sample**. It may not be representative because members of the group may only ask passers-by who seem approachable. There could also be something about the location – it could, for example, be near a school or a leisure centre – which might bias the kinds of people in the street at the time.

b This is a **systematic sample**. It may not be representative because it could be, with this relatively small sample, that the children chosen happen to be those who are keen on learning French.

c This is a **self-selecting sample**. It may not be representative because people who volunteer to take part in studies may be a particular type of person.

d This is an **opportunity sample**. It may not be representative for the same reasons as those given for (a).

12 **Independent measures:** order effects are eliminated; demand characteristics are reduced; fewer materials are required.

Repeated measures: individual differences are reduced, though not eliminated.

Drawbacks: the main drawback of the matched pairs design is the time involved in matching up participants, or indeed in finding participants who can be matched in this way. Complete matching is not really possible, and it may be that participants have not been matched on a characteristic which turns out to be important. If one participant drops out of the study, the nature of the design means that two participants are lost.

13 a interval (and ratio) level – for example, there is the same difference between people who make one contact and two contacts as there is between people who make five contacts and six contacts.

b nominal level – the first choice of each participant is assigned to a category by gender and by type of play.

c the amount of time spent is **interval (and ratio) level**. The grades are better reduced to ordinal level – it cannot be assumed that an essay given a B grade (8 marks) is exactly twice as good as one given a D grade (4 marks).

d possibly **interval level**, on the grounds that ten words, say, is twice as many as five. This could also be regarded as ordinal level data, since all the words might not be equally easy to remember, so there are not equal intervals between the points on the scale (i.e. one word, two words, three words, and so on.)

14 a the mean, median and mode are all 11.

b nobody actually has 2.4 children. The mode, i.e. the number of children a family is most likely to have, might be a more realistic way of putting this information across.

c the mode could be used. This would be a bimodal distribution, with modes at 18 and 31. On the other hand, there are a lot of scores which have different values from these. The mean could be used, but would give a rather distorted picture, since the score of 64 is extreme, well out of line with the other scores. The median would probably give the most accurate picture.

15 mean: advantages **b** (yes) and **c** (yes); disadvantages **a** (no) and **d** (yes).

median: advantages **d** (no) and **b** (yes); disadvantages **a** (only with an odd number of scores) and **c** (no).

mode: advantages **a** (yes) and **d** (no); disadvantages **b** (no) and **c** (no).

16 1 five words; **2** 26-30; **3** four participants.

17 1 kicking; **2** pushing; **3** seven times.

18 The scattergraph should look like this:

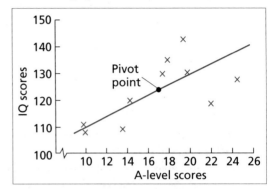

1 The line of best fit indicates a positive correlation.

2 Most of the points lie fairly close to the line of best fit, though there are some outliers.

3 This indicates a reasonable but not particularly strong positive correlation between IQ and A-level points scores.

REFERENCES

Abernathy EM (1940) The effect of changed environmental conditions upon the results of college examinations. *Journal of Psychology* **10** pp 293–301.

Adorno TW, Frenkel-Brunswick E, Levinson DJ and Sanford RN (1950) *The Authoritarian Personality*. New York: Harper & Row.

Ainsworth M, Blehar MC, Waters E and Wall S (1978) Patterns of Attachment: a Psychological Study of the Strange Situation. Hillsdale, New Jersey: Lawrence Erlbaum.

Allen VL and Levine JM (1968) Social support, dissent and conformity. *Sociometry* **31** pp 138–49.

Allen VL and Levine JM (1971) Social support and conformity: the role of independent assessment of reality. *Journal of Experimental Social Psychology* **7** pp 48–58.

Allport FH (1924) *Social Psychology*. Boston: Houghton Mifflin.

Andersson B-E (1992) Effects of day care on cognitive and socioemotional competence of thirteen-year-old Swedish schoolchildren. *Child Development* **63** pp 20–36.

Aronson E (1988) *The Social Animal* (5th edn). New York: Freeman.

Asch SE (1951) Effect of group pressure upon the modification and distortion of judgements. In Guetzkow H (ed) *Groups, Leadership and Men*. Pittsburgh, Pennsylvania: Carnegie Press.

Atkinson RL, Atkinson RC, Smith EE and Hilyard ER (1983) *Introduction to Psychology* (8th edn). New York: Harcourt Brace Jovanovich.

Atkinson RC and Shiffrin RM (1968) Human memory: a proposed system and its control processes. In Spence KW and Spence JT (eds) *The Psychology of Learning and Motivation*, vol. 2. London: Academic Press.

Atkinson RC and Shiffrin RM (1971) The control of short-term memory. *Scientific American* **224** pp 82–90.

Averbach E and Coriell AS (1961) Short-term memory in vision. *Bell System Technical Journal* **40** pp 309–328.

Baddeley AD (1966) The influence of acoustic and semantic similarity on long-term memory for word sequences. *Quarterly Journal of Experimental Psychology* **18** pp 302–309.

Baddeley AD and Hitch G (1974) Working memory. In Bower GA (ed) *Recent Advances in Learning and Motivation*, vol. 8. New York: Academic Press.

Baddeley AD, Thomson N and Buchanan M (1975) Word length and the structure of short-term memory. *Journal of Verbal Learning and Verbal Behavior* **14** pp 575–589.

Bahrick HP, Bahrick PO and Wittinger RP (1975) Fifty years of memory for names and faces: a cross-sectional approach. *Journal of Experimental Psychology: General* **104** pp 54–75.

Bandura A (1965) Influence of model's reinforcement contingencies on the acquisition of imitative responses. *Journal of Personality and Social Psychology* **1** pp 589–595.

Bandura A, Ross D and Ross SA (1963) Imitation of film-mediated aggressive models. *Journal of Abnormal and Social Psychology* **66** pp 3–11.

Baron RA and Ransberger VM (1978) Ambient temperature and the occurrence of collective violence: the "long hot summer" revisited. *Journal of Personality and Social Psychology* **36** pp 351–360.

Bartlett FC (1932) *Remembering*. Cambridge: Cambridge University Press.

Baumrind D (1964) Some thoughts on ethics of research: after reading Milgram's behavioural study of obedience. *American Psychologist* **19** pp 421–423.

Beck AT (1967) *Depression: Causes and Treatment*. Philadelphia: University of Philadelphia Press

Beck AT (1991a) Cognitive therapy: a 30-year perspective. *American Psychologist* **46(4)** pp 368–375.

Bekerian DA and Bowers JM (1983) Eye-witness testimony: Were we misled? *Journal of Experimental Psychology, Learning, Memory, and Cognition* **9** pp 139–45

Belsky J (1988) The "effects" of infant day care reconsidered. *Early Child Research Quarterly* **3** pp 235–272.

Bemis KM (1978) Current approaches to the etiology and treatment of anorexia nervosa. *Psychological Bulletin* **85** pp 593–617.

Berkowitz L and La Page A (1967) Weapons as aggression-eliciting stimuli. *Journal of Personality and Social Psychology* **7** pp 202–207.

Blakemore C (1988) *The Mind Machine*. London: BBC Publications.

Blumenthal JA, Burg MM, Barefoot J, Williams RB, Haney T and Zimet C (1987) Social support, Type A behavior, and coronary artery disease. *Psychosomatic Medicine* **49** pp 331–339.

Bogdonoff MD, Klein RF, Estes EH, Shaw DM and Back K (1961) The modifying effect of conforming behaviour upon lipid responses accompanying CNS arousal. *Clinical Research* **9** p 135.

Boulton MG (1983) *On Being a Mother: A Study of Women with Preschool Children*. London: Tavistock.

Bourne PG (1971) Altered adrenal function in two combat situatioins in Viet Nam. In Elefteriou BE and Scott JP (eds) *The Physiology of Aggression and Defeat*. New York: Plenum Press pp 256–290.

Bower GH, Monteiro KP and Gilligan SG (1978) Emotional mood as a context for learning and recall. *Journal of Verbal Learning and Verbal Behavior* **17** pp 573–585.

Bowlby J (1944) Forty-four juvenile thieves: their characters and home life. *International Journal of Psychoanalysis* **25** pp 1–57 and 207–228.

Bowlby J (1953) *Child Care and the Growth of Love*. Harmondsworth: Penguin.

Bowlby J (1969) *Attachment and Loss: attachment*. New York: Basic Books.

Brady JV (1958) Ulcers in 'executive monkeys'. *Scientific American* **199** pp 95–100.

Brehm JW (1956) Post-decision changes in the desirability of alternatives. *Journal of Abnormal and Social Psychology* **52** pp 384–389.

Brewer WF and Treyens JC (1981) Role of schemata in memory for places. *Cognitive Psychology* **13** pp 207–230.

Broverman IK, Broverman DM, Clarkson FE, Rosencrantz PS and Vogel SR (1981) Sex role stereotypes and clinical judgements of mental health. In Howell E and Boyes M (eds) *Women and Mental Health*. New York: Basic Books.

Brown R (1986) *Social Psychology* (2nd edn). New York: Free Press.

Brown R and Kulik J (1977) Flashbulb memories. *Cognition* **5** pp 73–99.

Bruch H (1973) *Eating Disorders*. New York: Basic Books.

Buckhout R (1974) Eyewitness testimony. *Scientific American* **231** pp 23–31.

Burton AM, Bruce V and Hancock PJB (1999) From pixels to people: a model of familiar face recognition. *Cognitive Science* **23** pp 1–31.

Buss AH and Plomin R (1984) *Temperament: Early Developing Personality Traits*. Hillsdale, New Jersey: Erlbaum.

Calhoun JB (1962) Population density and social pathology. *Scientific American* **206(2)** pp 139–148.

Campbell FA and Ramey CT (1991) *The Carolina Abecedarian Project*. Paper presented at the biennial meeting of the Society for Research in Child Development, Seattle, WA.

Cannon WB (1929) *Bodily Changes in Pain, Hunger, Fear and Rage*. New York: Appleton-Century-Crofts.

Carter R (1998) *Mapping the Mind. London*. Weidenfeld and Nicholson.

Ceci SJ, Ross DF and Toglia MP (1987) Suggestibility of children's memory: psycholegal implications. *Journal of Experimental Psychology: General* **116** pp 38–49.

Clarke-Stewart A (1988) The 'effects' of infant day care reconsidered: risks for parents, children and researchers. *Early Childhood Research Quarterly* **3** pp 292–318.

Clarke-Stewart KA and Fein GG (1983) Early Childhood Problems. in P.H. Mussen (ed) *Handbook of Child Psychology* **2**. New York: Wiley

Cochrane R (1977) Mental illness in immigrants to England and Wales: an analysis of mental hospital admissions, 1971. *Social Psychiatry* **12** pp 25–35.

Cohen S (1980) Aftereffects of stress on human performance and social behaviour: a review of research and theory. *Psychological Bulletin* **87** pp 578–604.

Cohen S and Williamson GM (1991) Stress and infectious disease in humans. *Psychological Bulletin* **109** pp 5–24.

Cohen S, Tyrell DAJ and Smith AP (1991) Psychological stress and susceptibility to the common cold. *The New England Journal of Medicine* **325** pp 606–612.

Collins AM and Loftus EF (1975) A spreading-activation theory of semantic processing. *Psychological Review* **82** pp 407–428.

Conrad R (1964) Acoustic confusion in immediate memory. *British Journal of Psychology* **55** pp 75–84.

Conway MA, Anderson SJ, Larsen SF, Donnelly CM, McDaniel MA, McClelland AGR and Rawles RE (1994) The formation of flashbulb memories. *Memory and Cognition* **22** pp 326–343.

Coolican H (1990) *Research Methods and Statistics in Psychology*. Sevenoaks: Hodder & Stoughton.

Cox T (1975) The nature and management of stress. *New Behaviour, September* 25 pp 493–495.

Cox T, Watts C R and Barnett A (1981) The experience and effects of task-inherent demand. *Final Technical Report to the US Army Research, Development and Standardisation Group, UK.*.

Craik F and Lockhart R (1972) Levels of processing. *Journal of Verbal Learning and Verbal Behaviour* **11** pp 671–684.

Craik F and Tulving E (1975) Depth of processing and the retention of words in episodic memory. *Journal of Experimental Psychology: General* **104** pp 268–294.

Craik F and Watkins M (1973) The role of rehearsal in short term memory. *Journal of Verbal Learning and Verbal Behaviour* **12** pp 599–607.

Crisp AH and Kalucy RS (1974) Aspects of perceptual disorder in anorexia nervosa. *British Journal of Medical Psychology* **47** pp 349–361.

Crutchfield RS (1954) A new technique for measuring individual differences in conformity to group judgement. *Proceedings of the Invitational Conference on Testing Problems*, pp 69–74.

Crutchfield RS (1955) Conformity and character. *American Psychologist* **10** pp 191–198.

Curtiss S (1977) *Genie: A Psycholinguistic Study of a Modern-Day 'Wild Child'*. London: Academic Press.

Cutts TF and Barrios BA (1986) Fear of weight gain among bulimic and non-disturbed females. *Behaviour Therapy* **17** pp 626–636.

Davis K (1947) Final note on a case of extreme isolation. *American Journal of Sociology* **52** pp 432–437.

Davison GC and Neale JM (1994) *Abnormal Psychology* (6th edn). New York: Wiley.

De Renzi E (1986) Current issues in prosopagnosia. In Ellis HD, Jeeves MA, Newcombe F and Young A (eds) *Aspects of Face Processing*. Dordrecht: Martinus Nijhoff.

Dembroski TM and Costa P (1988) Assessment of coronary-prone behaviour: a current overview. *Annals of Behavioral Medicine* **10** pp 60–63.

Den Heyer K and Barrett B (1971) Selective loss of visual and verbal information in short-term memory by means of visual and verbal interpolated tasks. *Psychonomic Science* **25** pp 100–102.

Dent HR (1988) Children's eyewitness evidence: a brief review. In Gruneberg MM, Morris PE and Sykes RN (eds) *Practical Aspects of Memory: Current Research and Issues* (vol. 1) pp 101–106. Chichester: Wiley.

Deutsch M and Gerard HB (1955) A study of normative and informational social influences upon individual judgement. *Journal of Abnormal and Social Psychology* **51** pp 629–636.

Devlin, Honourable Lord Patrick (chair) (1976) *Report to the Secretary of State for the Home Department of the Departmental Committee on Evidence of Identification in Criminal Cases*. London: Her Majesty's Stationery Office.

Dollard J and Miller NE (1950) *Personality and Psychotherapy*. New York: McGraw Hill.

Duncan SL (1976) Differential social perception and attribution of intergroup violence: testing the lower limits of stereotyping of blacks. *Journal of Personality and Social Psychology* **34** pp 590–598.

Dunn J and Kendrick C (1982) *Siblings: love, envy and understanding*. London: Grant McIntyre.

Ebbinghaus H (1885) *Concerning Memory*. New York: Teachers' College Press (published in 1913).

Elias CS and Perfetti CA (1973) Encoding task and recognition memory: the importance of semantic coding. *Journal of Experimental Psychology* **99(2)** pp 151–157.

Ellis H and Szulecka T (1996) The disguised lover: a case of Fregoli delusion. In Halligan PW and Marshall JC (eds) *Method in Madness: Case Studies in Cognitive Neuropsychiatry*. Hove: Psychology Press.

Ellis HD, Shepherd JW and Davies GM (1979) Identification of familiar and unfamiliar faces from internal and external features: some implications for theories of face recognition. *Perception* **8** pp 431–439.

Ellis HD, Shepherd JW, Shepherd J, Flin RH and Davies GM (1989) Identification from a computer-driven retrieval system compared with a traditional mug-shot album search: a new tool for police investigations. *Ergonomics* **32** pp 167–177.

Elms AC (1972) *Social Psychology and Social Relevance*. Boston: Brown.

Elms AC and Milgram S (1966) Personality characteristics associated with obedience and defiance towards authoritative command. *Journal of Experimental Research in Personality* **1** pp 282–289.

Epstein LC and Lasagna L (1969) Obtaining informed consent. *Archives of Internal Mesdicine* **123** pp 682–8

Erbeck J, Elfner L and Driggs D (1983) Reduction of blood pressure by indirect biofeedback. *Biofeedback and Self Regulation* **8(1)** pp 63–72.

Farina A, Holland CH and Ring K (1966) Role of stigma and set in interpersonal interaction. *Journal of Abnormal and Social Psychology* **71** pp 421–428.

Farrimond, T (1968) Retention and recall: incidental learning of visual and auditory material. *Journal of Genetic Psychology* **113** pp 155–165.

Fisher RP, Geiselman RE and Raymond DS (1987a) Critical analysis of police interview techniques. *Journal of Police Science and Administration* **15** pp 177–185.

Fisher RP, Geiselman RE and Raymond DS, Turkerich LM and Warhaftig ML (1987b) Enhancing enhanced eyewitness memory: refining the cognitive interior. *Journal of Police Science and Administration* **15** pp 291–297.

Fisher RP, Geiselman RE and Amador M (1990) Field test of the cognitive interior, reported in *The Psychologist*, Sept 1991.

French JRP, Caplan RD and Van Harrison R (1982) *The Mechanisms of Job Stress and Strain*. New York: Wiley.

Frenkel-Brunswik E (1942) Motivation and behaviour. *Genetic Psychology Monographs* **26** pp 121–265.

Freud A and Dann S (1951) An experiment in group upbringing. *Psychoanalytic Study of the Child* **6** pp 127–168.

Friedman M and Rosenman RH (1974) *Type A behaviour and your heart*. New York: Knopf.

Friedman M, Thoresen CE, Gill JJ, Ulmer D, Powell LH, Price VA, Brown B, Thompson L, Rabin D, Breall WS, Bourg E, Levy R and Dixon T (1986) Alteration of Type A behavior and its effects on cardiac recurrences in postmyocardial infarction patients: summary of The Recurrent Coronary Prevention Project. *American Heart Journal* **112** pp 653–665.

Gamson WB, Fireman B and Rytina S (1982) *Encounters with Unjust Authority*. Hounwood, Illinois: Dorsey Press.

Garfinkel PE and Garner DM (1982) *Anorexia Nervosa: A Multidimensional Perspective*. New York: Brunner/Mazel.

Garner DM, Garfinkel PE, Schwartz D and Thompson M (1980) Cultural expectations of thinness in women. *Psychological Reports* **47** pp 483–491.

Geiselman RE, Fisher RP, Firstenberg I, Hutton LA, Avetissian IV and Prosk AL (1984) Enhancement of eyewitness memory: an empirical evaluation of the cognitive interview. *Journal of Police Science and Administration* **12** pp 74–80.

Geiselman RE, Risher RP, MacKinnon DP and Holland HL (1986) Enhancement of eyewitness memory with the cognitive interview. *American Journal of Psychology* **99** pp 385–401.

Glanzer M and Cunitz AR (1966) Two storage mechanisms in free recall. *Journal of Verbal Learning and Verbal Behaviour* **5** pp 351–360.

Glass DC, Singer JE and Friedman LW (1969) Psychic cost of adaptation to an environmental stressor. *Journal of Personality and Social Psychology* **12** pp 200–210.

Godden DR and Baddeley AD (1975) Context-dependent memory in two natural environments: on land and under water. *British Journal of Psychology* **66** pp 325–331.

Gold D, Rogacz S, Bock N, and Tosteson, Tor-D. Rotating shift work, sleep and accidents related to sleepiness in hospital nurses. *American Journal of Public Health* **82** pp 1011–1014.

Goldfarb W (1943) The effects of early institutional care on adolescent personality. *Journal of Experimental Education* **12** pp 106–129.

Goldstein IB (1981) Assessment of hypertension. In Prokop CK and Bradley LA (eds) *Medical Psychology*. New York: Academic Press.

Goodwin DW, Powell B, Bremer D, Hoine H and Stern J (1969) Alcohol and recall: state-dependent effects in man. *Science* **163** p 1358.

Grasha AF (1983) *Practical Applications of Psychology* (2nd ed). Boston: Little, Brown & Co.

Greer A, Morris T and Pettingale KW (1979) Psychological response to breast cancer: effect on outcome. *Lancet* **13** pp 785–787.

Grossman K, Grossman KE, Spangler G, Suess G and Unzer L (1985) Maternal sensitivity and newborn's orientation responses. In Bretherton I and Waters E (eds) *Growing Points in Attachment Theory and Research*, Monographs of the Society for Research in Child Development **50** Serial No. 209 pp 3–35.

Hall K and Savery LK (1987) *Stress Management Management Decision* London.

Halmi KA, Goldberg SC and Cunningham S (1977) Perceptual distortion and body image in adolescent girls: distortion of body image in adolescence. *Psychological Medicine* **7** pp 253–257.

Harburg E, Erfurt JC, Hauenstein LS, Chape C, Schull WJ and Schork MA (1973) Socioecological stress, suppressed hostility, skin colour, and black-white male blood pressure: Detroit. *Psychosomatic Medicine* **35** pp 276–296.

Hargreaves DH (1967) *Social Relations in a Secondary School*. London: Routledge and Kegan Paul.

Harlow HF and Harlow MK (1962) Social deprivation in monkeys. *Scientific American* **207(5)** p 136.

Harlow HF and Zimmerman RR (1959) Affectional responses in the infant monkey. *Science* **130** pp 421–432.

Hay DC and Young AW (1982) The human face. In Ellis A (ed) *Normality and Pathology in Cognitive Functions*. New York: Academic Press.

Hazan C and Shaver P (1987) Romantic love conceptualized as an attachment process, *Journal of Personality and Social Psychology*, **52** 511–524.

Helman CG (1990) *Culture, Health and Illness*. Oxford: Butterworth Heinemann.

Hetherington EM, Cox MJ and Cox R (1979) Play and social interaction in children following divorce. *Journal of Social Issues* **35** pp 26–49.

Hetherington EM, Cox MJ and Cox R (1982) Effects of divorce on parents and children. In Lamb ME (ed) *Non-Traditional Families: Parenting and Child Development*. Hillsdale, New Jersey: Lawrence Erlbaum Associates.

Hiroto DS and Seligman MEP (1975) Generality of learned helplessness in man. *Journal of Personality and Social Psychology* **31** pp 311–327.

Hoffman LW (1974) Effects of maternal employment on the child – a review of the research. *Developmental Psychology* **10** pp 204–228.

Hofling KC, Brotzman E, Dalrymple S, Graves N and Pierce CM (1966) An experimental study in the nurse-physician relationship. *Journal of Nervous and Mental Disorders* **143** pp 171–180.

Holland AJ, Hall A, Murray R, Russell GFM and Crisp HH (1984) Anorexia nervosa: a study of 34 twin pairs and one set of triplets. *British Journal of Psychiatry* **145** pp 414–419.

Holmes TH and Rahe RH (1967) The social readjustment rating scale. *Journal of Psychosomatic Research* **11** pp 213–218.

House JS, Landis KR and Umberson D (1988) Social relationships and health. *Science* **241** pp 540–545.

Howes C (1990) Can the age of entry into child care and the quality of child care predict adjustment in kindergarten? *Developmental Psychology* **26** pp 292–303.

Hsu LK (1990) *Eating Disorders*. New York: Guilford.

Humphreys L (1970) *Tearoom Trade*. Chicago: Aldine.

Insko CA, Drenan S, Solomon MR, Smith R and Wade TJ (1983) Conformity as a function of the consistency of positive self-evaluation with being liked and being right. *Journal of Experimental Social Psychology* **19** pp 341–358.

Ivancevich JM, Matteson MT and Preston C. (1982) Occupational stress, Type A behaviour and physical well-being. *Academy of Management Journal* **25** pp 373–391.

Jacobs TJ and Charles E (1980) Life events and the occurrence of cancer in children. *Psychosomatic Medicine* **42** pp 11–24.

Jahoda M (1958) *Current Concepts of Positive Mental Health*. New York: Basic Books.

James W (1890) *Principles of Psychology*. New York: Holt.

Janis (1971) *Stress and Frustation*. New York: Harcourt.

Jemmott JB III, Borysenko M, McClelland DC, Chapman R, Meyer D and Benson H (1985) Academic stress, power motivation and decrease in salivery secretory immunoglubulin: a secretation rate. *Lancet* **I** pp 1400–1402.

Jenness, A (1932) The role of discussion in changing opinion regarding matter of fact. *Journal of Abnormal and Social Psychology* **27** pp 279–296.

Johnson JH and Sarason IG (1978) Life stress, depression and anxiety: internal/external control as a moderator variable. *Journal of Psychosomatic Research* **22(3)** pp 205–208.

Jones L and Cochrane R (1981) Stereotypes of mental illness: a test of the labelling hypothesis. *International Journal of Social Psychiatry* **27** pp 99–107.

Kadushin A (1970) *Adopting older children*. New York: Columbia University Press.

Kagan J, Kearsley RB and Zelazo P (1980) *Infancy: Its Place in Human Development* (2nd edn). Cambridge, Massachusetts: Harvard University Press.

Kanner AD, Coyne JC, Schaefer C and Lazarus RS (1981) Comparison of two modes of stress management: Daily hassles and uplifts versus major life events. *Journal of Behavioural Medicine* **4** pp1–39

Kant (1781) *Critique of Pure Reason*

Kelly GA (1955) *The Psychology of Personal Constructs*. New York: Norton.

Kelman HC (1958) Compliance, identification and internalization: three processes of attitude change. *Journal of Conflict Resolution* **2** pp 51–60.

Kelman HC (1967) Human use of human subjects: the problem of deception in social psychological experiments. *Psychological Bulletin* **67** pp 1–11.

Kendler KS, Maclean C, Neale M, Kessler R, Heath A and Eaves L (1991) The genetic epidemiology of bulimia nervosa. *American Journal of Psychiatry* **148** pp 1627–1637.

Kennedy (1997) in *The Times* (14 April)

Kilham W and Mann L (1974) Level of destructive obedience as a function of transmitter and executant roles in the Milgram obedience paradigm. *Journal of Personality and Social Psychology* **29** pp 696–702.

Kobasa SC (1979) Stressful life events, personality, and health: an enquiry into hardiness. *Journal of Personality and Social Psychology* **37** pp 1–11.

Kobasa SC, Maddi SR and Kahn S (1982) Hardiness and health: a prospective study. *Journal of Personality and Social Psychology* **42** pp 168–177.

Kudirka NK (1965) *Defiance of Authority under Peer Influence*. Unpublished doctoral dissertation, Yale University.

Laing RD (1965) *The Divided Self*. Harmondsworth, Middlesex: Penguin.

Laing, RD (1967) *The Politics of Experience and the Bird of Paradise*. Harmondsworth, Middlesex: Penguin.

Langer FJ, Janis IL and Wolfer JA (1975) Reduction of psychological stress in surgical patients. *Journal of Experimental Social Psychology* **11** pp 155–165.

Larsen KS (1974) Conformity in the Asch experiment. *Journal of Social Psychology* **94** pp 303–304.

Lazarus RS and Folkman S (1984) *Stress, Coping and Adaptation*. New York: Springer.

Leach P (1979) *Who Cares: A New Deal for Mothers and Their Small Children*. Harmondsworth: Penguin.

Lee MT and Ofshe R (1981) The impact of behavioral

style and status characteristics on social influence: a test of two competing theories. *Social Psychology Quarterly* **44** pp 73–82.

Lewis VJ and Blair A (1991) In Cochrane R and Carroll D (eds) *Psychology and Social Issues: A Tutorial Text*. Hove: Psychology Press.

Likert R (1932) A technique for the measurement of attitudes. *Archives of Psychology* **22** p 140.

Linton M (1979) I remember it well. *Psychology Today* July pp 81–86.

List J (1986) Age and schematic differences in the reliability of eyewitness testimony. *Developmental Psychology* **22** pp 50–57.

Loftus EF (1975) Leading questions and the eyewitness report. *Cognitive Psychology* **7** pp 560–572.

Loftus EF (1979) Reactions to blatantly contradictory information. *Memory and Cognition* **7** pp 368–374.

Loftus EF (1994) *The Myth of Repressed Memory*. New York: St Martin's Press.

Loftus EF and Burns (1982) Mental shock can produce retrograde amnesia. *Memory and Cognition* **10** pp 318–323.

Loftus EF and Palmer JC (1974) Reconstruction of automobile destruction: an example of the interaction between language and memory. *Journal of Verbal Learning and Verbal Behaviour* **13** pp 585–589.

Loftus EF, Levidow B and Duensing S (1991) Who remembers best? Individual differences in memory for events that occurred in a science museum. *Applied Cognitive Psychology*

Loftus EF, Schooler JW, Boone SM and Kline D (1987) Time went by so slowly: overestimation of event duration by males and females. *Applied Cognitive Psychology* **1** pp 3–13.

Loftus EF and Zanni G (1975) Eyewitness testimony: The influence of the wording of a question. *Bulletin of the Psychonomic Society* **5** pp 86–8.

Lopez S and Hernandez P (1986) How culture is considered in evaluations of psychopathology. *Journal of Nervous and Mental Disease* **176** pp 598–606.

Lydiard RB, Brewerton TD, Rossey MD, Laraia MT, Stuart G, Beinfield MC and Ballenger JC (1993) CSF cholecystokinin octapeptide in patients with bulimia nervosa and in comparison with normal subjects. *American Journal of Psychiatry* **150** pp 1099–1101.

Main M and Cassidy J (1988) Categories of response to reunion with the parent at age 6: predictable from infant classifications and stable over a 1-month period. *Developmental Psychology* **24** pp 415–426.

Main M and Goldwyn R (1984) Predicting rejection of her infant from mother's representation of her own experience: implications for the abused-abusing inter-generational cycle. *Child Abuse and Neglect* **8** pp 203–217.

Main M and Solomon J (1990) Procedures for identifying infants as disorganised/disoriented during the Ainsworth Strange Situation. In Greenberg MT, Cicchetti D and Cummings EM (eds) *Attachment in the Preschool Years*. Chicago, Illinois: University of Chicago Press.

Mantell DM (1971) The potential for violence in Germany. *Journal of Social Issues* **27** pp 101–112.

Marsh P (1978) *The Rules of Disorder*. London: Routledge & Kegan Paul.

Masling J (1966) Role-related behaviour of the subject and psychologist and its effect upon psychological data. In Levine, D (ed) *Nebraska Symposium on Motivation*. Lincoln, Neb.: University of Nebraska Press.

Mathews KA (1984) Assessment of type A, anger, and hostility in epidemiological studies of cardiovascular disease. In Ostfeld A and Eaker E (eds) *Measuring Psychosocial Variables in Epidemiologic Studies of Cardiovascular Disease*. Bethesda, Maryland: National Institute for Health.

McCartney K, Scarr S, Phillips D and Grajek S (1985) Day care as intervention: comparisons of varying quality programs. *Journal of Applied Developmental Psychology* **6** pp 247–260.

McCloskey M and Zaragoza M (1985) Misleading post-event information and memory for events: arguments and evidence against memory impairment hypotheses. *Journal of Experimental Psychology* **114** pp 1–16.

McCloskey M, Wible CG and Cohen NJ (1988) Is there a special flashbulb-memory mechanism? *Journal of Experimental Psychology: General* **117** pp 171–181.

McGeoch JA and Macdonald WT (1931) Meaningful relations and retroactive inhibition. *American Journal of Psychology* **43** pp 579–588.

McNeil JE and Warrington EK (1991) Prosopagnosia: a reclassification. *Quarterly Journal of Experimental Psychology* **A43:2** pp 267–287.

Meeus WHJ and Raaijmakers QAW (1986) Administrative obedience: carrying out orders to use psychological-administrative violence. *European Journal of Social Psychology* **16** pp 311–324.

Meichenbaum D (1985) *Stress Inoculation Training*. New York: Pergamon.

Melhuish EC, Mooney A, Martin S and Lloyd E (1990a) Type of childcare at 18 months – I. Differences in interactional experience. *Journal of Child Psychology and Psychiatry* **31** pp 849–859.

Melhuish EC, Mooney A, Martin S and Lloyd E (1990b) Type of childcare at 18 months – II. Relations with cognitive and language development. *Journal of Child Psychology and Psychiatry* **31** pp 861–870.

Menges RJ (1973) Openness and honesty versus coercion and deception in psychological research. *American Psychologist* **28** pp 1030–1034.

Mikulincer M, Florian V and Weller A (1993) Attachment styles, coping strategies, and post-traumatic psychological distress: the impact of the Gulf War in Israel. *Journal of Personality and Social Psychology* **64** pp 817–826.

Milgram S (1963) Behavioural study of obedience. *Journal of Abnormal and Social Psychology* **67** pp 391–398.

Milgram S (1964) Issues in the study of obedience: A reply to Baumrind. *American Psychologist* **19** pp 848–852.

Milgram S (1965) Some coditions of obedience and disobedience to authotity. *Human Realations* **18** pp 57–76

Miller GA (1956) The magical number seven, plus or minus two: some limits on our capacity for processing information. *Psychological Review* **63** pp 81–97.

Milner BR (1996) Amnesia following operation on temporal lobes, in CWN Whitty and OL Zangwill (eds) *Amnesia* London: Butterworth.

Minuchin S, Rosman B and Baker L (1978) *Psychosomatic Families*. Cambridge, Massachusetts: Harvard University Press.

Morris CD, Bransford JD and Franks JJ (1977) Levels of processing versus transfer appropriate processing. *Journal of Verbal Learning and Verbal Behaviour* **16** pp 519–533.

Morris PE, Tweedy M and Gruneberg MM (1985) Interest, knowledge and the memory of soccer scores. *British Journal of Psychology* **76** pp 417–425.

Moscovici S and Nemeth C (1974) Social influence II: minority influence. In Nemeth C (ed) *Social Psychology: Classic and Contemporary Integrations*. Chicago: Rand McNally.

Moscovici S, Lage E and Naffrechoux M (1969) Influence of a consistent minority on the response of a majority in a colour perception task. *Sociometry* **32** pp 365–379.

Mugny G (1984) The influence of minorities. In Tajfel H (ed) *The Social Dimension* vol. 2. Cambridge: Cambridge University Press.

National Association for the Education of Young Children (1991) *Accreditation criteria and procedures of the National Academy of Early Childhood Programs* (rev ed). Washington, DC: Author.

Nemeth C and Wachtler J (1973) Consistency and modification of judgement. *Journal of Experimental Social Psychology* **9** pp 65–79.

Orbach S (1978) *Fat is a Feminist Issue: How to Lose Weight Permanently Without Dieting*. London: Paddington Press.

Orne MT (1962) On the social psychology of the psychological experiment – with particular reference to demand characteristics and their implications. *American Psychologist* **17(1)** pp 776–783.

Orne MT and Holland CC (1968) On the ecological validity of laboratory deceptions. *International Journal of Psychiatry* **6** pp 282–293.

Orne MT, Soskis DA, Dinges DF and Orne EC (1984) Hypnotically induced testimony. In Wells G and Loftus E (eds) *Eyewitness Testimony: Psychological Perspectives*. Cambridge: Cambridge University Press.

Page MM and Scheidt RJ (1971) The elusive weapons effect. *Journal of Personality and Social Psychology* **20** pp 304–318.

Park RJ, Lawrie JM and Freeman CP (1995) Post-viral onset of anorexia nervosa. *British Journal of Psychology* **166** pp 386–389.

Parkin JR and Eagles JM (1993) Blood-letting in anorexia nervosa. *British Journal of Psychiatry* **162** pp 246–248.

Parry-Jones WL and Parry-Jones B (1993) Self-mutilation in four historical cases of bulimia. *British Journal of Psychiatry* **163** pp 394–402.

Pavlov IP (1927) *Conditioned Reflexes*. London: Oxford University Press.

Penfield W (1969) Consciousness, memory and man's conditioned reflexes. In Pribram K (ed) *On the Biology of Learning*. New York: Harcourt Brace Jovanovich.

Penry J (1971) *Looking at Faces and Remembering Them: A guide to Facial Identification*. London: Elek Books.

Perrin S and Spencer C (1981) Independence or conformity in the Asch experiment as a reflection of cultural and situational factors. *British Journal of Social Psychology* **20** pp 205–209.

Peters DP (1988) Eyewitness memory and arousal in a natural setting. In Gruneberg MM, Morris PE and Sykes RN (eds) *Practical Aspects of Memory: Current Research and Issues* (vol. 1) pp 89–94. Chichester: Wiley.

Peterson LR and Peterson MJ (1959) Short term retention of individual items. *Journal of Experimental Psychology* **58** pp 193–198.

Phillips DA, Voran M, Kisker E, Howes C and Whitebook M (1994) Child care for children in poverty: opportunity or inequity? *Child Development* **65** pp 472–492.

Pike KM and Rodin J (1991) Mothers, daughters, and

disordered eating. *Journal of Abnormal Psychology* **100** pp 198–204.

Pillemer DB (1984) Flashbulb memories of the assassination attempt on President Reagan. *Cognition* **16** pp 63–80.

Piran N, Kennedy S, Garfinkel PE and Owens M (1985) Affective disturbance in eating disorders. *Journal of Nervous and Mental Disease* **173** pp 395–400.

Pringle MLK and Bossio V (1960) Early prolonged separations and emotional adjustment. *Journal of Child Psychology and Psychiatry*, **1** pp 37–48.

Ragland DR and Brand RJ (1988) Type A behavior and mortality from coronary heart disease. *New England Journal of Medicine* **318** pp 65–69.

Rahe RH and Arthur RJ (1977) Life change patterns surrounding illness experience. In Monat A and Lazarus RS (eds) *Stress and Coping*. New York: Columbia University Press.

Ring K, Wallston K and Corey M (1970) Role of debriefing as a factor affecting subjective reaction to a Milgram type obedience experiment: an ethical enquiry. *Representative Research in Social Psychology* **1** pp 67–88.

Roberts A and Bruce V (1988) Feature saliency in judging the sex and familiarity of faces. *Perception* **17** pp 475–481.

Robertson J and Robertson J (1967–73) *Young Children In Brief Separation*. A film study.

Rosen S (1970) Noise, hearing and cardiovascular function. In Welch, B. and Welch, A. (eds) *Physiological effects of noise*. New York: Plenium.

Rosenhan DL and Seligman MEP (1989) *Abnormal Psychology* (2nd edn). London: Norton.

Rosenhan RH, Brand RJ, Jenkins CD, Friedman M, Strauss R and Wurm M (1975) Coronary heart disease in the Western Collaborative Group Study. *Journal of the American Medical Association* **233** pp 872–7

Rotter JB (1966) Generalized expectancies for internal versus external control of reinforcement. *Psychological Monographs* **30(1)** pp 1–26.

Rotton J, Frey J, Barry T, Milligan M and Fitzpatrick M (1978) The air pollution experience and physical aggression. *Journal of Applied Social Psychology* **9** pp 397–412.

Rubin DC and Kozin M (1984) Vivid memories. *Cognition* **16** pp 81–95.

Rutter M (1972) *Maternal Deprivation Reassessed*. Harmondsworth: Penguin.

Sacks O (1985) *The Man Who Mistook His Wife for a Hat*. New York: Summit Books.

Sameroff AJ (1991) The social context of development. In Woodhead M and Light P (eds) *Becoming a Person*. London: Routledge/The Open University.

Schaffer HR (1977) *Mothering*. London: Fontana.

Schaffer HR (1990) *Making Decisions about Children* Oxford: Blackwell.

Schaffer HR and Emerson PE (1964) The development of social attachments in infancy. *Monographs of the Society for Research in Child Development* **29** (whole no. 3).

Scheff TJ (1966) *Being Mentally Ill: A Sociological Theory*. Chicago: Aldine.

Seligman MEP, Maier SF and Solomon RL (1971) Unpredictable and uncontrollable aversive events. In Brush FR (ed) *Aversive Conditioning and Learning*. New York: Academic Press.

Seligman, MEP (1975) *Helplessness: On Depression, Development and Death*. San Francisco: W H Freeman.

Selye H (1956) *The Stress of Life*. New York: McGraw-Hill.

Selye H (1974) *Stress Without Distress*. New York: Harper & Row.

Sergent J (1984) Configural processing of faces in the left and the right cerebral hemispheres. *Journal of Experimental Psychology: Human Perception and Performance* **10** pp 554–572.

Shallice T (1967) Paper presented at NATO symposium on short-term memory, Cambridge, England.

Shallice T and Warrington EK (1970) Independent functioning of verbal memory stores: a neuropsychological study. *Quarterly Journal of Experimental Psychology* **22** pp 261–273.

Shapiro PN and Penrod S (1986) Meta-analysis of facial identification studies. *Psychological Bulletin* **100** pp 139–156.

Shepherd JW (1986) An interactive computer system for retrieving faces. In Ellis H, Jeeves M, Newcombe F and Young A (eds) *Aspects of Face Processing*. Dordrecht: Nijhoff.

Shepherd JW, Deregowski JB and Ellis HD (1974) A cross-cultural study of recognition memory for faces. *International Journal of Psychology* **9** pp 205–212.

Sheridan CL and King KG (1972) Obedience to authority with an authentic victim. *Proceedings of the 80th Annual Convention of the American Psychological Association* **7** pp 165–166.

Sherif M (1935) A study of sane factors in perception. *Archives of Psychology* **27** (whole no. 187)

Slade DD and Russell GFM (1973) Awareness of body dimensions in anorexia nervosa: cross-sectional and longitudinal studies. *Psychological Medicine* **3** pp 188–199.

Smith C and Lloyd BB (1978) Maternal behaviour and perceived sex of infant. *Child Development* **49** pp 1263–1265.

Solomon GF (1969) Emotions, stress, the CNS and immunity. *Annals of the New York Academy of Sciences* **164** pp 335–343.

Spector PE (1987) Interactive effects of percieved control and job stressors on alternative and health outcomes for clerical workers. *Work and Stress* **1** pp 155–162.

Spector PE, Dwyer DJ and Jex SM (1988) Relation of job stressors to affective, health and performance outcomes: a comparison of multiple data sources, *Journal of Applied Psychology* **73** pp 11–19

Sperling G (1960) The information available in brief visual presentation. *Psychological Monographs* **74** (whole no. 498).

Stacey M, Dearden R, Pill R and Robinson D (1970) *Hospitals, Children and Their Families: The Report of a Pilot Study*. London: Routledge & Kegan Paul.

Standing L (1973) Learning 10,000 pictures. *Quarterly Journal of Experimental Psychology* **25** pp 207–222.

Stang DJ (1973) Effects of interaction rate on ratings of leadership and liking. *Journal of Personality and Social Psychology* **27** pp 405–408.

Sui-Wah L (1989) Anorexia nervosa and Chinese food. *British Journal of Psychiatry* **155** p 568.

Suomi SJ and Harlow HF (1972) Social rehabilitation of isolate-reared monkeys. *Developmental Psychology* **6** pp 487–496.

Sweeney K (1995) Stay calm and heal better. *The Times* 21 December p 5.

Syer J and Connolly C (1988) *Sporting Body Sporting Mind: an athlete's guide to mental training*. Eaglewood Cliffs, NJ: Prentice Hall.

Szasz T (1972) *The Myth of Mental Illness*. London: Paladin.

Tache J, Selye H and Day S (1979) *Cancer, Stress, and Death*. New York: Plenum Press.

Tajfel H, Billig MG and Bundy RP (1971) Social categorization and intergroup behaviour. *European Journal of Social Psychology* **1(2)** pp 149–178.

Takahashi K (1990) Are the key assumptions of the 'strange situation' procedure universal? A view from Japanese research. *Human Development* **33** pp. 23–30.

Thompson RF (1986) The neurobiology of learning and memory. *Science* **233** pp 941–947.

Tizard B and Hodges J (1978) The effect of early institutional rearing on the behaviour problems and

affectional relationships of four-year-old children. *Journal of Child Psychology and Psychiatry* **16** pp 61–74.

Tizard B and Rees J (1975) The effect of early institutional rearing on the development of eight-year-old children. *Journal of Child Psychology and Psychiatry* **19** pp 99–118.

Tizard, B (1991) Working mothers and the care of young children. In Woodhead M, Light P and Carr R (eds) *Growing Up in a Changing Society*. London: Routledge.

Treisman AM (1964) Verbal cues, language, and meaning in selective attention. *American Journal of Psychology* **77** pp 206–219.

Tulving E (1962) Subjective organisation in free recall of 'unrelated' words. *Psychological Review* **69** 344–354.

Tulving E (1972) Episodic and semantic memory. In Tulving E and Donaldson W (eds) *Organisation of Memory*. London: Academic Press.

Tulving E (1974) Cue-dependent forgetting. *American Scientist* **62** pp 74–82.

Tyler SW, Hertel PT, McCallum MC and Ellis HC (1979). Cognitive effort and memory. *Journal of Experimental Psychology (Human Learning and Memory)* **5(b)** pp 607–617.

Tyszkowa M (1991) The role of grandparents in the development of grandchildren as perceived by adolescents and young adults in Poland. In Smith PK (ed) *The Psychology of Grandparenthood: an International Perspective*. London: Routledge.

US Bureau of the Census (1994) *Statistical abstract of the United States* (114th edn). Washington, DC: US Government Printing Office.

Van Ijzendoorn MH and Kroonenberg PM (1988) Cross-cultural patterns of attachment: a meta-analysis of the Strange Situation. *Child Development* **59** pp 147–156.

Visintainer M, Seligman M and Volpicelli J (1983) Helplessness, chronic stress and tumor development. *Psychosomatic Medicine* **45** pp 75–76.

Wade C and Tavris C (1993) *Psychology* (3rd edn). London: HarperCollins.

Wagenaar WA and Groeneweg J (1990) The memory of concentration camp survivors. *Applied Cognitive Psychology* **4** pp 77–87.

Waters E (1978) The reliability and stability of individual differences in infant-mother attachment. *Child Development* **49** pp 483–494.

Watson JB and Rayner R (1920) Conditioned emotional reactions. *Journal of Experimental Psychology* **3** pp 1–14.

Weiss JM (1972) Influence of psychological variables on stress induced pathology. In Knight J and Porter R (eds) *Phsiology, Education and Psychosomatic Illness*. Amsterdam: Elsevier.

Werner E (1991) Grandparent-grandchild relationships amongst US ethnic groups. In Smith PK (ed) *The Psychology of Grandparenthood: an International Perspective*. London: Routledge.

Whittaker JO Meak RD (1967) Sound pressure in the andification a nd distribution of judgement: a cross-cultural study. International *Journal of Psychology* **2** pp 109–113.

Whyte (1948) *Human Relations in the Restaurant Industry*, New York: McGrauer Hill

Wiesenthal DL, Endler NS, Coward TR and Edwards J (1976) Reversability of relative competence as a determinant of conformity across different perceptual tasks. *Representative Research in Social Psychology* **7** pp 35–43.

Wiggins JA, Dili F and Schwartz RD (1967) On 'status ability'. *Sociometry* **28** pp 197–209.

Wilkinson J (1988) Context effects in children's event memory. In Gruneberg MM, Morris PE and Sykes RN (eds) *Practical Aspects of Memory: Current Research and Issues* (vol 1) pp 107–111. Chichester: Wiley.

Williams RB (1984) Type A behavior and coronary heart disease: something old, something new. *Behavioral Medicine Update* **6(3)** pp 29–33.

Winnurst JAM, Buunk BP and Marcelissen FHG (1988) Social support and stress: perspectives and processes. In Fisher S and Reason J (eds) *Handbook of Life Stress, Cognition and Health*. New York: Wiley.

Wolfgang AP (1988) Job stress in the health professionals: a study of physicians, nurses and pharmacists. *Behavioural Medicine* **14** pp 43–7.

Yager J, Hatton CA and Lawrence M (1986) Anorexia nervosa in a woman totally blind since the age of two. *British Journal of Psychiatry* **149** pp 506–509.

Yarnell PP and Lynch S (1970) Retrograde memory immediately after concussion. *Lancet* **1** 863–865.

Yuille JC and Cutshall JL (1986) A case study of eyewitness memory of a crime. *Journal of Applied Psychology* **71** pp 291–301.

Zechmeister EB and Nyberg SE (1982) *Human Memory*. Monterey, California: Brooks/Cole.

Zigler EF and Gilman E (1993) Day care in America: what is needed? *Pediatrics* **91** pp 175–178.

Zimbardo PG, Banks WC, Craig H and Jaffe D (1973) A Pirandellian prison: the mind is a formidable jailor. *New York Times Magazine*

INDEX